KU-024-164

JUSTIN WYATT

High Concept

Movies and Marketing in Hollywood

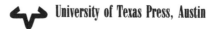 University of Texas Press, Austin

Copyright © 1994 by the University of
Texas Press
All rights reserved
Printed in the United States of America

Fifth paperback printing, 2006

Requests for permission to reproduce
material from this work should be sent to:
    Permissions
    University of Texas Press
    P.O. Box 7819
    Austin, TX 78713-7819
    www.utexas.edu/utpress/about/
        bpermission.html

⊗ The paper used in this book meets the
minimum requirements of ANSI/NISO
Z39.48-1992 (R1997) (Permanence of
Paper).

Library of Congress
Cataloging-in-Publication Data

Wyatt, Justin, date
    High concept : movies and marketing
in Hollywood / Justin Wyatt. - 1st ed.
        p.   cm. - (Texas film studies
series)
    Includes bibliographical references and
index.
    ISBN-13: 978-0-292-79091-9

    1. Motion pictures—United States—
Marketing. I. Title. II. Series.
PN1995.9.M29W9 1994
791.43'068'8-dc20   94-11131

014616868 Liverpool Univ

High Concept

University of Liverpool

Withdrawn from stock

Texas Film and Media Studies Series
Thomas Schatz, Editor

To Jeff and to the memory of Lindie Leigh

Contents

Acknowledgments

As this book has developed from doctoral research at UCLA, I would like to thank those faculty members who helped shape the initial project: Steve Mamber, Trudy Cameron, Howard Suber, Kathryn Montgomery, Carol Scott, and particularly Janet Bergstrom. Prior to UCLA, several teachers and professors fostered my interest in film, economics, and the intersection between the two: Erwin Diewert, Shelagh Heffernan, John Mills, A. J. Reynertson, John Weymark, and Joanne Yamaguchi.

I am also grateful for the generous feedback and encouragment which I have received over the years while developng high concept. Randy Rutsky, my co-author on an initial article in *Wide Angle* ("High Concept: Abstracting the Postmodern," *Wide Angle* 10, no. 4 (1988): 42–49), has been especially supportive. I also must thank many other colleagues for their comments and suggestions: J. M. Clarke, Jon Lewis, James Naremore, Victoria O'Donnell, Donald Mott, Bruce Austin, Kenneth White, Hamid Naficy, Nina Leibman, and Joanne Yamaguchi. At the University of North Texas, I have been blessed with wonderful colleagues, including Steve Fore, Don Staples, and Gerry Veeder, an impressive chairman, John Kuiper, and a tireless research assistant, Yoshiko Nabei.

Several members of the film and television industries graciously shared their views on matters related to high concept, including Peter Guber, Jerry Bruckheimer, Diana Widom, Maggie Young, Perry Katz, Peter McAlevey, Sid Kaufman, Adam Gold, Hilary Estey, Rob Jennings, and the late Mardi Marans.

The company and caring of friends have enabled me to write this book, and I am indebted to many, including Juan Morales, Rhona Berenstein, Alison Lloyd McKee, James Spottiswoode, Constance Meyer, Woods Gleason, Francis Gargani, Eric Prokesh, Todd Haynes, David Griffin, Steve Fore, Bob Helstrom, and Myra Walker.

Luke Ryan photographed stills and one-sheets for this book. A portion of Chapter 3 appears in an earlier version in "High Concept, Product Differentiation, and the Contemporary U.S. Film Industry," *Current Research in Film: Audiences, Economics, and Law,* vol. 5, ed. Bruce A. Austin (Norwood, N.J.: Ablex Publishing Corporation, 1991): 86–105. Reprinted with permission from Ablex Publishing Corporation.

At the University of Texas Press, Betsy Williams and Frankie Westbrook have been wonderful with their enthusiasm and measured advice.

Above all, I wish to thank my inspirational editor, Thomas Schatz, for his kindness, criticism, perseverance, and intellectual rigor.

High Concept

C H A P T E R 1

A Critical Redefinition: The Concept of High Concept

Consider two musicals from the late 1970s: *Grease* (1978), critically lambasted and adored by millions of teenagers, and *All That Jazz* (1979), critically lauded and admired by members of the Academy of Motion Picture Arts and Sciences (to the tune of nine Oscar nominations). While the films fit the musical genre, to the extent that both feature singing and dancing, differences in content, marketing, and reception between the two films illuminate one of the most significant forms of production in contemporary Hollywood. More to the point, these films embody the contrast between "high concept" and "low concept."

Grease was firmly within the mainstream of contemporary Hollywood. The potent marketing assets of the film easily distinguished it from other musicals, such as *All That Jazz*. These assets were driven first and foremost through *Grease*'s star power: John Travolta, directly after his rise to stardom in *Saturday Night Fever* (1977); pop star Olivia Newton-John; and, to attract an older audience, a host of media stars evoking the film's period of the '50s, including Frankie Avalon, Ed "Kookie" Byrnes, Eve Arden, and Sid Caesar. Of these media icons, Travolta was the most significant. Indeed, he was perhaps the industry's hottest star at that time. With *Grease* released only six months after *Fever*'s debut, the association with *Saturday Night Fever* was fresh. In addition, with a recent nomination as Best Actor, Travolta was validated critically.

The mixture of elements within the star "package" explains the rationale behind *Grease*'s marketing formula, which could be articulated as

Marketing through star power: John Travolta and Olivia Newton-John (Grease, Paramount, 1978).

Frankie Avalon in the Beauty School Dropout number: tapping an older audience segment (Grease, Paramount, 1978). Copyright © MCMLXXVII by Paramount Pictures Corporation.

a focus both on the young, drawn to Travolta and the subject of teen romance/music, and on the older audience segments, drawn to the nostalgia. Critic David Ansen identified this double focus in commenting, "The success of *Grease* with teen audiences, who often dance on their seats as if at a concert, can have little to do with '50s nostalgia. The movie, like *Saturday Night Fever* before it, is a Dionysian celebration of middle-class values."[1] Each element of the marketing package served this formula of young and old. For instance, the merchandising—T-shirts, tie-in novels, posters—normally reserved for the young, also attempted to appeal to an older crowd. "Remember the music, the gang, the feeling? *Grease* is Paramount Pictures' smash hit musical that captures the life and times of the '50s. . . . You can share in the nostalgia too!" enthused a merchandising insert to the double-album soundtrack. The nostalgia suggested in the promo extended to the soundtrack, which included several songs by retro-'50s band Sha-Na-Na, along with

"Love Is a Many Splendored Thing" and "Look at Me, I'm Sandra Dee" (an icon certainly lost on the youth of 1978). The hit singles from the film, such as "You're the One That I Want" and "Hopelessly Devoted to You," however, had a "contemporary" '70s sound, and were, in fact, added to the original Broadway score for the film. Both decades coalesced in the new theme "Grease," sung by Franki Valli, and written and produced by Barry Gibb of the Bee Gees, the most popular group at the time, thanks to their disco songs in *Saturday Night Fever*. The mix between old and new even influenced the visual style of the film, with director Randal Kleiser commenting at the time of the release, "Stylistically, the actors will stop and break into song — that's old — but we are using all the '70s film techniques we can muster, like split screens and high-powered sound."[2]

In addition to the stars, the music, and the merchandising, *Grease* also had the marketing advantage of being a pre-sold property, based on the long-running musical (playing a run of 3,388 performances on Broadway).[3] The film's producers, Robert Stigwood and Allan Carr, discarded half of the "strictly '50s" Broadway score, choosing to entice a younger crowd to the film.[4] In a move that certainly enhanced the film's marketability, the dialogue in the sometimes rough theatrical musical also was pared down, and the setting moved from the urban inner city to a more innocuous Southern California locale. The result was a Disney-like musical with the traditional "bad guys" (i.e., the hoods and greasers) as heroes.

Finally, the film was represented throughout the media — in the one-sheet, soundtrack, novelizations, trailer, and other marketing forms — with an identifiable logo: a small car containing the word "GREASE" written in a fluid, grease-like style. The logo served to identify the film visually in large part since the marketers were consistent in using this logo at every possible opportunity. All these marketing assets permitted a wide opening, at that time, of 902 theaters and a strong opening weekend gross of $9.31 million. The film continued to play very well across the summer, eventually garnering rentals to Paramount of $96.3 million.[5]

On the other hand, *All That Jazz*, while still ostensibly a musical, could hardly be described as having the same marketing assets as *Grease*. Bob Fosse's film borrowed heavily from the art cinema, particularly Fellini's 8½ (1963), to tell the strongly autobiographical tale of an over-committed director whose personal and professional lives are derailed by a series of heart attacks, culminating in the director-protagonist's death. Such a "difficult" subject seems unlikely fare for a musical and, indeed, the film clearly was interested in examining and deconstructing

Roy Scheider as Fosse-like choreographer Joe Gideon and Bob Fosse, co-author, director, and choreographer of All That Jazz *(All That Jazz, Twentieth Century Fox and Columbia, 1979).*

this genre.[6] Richard Dyer's analysis of Fosse's first film, *Sweet Charity*, aptly summarizes Fosse's approach in *All That Jazz*: "[*Sweet Charity*] uses every trick in the cinematic book to embody the musical qualities of rhythm, melody and tone, and uses its total visual, aural, and choreographic musicality to express a cynically wise view of the limitations of the musical genre."[7] *All That Jazz* actually inverted several cornerstones of the musical, including the movement toward unification and community within the world of the film musical.

Fosse was clearly aware of the manner in which his film strayed from the traditional genre and, in fact, he stated at the time of release, "It doesn't fit into any category. You can like it or not like it, but it isn't a copy of anything else, and I'm proud of that."[8] The commercial implications of "not fitting into any category" were numerous. Even during production, the financial risk of the film scared the distributor, Columbia, to the extent that a co-distributor, Twentieth Century–Fox, was added when Fosse exceeded his original budget by more than $4 million.[9] Both distributors understandably were concerned, since the film had low marketability. While leading actor Roy Scheider had appeared

*Low marketability and deconstruction of the musical genre (*All That Jazz, Twentieth Century–Fox and Columbia, 1979). Copyright © 1979 20th Century–Fox Film).*

in financially successful films, such as *The French Connection* and *Jaws*, his name alone certainly could not "open" a film at the boxoffice. Apart from the lack of star power, the diverse themes and complex narrative defied translation into a simple marketing approach. Indeed, the one-sheet for the film lacked a focus: the graphic showed the film's title in lights and the copy offered variations on the theme, "All that . . ." (All that work. All that glitter. All that pain. All that love. All that crazy rhythm. All that jazz.) The ad is problematic, since it conveys little about the film's plot in its attempts to suggest the diversity of the film. Tellingly, the novelization released in conjunction with the film used a different title graphic and copy ("What makes Joe Gideon dance? Power, sex, and . . . All That Jazz"), thereby breaking continuity in the marketing and public identification with the film. In terms of the soundtrack, the film featured standards such as "Bye, Bye, Love" and "After You're Gone," hardly marketable in the age of the Bee Gees and disco. Consequently, the film had no marketing hooks, except for its high quality credentials which would place the film commercially into the marginalized "art house" category. As Fosse biographer Kevin Boyd Grubb commented on the commercial performance of the film, "Not surprisingly, *All That Jazz* fared better with European audiences and critics than it did in America."[10] Even classic musical fans could be alienated by the film's generic deconstruction, not to mention the frank language, nudity, and suggestiveness.

Whereas *All That Jazz* was produced despite the lack of inherent marketing opportunities, *Grease*, with its target of young and old, could be defined by its marketing possibilities. The latter film's marketing hooks are numerous and strong. In addition, the dependence of *Grease* on marketing through stars, a pre-sold property, music, merchandising, and a single image has become increasingly significant as a marketing approach. This approach can be succinctly described in a "pitch" or a one-line concept: "John Travolta and Olivia Newton-John star as the '50s greaser and the 'good girl' in the screen adaptation of the hit stage musical *Grease*." In contrast, the disparate themes and complexity of *All That Jazz* cannot be reduced readily to a concept or a single ad-line.

These differences might be articulated by describing *Grease* as a relatively high concept project, while *All That Jazz* would fall into the low concept category. This classification offers an entry point into an understanding of a significant focus for mainstream studio motion picture production. The term "high concept" originated in the television and film industries, but it was soon adopted by the popular presses, who seized the term as an indictment of Hollywood's privileging those films which seemed most likely to reap huge dollars at the boxoffice. Clearly the studios *are* most interested in those films with an increased likelihood of a solid return, and high concept has been used as one catch phrase to describe any number of commercial projects. I propose to offer a more precise definition of high concept through tracing the historical, institutional, and economic forces which have helped to shape this particular kind of commercial filmmaking. Through an awareness of these forces, high concept can be considered as a form of differentiated product within the mainstream film industry. This differentiation occurs in two major ways: through an emphasis on style within the films, and through an integration with marketing and merchandising.

Positing high concept as a kind or style of filmmaking in the contemporary film industry has implications for understanding not only the determinants of commercial filmmaking, but also film historiography. Indeed, in terms of film history, the period of "classical Hollywood" is marked by the mature studio system and a style of filmmaking centered on continuity; however, the traits of the "post-classical" period (i.e., after the postwar disintegration of the studio system and the concurrent rise of television) have been suggested, but not formalized. Most frequently, a "post-classical" period is aligned with the "New Hollywood" of the '60s and '70s, a period characterized by auteurs and the media conglomeration of the film industry. High concept can be considered as one central development—and perhaps *the* central development—within post-classical cinema, a style of filmmaking molded by economic and institutional forces. Through high concept, the diverse manner through which economics and aesthetics are joined together can be understood, and even appreciated, at one particular time in American film history.

The Entertainment Industries on High Concept

According to the folklore of the entertainment industry, high concept as a term was first associated with Barry Diller, during his tenure in the early 1970s as a programming executive at ABC.[11] Diller received much credit for bolstering the network's poor ratings, partly through the introduction of the made-for-television movie format.[12] Since Diller needed stories which could be easily summarized for a thirty-second television spot, he approved those projects which could be sold in a single sentence. This sentence would then appear in the advertising spots and in *TV Guide* synopses. The result produced television movies, like *Brian's Song* (1971) and *That Certain Summer* (1972), whose themes and appeal were immediately obvious. Thus the demand for a marketable theme or plot became associated with the term high concept.

Instead of crediting Diller, Disney president Jeffrey Katzenberg, on the other hand, attributes the term *high concept* to Michael Eisner.[13] According to Katzenberg, Eisner used high concept while working as a creative executive at Paramount to describe a unique idea whose originality could be conveyed briefly. Similarly, Columbia Pictures Entertainment President Peter Guber defines high concept in narrative terms. Rather than stressing the uniqueness of the idea, Guber states that high concept can be understood as a narrative which is very straightforward, easily communicated, and easily comprehended.[14]

The emphasis on narrative as the driving force behind high concept masks another aspect to the usage of the term within both the film and television industries.[15] While the idea must be easily communicated and summarized, the concept must also be marketable in two significant ways: through the initial "pitch" for the project, and through the marketing, the "pitch" to the public. Clearly there are many films which might be summarized briefly, yet which would not be described as high concept within the film industry. Consider, for example, the concepts

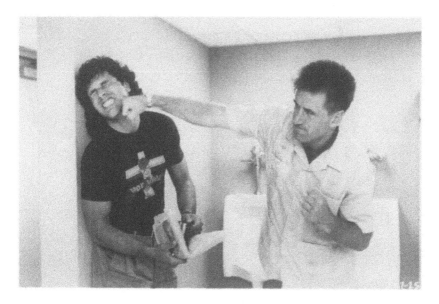

Miami Blues: *a concept lacking broad-based appeal* (Miami Blues, Orion, 1990). *Photo by Zade Rosenthal,* © *1990 Orion Pictures Corporation.*

which might be used to pitch *Everybody's All American* (1988: a football star and his glamorous wife face the difficulties of life after the fame fades), *Shirley Valentine* (1989: bored housewife starts a new life by running away to Greece), or *Miami Blues* (1990: charismatic, yet psychopathic, ex-con impersonates a detective to pull off some heists). All three films suggest concepts which lack broad marketability through being too limited in audience appeal: *Shirley Valentine* and *Everybody's All American* would appeal primarily to an older audience segment (particularly mature females), while *Miami Blues* lacks broad-based appeal since it is not substantively different from other cop television shows and films.

Indeed, the connection between marketability and high concept seems to be very strong in the entertainment industries. Brandon Stoddard, president of ABC Entertainment, suggests that a one-sentence high concept is nothing more than the ad line that would show up in a marketing campaign.[16] Former Columbia Pictures president Dawn Steel also stresses a simple, marketable theme as central to high concept: "[The movie business in 1978] was all about capturing the spirit of the times with high-concept pictures geared to the youth audience—movies

Everybody's All American: *the dramatic and domestic problems for a couple after the fame has vanished (*Everybody's All American, *Warner Bros., 1988). Copyright © 1988 Warner Bros. Inc.*

whose themes could be explained in a sentence or two. These were movies like *Saturday Night Fever* that were, as they were called at the time, critic-proof, so that they could bypass all the old ways of thinking.''[17] Following this premise, those films which are high concept could be matched by marketing campaigns that accurately represent their content, while marketing for low concept films would be more problematic, since the marketing, which inevitably operates through a reduction of the film's narrative, misrepresents the film as a whole.

Star power is one way through which a project might develop a broader marketability. In fact, another aspect of high concept within the industry is the linkage of a star's persona with a concept; for example, Clint Eastwood in a crime thriller implies a high concept project. As a qualification to this principle, it is not always true that a star ensures that a project will be high concept. When a star's persona is directly linked with a genre and the project under consideration adheres to this genre, then the film generally falls into the high concept category. For example, Clint Eastwood and Charlie Sheen as a seasoned cop and trainee in *The Rookie* (1990) would undoubtedly be described as high concept, while Clint Eastwood as an eccentric and obsessive film director in Africa in *White Hunter, Black Heart* (1990) would not. As a condition of this principle, a star working directly *against* his image may also suggest high concept. For instance, consider the possibilities of tough guy Arnold Schwarzenegger as the tooth fairy as described in this

Star power and high concept: Clint Eastwood and Charlie Sheen in The Rookie *(The Rookie, Warner Bros., 1990). Copyright © 1990 Warner Bros. Inc.*

announcement from *Variety*: "Norman Lear's Act III Communications and Columbia Pictures are developing *Sweet Tooth*, a so-called high-concept comedy, as a starring vehicle for Arnold Schwarzenegger. Schwarzenegger is being primed to play the tooth fairy in the script crafted over the past two years by writer Holly Sloan — with input from Lear — for Act III Communications."[18]

Following a similar line of argument, Diana Widom, former Senior Vice-President of Publicity and Promotion at Paramount Pictures, defines high concept through star persona with her description of a fictitious film based on this concept: "Eddie Murphy (as Axel Foley) meets Prince Charles." The juxtaposition of Murphy with royalty immediately sets up a series of oppositions which define the concept: the difference between rich and poor, America and Britain, black and white, brazen and reserved. All these oppositions develop from the simple one-line concept. Also, as the example indicates, the concept places a familiar, commercial element — in this case, a star working within his genre (comedy) — in a slightly altered context. This play of familiarity and difference seems essential to many definitions of high concept.

A final aspect to the usage of the term high concept is the tendency to describe such projects as dealing with timely or fashionable subjects. Since high concept often describes the most commercial type of film, the term necessarily has become connected to projects which offer subject matter "in vogue." This factor sometimes results in cycles of films which deal with similar high concepts. Consider, for example, the consecutive releases of *Raising Arizona* (1987), *Three Men and a Baby* (1987), *Baby Boom* (1987), and *She's Having a Baby* (1988) which led critics to label the trend combining yuppies and babies as high concept. Alternately, the "switching bodies" films (*Like Father, Like Son* [1987], *Vice Versa* [1987], *Big* [1988], *Dream a Little Dream* [1989]) have been treated as variations on a single high concept. A clear example of a film whose concept depends upon a trendy issue would be the John Travolta/Jamie Lee Curtis film *Perfect* in 1985. Seizing upon the health club phenomenon of the early 1980s, the film was motivated almost entirely by the notion that health clubs have become the new singles bars. However, as Stuart Byron and Anne Thompson astutely comment, the film is also a perfect example of a "dated-concept movie," since the fashionable subject had been completely exhausted through news and the popular presses by the time of the film's release.[19]

Therefore, within the film and television industries, high concept most frequently is associated with narrative and, in particular, a form of narrative which is highly marketable. This marketability might be based upon stars, the match between a star and a premise, or a subject matter which is fashionable. In practice, the locus of this marketability and concept in the contemporary industry is the "pitch." In fact, in order to pitch a project succinctly the film must be high concept; consider Steven Spielberg's comment: "If a person can tell me the idea in 25 words or less, it's going to make a pretty good movie. I like ideas, especially movie ideas, that you can hold in your hand."[20] Spielberg's opinion relates well to the vision of high concept expressed by other Hollywood representatives: a striking, easily reducible narrative which also offers a high degree of marketability.

The Critics on High Concept

Although narrative is still a focus, high concept suggests another set of meanings to the popular presses and analysts of Hollywood. These meanings are summarized aptly by Richard Schickel, who points out that with the term high concept, "high" is actually a misnomer: "What the phrase really means is that the concept is so low it can be summarized and sold on the basis of a single sentence."[21] During the past decade, high concept has appeared with ever increasing frequency in the popular discourses of the industry: trade journals such as *Variety, The Hollywood Reporter, Boxoffice, Paul Kagan* newsletters, and the entertainment sections of leading news magazines. Frequently the term is used as ammunition in an indictment against the contemporary industry, suggesting a bankruptcy of creativity within Hollywood. Whereas creative executives such as Katzenberg would stress the originality of a high concept idea, media critics would suggest that high concept actually represents the zero point of creativity.

As opposed to developing new ideas, critics describe high concept as relying heavily upon the replication and combination of previously successful narratives. In the extreme, critics describe high concept films as merely combinations of other films; the *Los Angeles Times*, for instance, presented a High Concept Match Game in which *RoboCop* was defined as *Terminator* meets *Dirty Harry* and *Harry and the Hendersons* as *Gentle Ben* meets *E.T.*[22] To a lesser extent, this replication can involve "revitalizing" past successes through a star or shift in emphasis. At the time of release for *Flashdance* (1983), Jon Peters remarked that he was certain of the boxoffice success of the film since *Flashdance* was, in essence, a *Rocky* (1976) for women.[23] Of course, this replication and recombination has a strong economic motive: audiences have a point of reference for the new film due to their familiarity with the other sources. A film recombining other financially successful films possesses built-in marketing hooks. This privileging of the marketing apparatus is viewed by the media as Hollywood focusing on commerce rather than art, placing an emphasis on marketable stories rather than "original" stories.

Consequently, critics describe high concept as Hollywood crassly privileging business over any consideration of creativity or artistic expression. While some critics sympathetically attribute high concept to concerns of fiscal responsibility and accountability, the majority simply utilize the term to denigrate contemporary Hollywood.[24] In fact, the term has gained such a negative connotation that high concept is often associated with the most sensationalist material. Consider critic Michael Wilmington's condemnation of the term in his review of *Nice Girls Don't Explode* (1987): "In an era of witless, tasteless high concepts, the one in *Nice Girls Don't Explode* ought to be eligible for some kind of award: maybe the Golden Bomb as *Terms of Endearment* collides with *Carrie*."[25]

Inherent in the media's usage of the term is the importance of not just summarizing, but also selling the film through the concept. In fact, Timothy Noah foregrounds this aspect in his definition of high concept: "The 'high concept' approach is favored by the seller—say, a producer trying to convince a studio to put up money for his movie—because it renders a proposal misunderstanding-proof. High concept proposals are by definition easily grasped by the studio executives on the run and, further down the road, by the movie audiences, who are given only a week or two from a film's opening to determine whether it will stay in theaters."[26] This "shorthand" form of communication between industry and audience occurs through the marketing of the high concept, which is aided by the simplicity and directness of the concept. Consequently, these films are designed to be sold; as critic Owen Gleiberman describes in his review of the John Goodman film *King Ralph* (1991), "This is the sort of high-concept comedy in which the jokes seem to have been designed primarily for use in the film's trailer."[27]

The understanding of high concept among the media critics actually parallels usage within the industry in many respects. Both the critics and the industry "practitioners" emphasize marketing and narrative in their definitions of high concept. But whereas the industry focuses on the uniqueness and originality of the concept, the media critics stress its creative bankruptcy. In effect, the industry utilizes high concept in a prescriptive manner—one "rule" toward a financially successful project—while the media uses the term in an evaluative sense, with high concept inevitably synonymous with being aesthetically suspect or tainted. Undoubtably as a reaction to the negative connotation of high concept within the media, the creative community of Hollywood distances itself, in a self-serving manner, from all projects which might be termed high concept. In a 1987 article about the development of United Artists, Jack Matthews states that "eighteen months ago, UA executives were talking about making high concept films that can be made with fiscal responsibility." Pointedly, Matthews claims that (now former) United Artists chairman Tony Thomopolous talks less about concepts ("It's *High Noon* in outer space"), and more about executing good stories.[28] One studio production executive, who wished to remain anonymous, recalled that the term *high concept* had been used frequently within the industry in the early 1980s, but has since been seized upon and utilized in a pejorative manner by critics: "People are amused by the algebra and vocabulary of the industry. 'High concept' is now used by some effete critic to describe a movie he doesn't like."[29]

Economics, Aesthetics, and High Concept as "Post" Classical Cinema

At the most basic level, high concept can be considered as one result of the tension between the economics and aesthetics on which commercial studio filmmaking is based. All mainstream Hollywood filmmaking is economically oriented, through the minimization of production cost and maximization of potential boxoffice revenue. However, the connection between economics and high concept is particularly strong, since high concept appears to be the most market-driven type of film being produced. This relation can be conceptualized in two different forms. First, as Douglas Gomery and Robert Allen suggest, production practices within the film industry are influenced by shifts in the industrial structure of Hollywood. Gomery and Allen describe the relationship between an industrial mode of production (i.e., the methods through which the human, technological, and aesthetic "raw materials" are transformed into film) and the cultural product, film, in the following terms: "Each mode of production produces its own set of production practices: normative conceptions of how a particular kind of film 'should' look and sound."[30] Historically, as the forces forming the mode of production change across time, so does the product of film, privileging a certain "look and sound" within filmmaking. This new "look and sound" is evident in the style of the high concept picture. Second, the relation between economics and high concept exists at the level of marketing: the high concept film is designed to maximize marketability and, consequently, the economic potential at the boxoffice. This marketability is based upon such factors as stars, the match between a star and a project, a pre-sold premise (such as a remake or adaptation of a best-selling novel), and a concept which taps into a national trend or sentiment.

This relationship between economics and aesthetics, which I am positing as integral to an understanding of high concept, also possesses an important temporal dimension. High concept can be considered as a style of filmmaking which developed at a particular point in the history of postwar Hollywood. More specifically, high concept represents one strand of post-classical Hollywood cinema: a style with strong ties to the classical cinema, yet with some significant deviations in terms of composition. Theories of the classical Hollywood cinema have been a significant recent development in the field of film studies, and film scholars have utilized many different methodological and theoretical approaches to the subject. Certainly one of the most influential approaches has been the work of David Bordwell, Janet Staiger, and Kristin Thompson, who develop classical Hollywood cinema as a particular stylistic system with clear economic and aesthetic determinants.[31] Characterizing the style of classic filmmaking as the result of several interconnecting causal factors, the authors are able to provide a substantial argument for the classical Hollywood cinema as a period with distinct breaks from primitive cinema. Understandably, given their focus, Bordwell, Staiger, and Thompson do not consider the influence of economic and institutional changes since 1960 — many of which have irrevocably altered the forms of product from Hollywood. High concept addresses how these economic and institutional changes — including the conglomeration of the film industry and the rise of television, new marketing methods, and changing distribution strategies — have extended and modified some significant traits of the classical model.

Micro- and Macro-Analysis: Style, Marketing, and Differentiation of Product

The analysis of high concept will begin at the "micro" level of the film, isolating and identifying the traits of the high concept film. The abstracted images which are the basis for the extensive marketing campaigns are derived, at least partially, from the unique style of the high concept films. This style becomes codified across successive films, so that one can identify the ways in which the style offers several modifications from the classical Hollywood cinema. More specifically this style is based upon two major components: a simplification of character and narrative, and a strong match between image and music soundtrack throughout the film. In the high concept film, the narrative frequently is composed of stock situations firmly set within the bounds of genre and viewer expectation. In fact, with the high concept film, one can see the movement of the narrative from the single-sentence concept. So, for example, *"Top Gun* (1986) in race cars" aptly describes the narrative trajectory of *Days of Thunder* (1990): the concept encapsulizes the establishment, animation, intensification, and resolution of the plot structure, as well as the star, the style, and genre of the film.[32] Conversely, a description for a film which is not high concept fails to offer a fair representation of the narrative trajectory. *Terms of Endearment* (1983) could be described as "the turbulent, but loving, relationship between a mother and daughter across three decades," but this concept fails to offer the viewer a sense of the film's overall narrative development. Consequently, the film cannot be captured by a single image through the marketing campaign in a manner similar to the selling of the high concept films.

Perhaps the most important component of this style is the relation of the image to the soundtrack, since frequently a major portion of these films is composed of extended montages which are, in effect, music video sequences. These musical sequences serve as modular set pieces which fragment the narrative. The soundtrack also accompanies a set of formal techniques which often hamper or actually halt the narrative progression: these techniques include extreme backlighting, a minimal (often almost black-and-white) color scheme, a predominance of reflected images and a tendency toward settings of high technology and industrial design. Consider just one of the "modules" from *Flashdance*: Jennifer Beals and Michael Nouri wandering hand-in-hand through an abandoned railway yard set against the song "Lady, Lady, Lady." The song matches the action only in its romantic mood, and the image of the striking couple in the perfectly lit industrial wasteland encourages a contemplation completely unconnected to the ostensible narrative. This tendency is bolstered also by the superficial narrative and characters. In some cases, the style of the productions seems to seep through onto the narrative; issues of style or image become crucial to the functioning of the characters and the development of the narrative. Consider, for example, the importance of style in performance to *Flashdance*, style in aviation to *Top Gun*, or personal style to *American Gigolo* (1980). The narrative of each film relies on style in order to progress: Alex's unique dancing style places her outside the world of both the strip clubs and the ballet, Maverick's renegade flying style causes his disciplinary problems with his superiors in *Top Gun*, and Julian Kay's choice of clothes and image separates him from all the other gigolos in Los Angeles. Furthermore, the reliance on bold images in the films reinforces the extraction of these images from the film for the film's marketing and merchandising. The reduced narrative and emphasis upon style, which often has a potent visual representation, permit, even en-

*Style in the narrative, style in the production
(*Flashdance, *Paramount, 1983). Copyright
© MCMLXXXIII by Paramount Pictures
Corporation.*

courage, the extensive reproduction of these key images from the film in mass marketing.

If high concept can be described as a style of filmmaking at a particular point in film history, there are causal mechanisms creating and demarcating this period. The larger structural changes within the industry—such as conglomeration, the development of new technologies, and the rise in marketing and merchandising—operate to privilege films which can be summarized and sold in a single sentence. These structural changes one-by-one cannot be assigned causation of the high concept films, however. While these changes can be correlated with the development of high concept, high concept as a style of filmmaking is created by myriad forces, including important aesthetic ties to the classical cinema. Perhaps it is best to consider high concept as only one aesthetic and economic way in which cinema has developed after the classical period.

The analysis of the aesthetic qualities of high concept leads into the larger "macro" factors molding this style of filmmaking. At the broadest macro-level, the high concept film has been influenced greatly by changes in the marketplace for film during the past twenty years. An examination of the reconfigured marketplace anchors my investigation of high concept. Following one of the basic tenets of industrial organization theory, firm behavior is affected by market structure. Therefore, as Gomery and Allen demonstrate, the film "product" invariably is shaped by the changing marketplace in which it is produced and consumed. High concept is definitely connected to two forces which have shaped the market for film powerfully in recent years: the development of new media (such as home video and cable) and the concurrent ownership changes within the film industry. These forces have minimized the boundaries between economic agents and their separate domains, splintering the marketplace for film. Two of the principal methods through which the most successful studios have responded to the changing marketplace have been the differentiation of product and the entry into the market created by new delivery systems. High concept can be seen as one of the major forms of product differentiation within the current industry. By producing high concept films, studios have been able to identify and exploit particular market segments. In this fashion, the changing economic parameters of the marketplace have helped to configure the high concept film.

High concept functions as a form of differentiated product primarily through two routes: through an integration with marketing and merchandising and through an emphasis on style. The connection between high concept and marketing begins at the level of the pitch. Recall that a pitch for a high concept product should be summed up and sold in a single sentence. The emphasis on marketing also extends through the entry of the film into the marketplace: the high concept films are accompanied by strikingly graphic print and television advertising campaigns, with many films also accompanied by merchandised product derived from the film. High concept films lend themselves to merchandising and marketing by their abstraction of a key image from the film (e.g., the hot rod forming the *Grease* logo) and through the manipulation of this image to extend the "shelf life" of the motion picture. The image, which is replicated through the advertising materials and product tie-ins, can be seen as the expression of the most commercial elements of the high concept film.

In addition to the reliance on striking images and their replication in marketing and merchandising (product tie-in) campaigns, other innovations in marketing blossomed at the same time as high concept. Consider, for example, the movement toward saturation releases utilizing television commercials, the widespread adoption of marketing research as a pre- and post-production tool, and the utilization of music soundtracks as a primary marketing focus. All these marketing methods became common practice throughout the 1970s and '80s, correlating with the development of high concept. Again, *Grease* can be seen as a paradigm for the marketing possibilities offered through high concept—the wide (and successful) opening of *Grease* was completely dependent on the strong marketing potential built into the film. It is impossible to overestimate the importance of marketing to the operation of high concept. High concept films, which could be described as the most market-driven projects in Hollywood, are narrated as much by their marketing as by their ostensible story. In this regard, Janet Staiger and Barbara Klinger have offered persuasive arguments for the importance of promotion (which includes both marketing and merchandising) to the content, style, and reception of the Hollywood film.[33] The relationship which they posit among promotion, the film text, and reception would seem to be even more pivotal to the market-driven high concept films.

Since high concept films are conceived as highly marketable, one might wonder about the actual commercial performance of these films within the marketplace. After my investigation of the marketing strategies in the high concept films and their impact upon the films' reception, the links between this commercial style of filmmaking and their actual popularity at the boxoffice will be investigated. A statistical model accounting for boxoffice revenue will be developed, with an eye toward explaining the commercial success or failure of the high concept films. This project also reflects the increased role that market research (including forecasting) has played in the contemporary film industry, a factor which reinforces the development of high concept. Barry Litman's study, "Predicting Success of Theatrical Movies: New Empirical Evidence," offers a model for such an analysis.[34] As part of this analysis, the relationship between boxoffice revenue and the subset of films fitting the criteria for high concept will be analyzed. Given their marketability and the reliance upon past successes, it is probable that the high concept films would be more popular than other films. In addition, given their modularity and "recycled" quality, statistical modeling, based upon coding the film into several constitutive variables, might be able to predict their boxoffice performance with more precision than that for the "low concept" films. If high concept functions as product differentiation, as I have posited, the financial success or failure of this differentiation in the actual marketplace is a significant aspect of high concept in practice to be accounted for.

"The Look, the Hook, and the Book"

High concept can be conceived, therefore, as a product differentiated through the emphasis on style in production and through the integration of the film with its marketing.

Table 1. The Spectrum of High Concept

This table lists some examples of high concept, that is, films which illustrate allegiance to one or more traits ("the look, the hook, and the book") of high concept. This is not intended to offer an exhaustive accounting of all high concept films over the past three decades, but rather merely a suggestion of the diverse set of films which could be supported as high concept.

Jaws (1975)
The Omen (1976)
King Kong (1976)
Star Wars (1977)
The Deep (1977)
Saturday Night Fever (1977)
Grease (1978)
Superman (1978)
The Main Event (1979)
The Jerk (1980)
The Blues Brothers (1980)
Caddyshack (1980)
The Empire Strikes Back (1980)
Urban Cowboy (1980)
American Gigolo (1980)
Flash Gordon (1980)
Superman II (1981)
Endless Love (1981)
Thief (1981)
Cat People (1982)
Star Trek II: The Wrath of Khan (1982)
E.T. the Extra-Terrestrial (1982)
Blue Thunder (1983)
Flashdance (1983)
Return of the Jedi (1983)
Trading Places (1984)
Staying Alive (1984)
Indiana Jones/Temple Doom (1984)
The Terminator (1984)
The Natural (1984)
The Keep (1984)
Footloose (1984)
Reckless (1984)
Thief of Hearts (1984)
Purple Rain (1984)
Streets of Fire (1984)
Gremlins (1984)
Beverly Hills Cop (1984)
Ghostbusters (1984)
St. Elmo's Fire (1985)
Commando (1985)

Mad Max beyond Thunderdome (1985)
Weird Science (1985)
To Live and Die in L.A. (1985)
9½ Weeks (1986)
Quicksilver (1986)
The Fly (1986)
American Anthem (1986)
Manhunter (1986)
Howard the Duck (1986)
Pretty in Pink (1986)
Ferris Bueller's Day Off (1986)
Ruthless People (1986)
Top Gun (1986)
The Lost Boys (1987)
Dragnet (1987)
The Witches of Eastwick (1987)
Mannequin (1987)
The Untouchables (1987)
Fatal Attraction (1987)
Beverly Hills Cop II (1987)
Cocktail (1988)
D.O.A. (1988)
Twins (1988)
Coming to America (1988)
Black Rain (1989)
Batman (1989)
Harlem Nights (1989)
Days of Thunder (1990)
Flatliners (1990)
The Hunt for Red October (1990)
Dick Tracy (1990)
Pretty Woman (1990)
Total Recall (1990)
Another 48 Hrs. (1990)
Kindergarten Cop (1990)
Hook (1991)
Robin Hood: Prince of Thieves (1991)
The Addams Family (1991)
Wayne's World (1992)
Batman Returns (1992)

This definition encompasses several aspects of high concept; to gather these aspects together in an appropriately high concept fashion, one can think of high concept as comprising "the look, the hook, and the book." The look of the images, the marketing hooks, and the reduced narratives form the cornerstones of high concept. High concept can be described most fruitfully as a spectrum based upon these three parameters: all Hollywood films fall along the scale, some falling toward the low end of the spectrum (the low concept films), while some fall toward the high end of the spectrum (the high concept films). Few films would actually fall at either end of the spectrum—either purely low concept or purely high concept. Following from this model, films could be classified more accurately in relative, rather than absolute, terms: for example, although both projects are star-driven, the straightforward comedy *Coming to America* (1988) is more high concept than the darkly comic satire *The War of the Roses* (1989).

The attempt to construct this model of high concept should neither be viewed as an academic spin on the critics' condemnation of commercial filmmaking, nor as an attempt to glorify the popular. Rather, the project addresses the initially curious supposition that *Grease*, along with *Jaws* (1975), *Star Wars* (1977), and *Saturday Night Fever*, is of much greater significance to American film history than the critically and institutionally recognized films of the period, such as *All That Jazz*, *Network* (1976), *One Flew over the Cuckoo's Nest* (1975), and *Kramer vs. Kramer* (1979). While this statement may alarm "canon" builders already periodizing the last three decades of American film, I believe that through understanding the commercial recipe and economic determinants of a film like *Grease*, one can gain a true appreciation of the contemporary landscape of American film—a landscape which has nurtured and privileged the high concept film.

2 Construction of the Image and the High Concept Style

High concept films are differentiated within the marketplace through an emphasis on style and through an integration with their marketing. These two factors are not mutually exclusive. The tie between marketing and high concept is centered on a concept which is marketable (i.e., that contains an exploitable premise or pre-sold properties, such as stars). The marketability of the concept must possess a *visual* form, presentable in television spots, trailers, and print ads. The high concept films therefore depend upon the visual representation of their marketable concepts in advertising. Advertising is key to the commercial success of these films through representing the marketable concepts of the films, but, more basically, advertising as a medium of expression is fundamental to the very construction of the high concept films. Indeed, the style of the films reflects, in many respects, the graphic design and print layouts associated with contemporary consumer goods advertising.

By style, I am referring to the usage of techniques within the film that become characteristic of the film. Extending the common usage of the term, which relates to cinematic techniques and capabilities, I am also including as style those elements within the film (such as stars and music) which are central to the film's operation (and marketing). Style is a defining characteristic of high concept, and its importance to an understanding of both the aesthetics and economics behind these films cannot be overestimated. The style shared within high concept cuts across a wide range of genres. In this manner, the high concept style parallels the conception of *film noir* as a style of filmmaking evident not just in the crime or gangster genres, but also in the melodrama or the musical.[1] The high concept style has several components: a high concept "look" (through the production design and cinematography), stars, music, music tie-ins, character, and genre all form patterns in the high concept films. While every film exhibits aspects of the style, it is rare for *all* traits of the style to be present in a single film. Generally, the aspects of the style foregrounded in the film depend on how the style can be integrated into the marketing and merchandising. For instance, a light comedy-drama driven by its star (e.g., *Cocktail* [1988], with Tom Cruise) foregrounds the mix of star and music within the film, which can then be exploited through music videos and advertising. On the other hand, the science-fiction thriller *The Terminator* (1984) benefits more through stressing the film's high concept look, the genre narrative, and the visually striking Arnold Schwarzenegger.

This chapter examines the construction of the high concept style through an analysis of the style's five major elements: the high concept "look," stars, music, character, and genre. The juxtaposition of these components occasionally "exceeds" the narrative of the film, leading to moments which seem excessive given the story's development. These are the moments which tend to be extracted and used for advertising due to their striking aesthetic quality. Since each of the style's components is ultimately driven by the film's marketing, before an analysis of the high concept style, I will consider the diverse ways through which advertising has influenced this style of filmmaking.

Advertising as an Influence on Style

With the marketable properties of the high concept films, the films already have a certain pre-sold identity, such as "the new thriller starring Clint Eastwood" or "the new action-adventure from Steven Spielberg." The function of advertising is to establish this identity with the public by the time of opening. The pre-sold nature of high concept permits an advertising approach which frequently utilizes simple and graphically striking image and copy; the simplicity of the ad aids recall by the moviegoer. In advertising terms, many of the high concept campaigns follow the design specifications of corporate communications, in which the designer seeks to create and maintain consistent identities across advertising campaigns for corporations.[2] The designer fulfills this task through economical and unadorned graphics, sometimes with an accent which suggests movement or change. Consider the many striking graphic representations of high concept: the laser bars which form the word "ALIEN" set against a throbbing futuristic egg, say, or the extraordinary campaigns for the John Hughes films which depend on the title matched with a simple logo. The Hughes campaigns even seek to define the films on a secondary level, reducing *Ferris Bueller's Day Off* (1986) to "FBDO" or *Some Kind of Wonderful* (1987) to "SKOW" in print ads through replicating a distinctive graphic design and logo from the ad campaign.

If the advertising campaigns for the high concept films might be described as graphically bold and stylish, these qualities reflect the content of the actual films. Indeed, style is central to many of the high concept films. To be more precise regarding the function of this style, recall Stuart Ewen's description of style as a social factor: "We see that style is about beautiful, mouth-watering surfaces, but we see more. Beyond displaying surfaces, the uninterrupted message of the television programme is that style makes up a way of life, a utopian way of life."[3] Ewen's analysis is especially apt for considering the high concept films. On the one hand, high concept can be identified through the surface appearance of the films: a high-tech visual style and production design which are self-conscious to the extent that the physical perfection of the films' visuals sometimes "freezes" the narrative in its tracks. Matching the surface perfection of the films' style, these films also privilege style as a way of life; many of the high concept films are driven by the style exhibited by the characters as each moves through the narrative. This style exemplifies a lifestyle, an approach to life, or "a way of life," in Ewen's terms, which, while not utopian perhaps, certainly replicates the superior, upscale lifestyles promised in many ads.

Fashion layouts and ads are designed to manipulate the consumer into buying not just a product, but also a lifestyle into which the product permits entry. This slippage from the selling of a product to the selling of a lifestyle depends, in part, on the physical perfection of the ad images — a perfection which encourages an appreciation beyond its organization around a particular product. Consider Janet Bergstrom's "reading" of a Calvin Klein ad which examines three androgynous models (two male, one female) strewn across a bed.[4] Bergstrom demonstrates that the image encourages multiple interpretations. Focusing on the image within the ad, the colors, textures, and design suggest a lifestyle centered on sexual attraction and seduction. Even further, it is important to note that the ad powerfully underlines Bergstrom's attempt to trace the development of androgyny in the contemporary media. Associated with this reading of the image, the models of the ad function inherently as models of behavior. The models live in the imaginary world constructed by the fashion and advertising industries. Especially considering the lack of copy directly advertising the product, the ad more potently suggests a way of living rather than how a product might change one's life.

"You've Got the Look": Perfect Images in High Concept

These qualities of the advertising image — the physical perfection, the attempt to sell both a product and a lifestyle — parallel the style of the high concept films. The connection between the style of the films and the style of advertising is not coincidental, however. Many of the directors most often associated with this high-tech style (e.g., Adrian Lyne, Ridley Scott, Tony Scott, and Hugh Hudson) began their careers directing television commercials, with many working in Europe, where television advertising often guides mass and popular culture.[5] The impact of these advertising-oriented directors on high concept is most significant. Consider, for example, the career of Tony Scott. After directing television commercials in partnership with brother Ridley, Tony Scott directed *The Hunger* (1983), a horror movie set in contemporary New York about vampirism and immortality starring Catherine Deneuve, Susan Sarandon, and David Bowie. This one-line synopsis seems woefully inadequate, however, to convey an impression of the film, since the movie actually functions as a combination of visually arresting images which overwhelm their narrative function. Appropriately, perhaps, Howard Kissel of the fashion magazine *Women's Wear Daily* sensed that the film's narrative was actually a slave to these images: "Tony Scott's *The Hunger* is supposed to be about such themes as death, immortality, violence and love, but it's really about art direction — the way blood looks splattered elegantly against a page of music; the way Catherine Deneuve's face looks lit from underneath by flames; the way a very fine lens can capture a tear moving slowly down her cheek; the way David Bowie and Susan Sarandon can be photographed to resemble each other; the way Sarandon can be reflected on the smooth surface of an immaculately polished pay phone."[6]

Considering the commercial failure of *The Hunger*, it is somewhat surprising that Scott was assigned by producers Don Simpson and Jerry Bruckheimer to direct the big-budget, high-profile *Top Gun*. Simpson and Bruckheimer's choice was motivated by their conception of the film in primarily visual terms. After seeing photos in *California* magazine showing supersonic aerial combat at the Miramar Naval Air Station, the producers decided to develop a motion picture to match the images of the jets and flyboys in combat.[7] For Bruckheimer and Simpson, Scott's visual style in *The Hunger* and his background in television advertising made him a logical choice to direct *Top Gun*.

The Hunger: *Catherine Deneuve and David Bowie . . . "It's really about art direction"* (The Hunger, *MGM/UA, 1983*).

The appropriation and adaptation of advertising aesthetics by film-makers create moments within the film which seem to work against the developing story, encouraging an appreciation for the film's formal composition. This tendency could be described in terms of "excess" within the film. Following Kristin Thompson's conception of the term, style is composed of techniques which are repeated and become characteristic of the film, whereas excess can be understood as those techniques which do not form specific patterns across the film.[8] While style tends to be justified by the viewer through understanding the film as the work of an artist—or, to use Thompson's term, through compositional motivation — excess cannot be reconciled in a similar manner. Excess implies a gap in the motivation of the work.[9]

On the level of formal composition, the high concept films are linked by a set of production techniques composed of extreme backlighting, a minimal (often almost black-and-white) color scheme, a predominance of reflected images, and a tendency toward settings of high technology and industrial design. At times, these techniques combine to freeze the narrative, creating an excess within the film. Consider, for example, the opening of *Flashdance*. The credits are set against the Irene Cara song "Flashdance . . . What a Feeling," which conveys a vaguely inspirational message, telling the viewer "to take your passion and make it happen." In addition, the song initiates the situation of Alex (Jennifer Beals) using her dancing to change her life, as the lyrics describe, "now I'm dancing for my life." The song plays over the image of a young woman, Alex, cycling along a bridge in long shot. Just as the song segues into a hard-driving instrumental backbeat, the scene cuts to a construction yard — although the location is hardly recognizable as such due to the extreme backlighting which extends the shadows of the figures within the frame and which creates high contrast in the images within the frame. In fact, the entire scene of industrial machinery, construction site, and workers appears to be black-and-white, except for the occasional red warning lights on the periphery of the frame. The look of the scene makes an everyday, banal sight aesthetically pleasing or at least aesthetically striking. This transformation is, at first, disorienting, causing the viewer to contemplate the strangeness of the image, rather than how the image fits into the developing story.

This type of image — aesthetically bold, often in a setting of high technology or industry — can be located through many of the high concept films. For instance, images in the thriller *Flatliners* (1990) fulfill a function similar to the one from *Flashdance*. The film, which is centered on a group of medical students inducing and experiencing near-death experiences, places much of the major action in a cavernous building undergoing construction, supposedly close to the medical school on campus. The huge building is largely bare — except for its gothic architecture and abandoned ornamentation, such as the large, sculpted head of a goddess. Light enters through windows cut like slits, creating intense backlighting reminiscent of *Flashdance*. The lighting is manipulated to create a black (or dark blue) and white scheme for all action in this building. The image is accompanied by a heavenly choir on the soundtrack. The effect of the lighting, production design, and soundtrack is to create an other-worldly environment appropriate for the "flatlining" medical students (a reference to the steady line on the EKG

The university building setting for the Flatliners *experiments: stylized and formal (* Flatliners, Columbia, 1990). Copyright © 1990
Columbia Pictures Industries, Inc.

showing the onset of death). Compared to the realistic depiction of the students' living environments, the scenes shot in the medical experimentation room seem stylized and formal. These scenes are excessive, since the look of the operating room sequences overwhelms their narrative function. In a fashion similar to *Flashdance, Flatliners* aestheticizes the environment through its "excessive" images.

Both of the environments in these scenes—the construction site and the renovated medical building—illustrate the allegiance of the high concept films to settings of high technology. The high concept films tend toward sleek, modern environments mirroring the post-industrial age through austere and reflective surfaces. Consider the high-tech dance club Mawby's in *Flashdance*, the spare, white apartment owned by Kiefer Sutherland in *Flatliners*, the conservative, monochromatic business worlds of *9½ Weeks* (1986), *Baby Boom* (1987), and *Wall Street* (1987), the Rodeo Drive art world of *Beverly Hills Cop* (1984), and the neon-drenched apartments and renovated warehouses turned into young yuppie homes in *St. Elmo's Fire* (1985).[10] The environments function also on the level of style within the narrative, with the modern architecture and interiors most frequently associated with urban, upwardly mobile characters.

A sleek, visually stunning "look" alone does not suggest that a film is high concept, however. While the look may aid the film's representation through the advertising, a look cannot sell a film if separated from the other aspects of high concept. Indeed, the image of the film must be connected to a concept that is marketable and exploitable. Two commercial "experiments" with strikingly different looks illuminate this lesson. Francis Coppola's *One from the Heart* (1982) offers Las Vegas completely re-created in all its neon splendor on Coppola's Zoetrope soundstages. This "Las Vegas of the mind," as described by former Zoetrope executive Lucy Fisher, depended on an elaborate theatricality in constructing an environment overwhelmed by sensuous colors, flashing lights, and neon.[11] Clearly Coppola's revival of the artificial mise-en-scene associated with classic musicals distinguished his film at the time of release. Still, the film did not foreground any other assets that could be marketed: the romantic plot was routine, the major players were not stars, but character actors, and the soundtrack was done by the commercial mismatch of gravelly voiced Tom Waits and country siren Crystal Gayle.

Although hardly utilizing a high concept look, Warren Beatty's *Dick Tracy* (1990), like Coppola's film, was also marked by an eye-catching look, inspired by its comic book source. The film's controlled color scheme and artificial sets were derived from the comic book source:

"Encouraged by Beatty to stick to the vibrant primary colors of the Sunday comic pages, costume designer [Milena] Canonero proposed that the movie's entire palette be restricted to red, yellow, orange, blue, green, fuchsia, purple, cyan, black and white."[12] Unlike *One from the Heart*, though, the look of Beatty's film is augmented by several strong marketing hooks: the comic book property, stars (Beatty, Madonna, Al Pacino, and guest cameos), and a coordinated merchandising campaign (including the release of three albums associated with the film). The result is a high concept film which is marketable primarily due to factors other than the look of the film.

Stars and Style

Apart from the formal composition, other factors within the high concept films, particularly pre-sold aspects, also generate excess within the films. Perhaps the most significant pre-sold property from a commercial standpoint is the human capital, the star, which is attached to a project. Economically, stardom can be conceived as the patent on a unique set of individual human characteristics. These characteristics would include purely physical aspects, with many stars defined first and foremost through their beauty. The uniqueness of the star can similarly motivate moments which are excessive within the films.

Consider Jack Nicholson's function in the high concept *Batman* (1989). While Nicholson's persona need not overwhelm a film (recall his understated supporting performance as Eugene O'Neill in *Reds* [1981] or his naturalistic performance in *The Border* [1982]), many of the more recent Nicholson performances operate in just the opposite direction. To a certain extent, Nicholson's star persona is the iconoclast, the nonconformist whose energy and mischievousness are infectious and appealing. While this image was formed in the 1960s and 1970s in such dramas as *Easy Rider* (1969), *Five Easy Pieces* (1970), *The Last Detail* (1973), *Chinatown* (1974), and *One Flew over the Cuckoo's Nest* (1975), by the 1980s this image had become so established that Nicholson could offer self-parodies in supporting roles in films such as *Terms of Endearment* and, in particular, *The Witches of Eastwick* (1987). *The Shining*, Stanley Kubrick's horror film released in 1980, can be considered as a transition in Nicholson's career in which the tendency toward self-parody begins to undermine a coherent, naturalistic leading performance. Pauline Kael's evaluation of Nicholson in *The Shining* locates this tension between Nicholson as star and Nicholson playing a role: "Nicholson's acting, though, suffers the most, because there are so many shots of him looking diabolic — and so many echoes of his other

*A curious match between Nicholson-as-star and Nicholson-as-character: Jack Nicholson as Jack Napier, the Joker (*Batman, Warner Bros., 1989).

freaks in *Carnal Knowledge* and *The Fortune* and *Goin' South.* . . . The tone of Nicholson's performance seems too grinningly rabid for the movie he's in: axe in hand and slavering, with his tongue darting about in his mouth, he seems to have stumbled in from an old A.I.P. picture."[13] While many scenes are played by Nicholson with a reserved naturalism, his persona fractures the world of the film at other times, suggesting a level of meaning beyond the fictional character. Indeed, the most memorable scene from the film — Nicholson coos "Here's Johnny" while axing down the bathroom door to attack his wife — works primarily due to the humor and self-deprecation associated with Nicholson's "bad boy" persona.

This excessiveness is especially evident in *Batman*, which foregrounds Nicholson's star persona. Recall that Nicholson's character, the Joker, is actually Jack Napier, and thus characters are constantly referring to Nicholson within the film as "Jack." The effect is a curious match between Nicholson-as-star and Nicholson-as-character which maximizes his star status. In the dour, oppressive world of *Batman*, Nicholson destroys the unity of each of his scenes: partly through his garish costuming (mixing purples, blues, and oranges) and his makeup (the permanent smile of his disfigured face as the Joker), but primarily through his broad, ostentatious acting, strongly dependent on gesture, which contrasts dramatically with the more naturalistic performances of the other cast members. This acting style also relies heavily on our identification with Nicholson's star persona, which gives a context to his "bad boy" actions as the Joker.

Typical of Nicholson's appearance in the film is his introduction to Vicki Vale. After arranging to meet Vale at the Gotham City art gallery, Jack and gang arrive, dancing to Prince's "Partyman," defacing the artworks with spray paint. After introducing himself as a "homicidal artist," Jack responds to Vale's questions in an off-the-cuff fashion (e.g., V: "What do you want?" J: "My face on the $1 bill"), utilizing wildly expressive gestures ("What do you know about . . . ," followed by Jack sucking in his cheeks and making small flying motions with his arms, thus referencing Batman). Even for a character named Jack, Nicholson's actions seem too grand, too self-consciously amusing. The encounter is capped with Vale trying to escape from Jack by throwing water in his face; Jack crouches, crying out "I'm melting" like the Wicked Witch in *The Wizard of Oz* (1939).[14] When Vale goes to comfort him, he cries "Boo" and laughs uproariously. While this series of actions would seem wild from any actor, the close fit between Nicholson's star persona, the role of the Joker, and the ostentatious mode of acting ruptures the coherence of the story and character. In the high concept films, therefore, excess may be motivated through the pre-sold elements, such as the stars, as much as through the perfection of the film's composition.

Like Nicholson, certain comedy stars — particularly Bill Murray and Eddie Murphy — function as excess at points within their films by appearing to be detached in a cynical and wry manner from the rest of the film. Murphy's performance in *Beverly Hills Cop* breaks the development of the story at several occasions due to Murphy's extraordinary "transformations." In order to gain access to information, Murphy, playing Detective Axel Foley, assumes strikingly different identities: from an irate *Rolling Stone* reporter to a dedicated floral delivery man to an effeminate gay lover. Each of these transformations is accomplished solely through Murphy's acting: through his speech patterns, gestures, and manner of presentation, rather than through physical disguises. The abruptness with which Murphy assumes each new character, along with the apparently arbitrary choice of persona, serves to break the world of the film. Murphy's performance, composed of these psychological transformations, explodes the banal detective story at these points, taking precedence over any narrative development.

The excess within high concept differs from the heavily coded moments of excess identified within the classical family melodramas from directors such as Douglas Sirk and Nicholas Ray. Consider Ray's 1956 melodrama *Bigger Than Life*, detailing the disastrous effects of a new "wonder drug" (cortisone) on one man and his family. As Ed (James Mason) begins to unravel, the film's style matches his delusions of grandeur. A key scene in which Ed bullies his son while the boy solves a math problem is shot from a very low angle, creating a "bigger than life" image for Ed and a huge shadow which symbolically engulfs the boy. The excess suggested in the image corresponds to the plot and character development in this case. Whereas Sirk and Ray created moments of excess in the visual style which directly related to the repression evidenced in the melodramatic plots, the excess in high concept cannot be reconciled in a similar fashion. Similarly, the style of the high concept films differs from the excessive style of the "New Hollywood" directors, such as Martin Scorsese, Brian De Palma, Steven Spielberg, and Robert Altman. While the new Hollywood directors have been accused of derivative style (e.g., De Palma's appropriation of Hitchcockian narrational devices in *Obsession* [1976] and *Dressed to Kill* [1980]), the style of these directors has been unified and patterned across successive films and, even more significantly, sewn into the fabric of the films' narrative: consider, for instance, Altman's innovative, realistic, and overlapping sound responding directly to the director's desire for verisimilitude in his characters' world.[15]

With high concept, however, the excess fostered by advertising creates films which illustrate the "danger" to traditional classical-realist aesthetics of unmotivated style or excess. Peter Lloyd's description of the 1960s Hollywood protest films (such as *The Strawberry Statement* [1970] and *Medium Cool* [1969]) is certainly applicable in this context: "No engagement with the subject-matter can be possible if the 'style' is directed towards such superficial ends, without any sense of structure or the organic relation of every frame to the total conception of the movie itself."[16] Richard T. Jameson extends Lloyd's position even further, suggesting that excessive style indicates a lack of personal vision on the part of the filmmaker: "No forms have been imposed here, no stylistic tradition invoked to cover for a lack of stylistic conviction on the part of the filmmaker. Style is absolute, personal and direct."[17] Since the excess represented in the high concept films is not driven by a personal vision, the logic of the marketplace is clearly the author of the style. The excess encourages extraction from the film for marketing

The style of Douglas Sirk: James Mason and
Barbara Rush in Bigger Than Life *(*Bigger
Than Life, *Twentieth Century–Fox, 1956).*
Copyright © 1956, 20th Century Fox Film
Corp.

purposes, as is the case with Tony Scott's images in *The Hunger* and *Top Gun*.

Certainly the physical design or "the look" of the film can be viewed as excess which can easily be replicated in the high-tech trailers or television commercials. Similarly, the high concept films are perfect for the publicist: the physical design matched with the characters as models and adherence to genre allow for publicity stills which, on the one hand, are aesthetically striking and, on the other hand, accurately represent the film. Unlike the still for *Ivan the Terrible* (1943) which commands the attention of Roland Barthes with its promise of a "third meaning," a level of discourse beyond the dramatic meaning of the still, the stills from high concept films encourage a singular reading.[18] Consider the posed "glamour" still from *Top Gun* as dark, masculine Tom Cruise strikes a macho pose against a jet, while blonde, voluptuous Kelly McGillis hangs from him. The image encapsulates the sexual dynamics and genre (adventure with romance), both marketing focuses for the film. In a parallel fashion, a still from the *9½ Weeks* press kit also works strongly as a marketing tool through representing the excess within the film: Kim Basinger looking submissively downward, while hiking her lingerie up her thigh and clutching the edge of a wall, which is split into light and dark. The still in its physical perfection and its strong sensuality in the figure of Basinger equals upscale sex; the excess of the film creates a still which could just as easily be "read" as a lingerie ad from an upscale fashion magazine as the representation of a motion picture. As a contrast to the stills from high concept films, consider a still from *The Sheltering Sky* (1990), a film which certainly falls outside the category of high concept due to the lack of marketing hooks and to the complexity of the narrative and its themes. With John Malkovich comforting a weary Debra Winger, the still seems to suggest a myriad number of possible storylines: Winger's haunted look and Malkovich's gaze to the outside suggest a troubled romance, or maybe an attempted seduction or someone helping a sick friend. The ambiguity of the image recalls Barthes's reading of the *Ivan the Terrible* still; unlike the high concept films, a movie such as *The Sheltering Sky* cannot be reduced to a publicity still. The style of this film does not permit its reduction to a tool of marketing.[19]

Music as an Element of Style

While the physical design and stars of the film can be represented visually, with ease, within the marketing, perhaps the most significant element of the high concept films' style for marketing/merchandising purposes is the music within the films.

Sex and genre in publicity (Top Gun, Paramount, 1986).

The commercial applications of music within film (e.g., music video, soundtrack) aid their separation from the rest of the film's elements. As Kristin Thompson suggests, the sound/image relationship, particularly the combination of image and music, is an especially disruptive element to the unity of a film: "Music has a great potential to call attention to its own formal qualities apart from its immediate function in relation to the image track."[20]

The excess of the film: Kim Basinger in 9½ Weeks (9½ Weeks, MGM/UA, 1986). © 1985 Jonesfilm.

*Low concept, ambiguous images: Debra
Winger and John Malkovich in* The Sheltering Sky *(The Sheltering Sky, Warner Bros.,
1990). Copyright © 1990 Warner Bros. Inc.*

In the era of post-classical Hollywood, music has become an increasingly significant marketing focus. As Alexander Doty notes, "Perhaps
Hollywood's growing awareness of a large and monied 'youth market'
finally led industry publicists to fully recognize the potential for music-
and-movie exploitation implicit in the conglomerate entertainment
networks."[21] There are several examples of films after the classical era,
but before high concept, which utilized music within the film and
within the marketing. For instance, *The Graduate* (1967) and *American
Graffiti* (1973) illustrate the different forms of integration between music and film in this period. *The Graduate* offers an amazing juxtaposition
of story and soundtrack so that Simon and Garfunkel's songs (such as
"The Sounds of Silence," "Scarborough Fair," "Mrs. Robinson") not
only comment on the action, but also lead the action through suggesting interpretations of the images. Indeed, the final shots of Ben and
Elaine in the bus, after running from the wedding, suggest a strong
sense of melancholy mainly through "The Sounds of Silence." In this
sense, the songs are integral to the development of the narrative and
the viewer's reception of the film. At the other extreme, *American Graffiti* uses music as a constant background to the main action, without

having songs integrated directly into the story. With forty-one vintage rock songs in the film, most heard on car radios tuned to the Wolfman Jack station, the music is most significant in creating a sense of verisimilitude. Nevertheless, the songs remain largely separate from the narrative, present mainly as an anchor to a specific historical period.

These examples differ from the usage of music in high concept mainly in terms of context. With the high concept films, the music is matched to a marketable concept behind the overall film. In addition, high concept is marked not only by music and a marketable concept, but also by the other traits of the style (i.e., the particular look and the other pre-sold elements, such as stars and narrative with marketing hooks). This configuration of elements distinguishes music in high concept, reinforcing the inherent marketability of placing music in the film which other post-classical films have realized.

The most obvious examples of high concept films driven by music are films such as *Flashdance, Footloose* (1984), *Purple Rain* (1984), *Staying Alive* (1983), and *The Bodyguard* (1992). With these music movies, the excess created by the conjunction of music and image creates a module separate from the narrative, working against the sequential structuring of the film. Due to the importance of music to these films' marketing and merchandising, the songs are presented in a fairly complete manner within the films. The difference between this structuring and the classical musical, which also relies on set pieces separate from the main action, derives from the high concept films' emphasis on frenetic editing, rather than continuous action in a low number of shots, and a lack of dramatic purpose to the musical numbers. In *Flashdance*, the set pieces are centered around Alex dancing: at Mawby's Bar (set to "He's a Dream" and "In the Pocket"), in her apartment ("Maniac"), at the audition ("Flashdance . . . What a Feeling"), and with her friends ("I Love Rock'n'Roll"). The songs may vaguely comment on the narrative (e.g., the theme song), but more often connect to the lifestyle of her friends ("I Love Rock'n'Roll" is an obvious anthem; "Maniac" tells of a "maniac" on the dance floor; "He's a Dream" and "In the Pocket" spin tales of male/female seduction).[22] Significantly, the majority of the songs are only peripherally associated with the film's central enigma (i.e., whether Alex can be successful as a legitimate dancer).

Since *Flashdance* was marketed as a musical, albeit a modern, rock musical, viewers might expect moments of excess, in which characters are able to transcend their mundane circumstances through music and dance as a form of expression. Clearly, in this respect, *Flashdance* is similar to the classical musicals. As Rick Altman points out, the excess within these musicals does become structured almost on a secondary textual level: "Unmotivated events, rhythmic montage, highlighted parallel-ism, overlong spectacles — these are the excesses in the classical narra-tive system that alert us to the existence of a competing logic, a second voice."[23] So, in some ways, the excess of the music and production "modules" can be reconciled by the viewer's previous experience read-ing musicals.

Many high concept films cannot appeal to the musical genre as an explanation for their excess. Indeed, some high concept films utilize music without being typed generically as musicals. The relationship of the soundtrack to the image is different in these cases, compared to the musical set pieces, since the viewer still tries to follow the narrative, despite the excess suggested by the music. In these cases, the music is not patterned throughout the film, but rather acts as an explosion which only momentarily disturbs the equilibrium of the film. Such mu-sical "explosions" are present in many post-classical Hollywood films — both high and low concept — across the decades; consider *The Black-board Jungle* (1955), *Easy Rider* (1969), *Coming Home* (1978), *The Big Chill* (1983), and *My Own Private Idaho* (1991). However, the high concept films tend to privilege these moments to a greater extent than other post-classical Hollywood films; recall significant musical scenes, repli-cated in the selling of the films, from such high concept movies as *Bat-man*, *Pretty Woman* (1990), *Risky Business* (1983), *Cocktail* (1988), and *Wayne's World* (1992).

The songs frequently occur in the openings of films, either over the credits or over the first scenes. Narrative information is usually highly concentrated in these opening moments regardless; as David Bordwell comments, "Credit sequences are very important narrational gestures. These extra fictional passages usually present information in a highly self-conscious and omniscient fashion."[24] Paul Schrader's *American Gigolo* (1980) offers a textbook example of this strategy. Basically the first scenes of the film illustrate the day-to-day existence of Julian Kay (Richard Gere), a high-priced gigolo in Los Angeles. Set against the song "Call Me" by Blondie, the scenes become resonant: shots of Gere driv-ing in his Mercedes, buying clothes, and escorting older women are energized through the synthesized Giorgio Moroder/Blondie song, with lyrics that could be interpreted as the pleas from an admirer of the gigolo. In fact, the lyrics outline the protagonist in detail; the line "you speak the language of love" from the song actually becomes a signifi-cant narrative point, with Julian's command of several languages, in-cluding the language of love, centering his first encounter with the film's heroine Michelle.

Similarly, the credits for *Pretty in Pink* (1986) illustrate the day-to-day existence of the film's heroine, Andie (Molly Ringwald). Against the Psychedelic Furs' "Pretty in Pink," in extreme close-up, Andie dresses and makes-up in the morning. Her clothes, accessories, and sense of style are integral to the development of the plot (these items separate her from the other characters), and the song comments directly on this difference ("Walking around in this dress that she wore"). In sum, in these high concept films, along with others such as *Top Gun, Beverly Hills Cop,* and *Breathless* (1983), music functions to create an excess in the opening, which traditionally has always privileged self-conscious and concentrated narrative information.

Outside the opening, music can reappear in the high concept film in a localized sense: a song accompanies a sequence, with the music creating a distinct sequence in the film. In practice the degree of interaction between the music and the narrative varies from film to film. *Eyes of Laura Mars* (1978), for example, utilizes songs only under the scenes of photographer Laura shooting her violent and sexual images: with two models dressed in lingerie catfighting against two burning cars in the streets of New York, the viewer hears "Burn," by Michalski & Oosterveen, a quasi-punk song describing the beauty of a fire burning. The song, with its anarchic and shrill vocals and rhythm, thus matches the intense visual imagery. Similarly, as Laura sets up an elaborate shoot juxtaposing murder and high fashion, director Irvin Kershner scores the scene with the disco song "Let's All Chant" by the Michael Zager Band. Unlike the previous case, though, the song relates to the images only in a thematic sense: the disco beat and "party" lyrics (consisting of different chants set to the disco rhythm) mirror the high spirits and dancing of the models in the scene.

However, music can be integrated into the narrative in these localized segments, with the song actually breaking the diegesis of the film. Consider Brian De Palma's *Body Double* (1984), a thriller centered around the seamy world of underground pornography. In the middle of the film, the hero, Jake (Craig Wasson), acts in a hardcore movie to meet porno actress Holly Body (Melanie Griffith). After Jake auditions for the role, De Palma cuts directly to Jake standing on the landing of an opulent club. The viewer is left unanchored in space and time given the preceding action. Jake is greeted by a sinister escort—Holly Johnson, the lead singer from Frankie Goes to Hollywood, singing "Relax," a song with thinly veiled sexual connotation. Through the singing, Johnson is able to lure Jake into the club, where Jake is exposed to a wide variety of deviant sexual practices. At the end of the sequence, however, Jake is revealed to be filming a scene from a hardcore video. A motivation for the song and vivid imagery (such as Jake's imagination or hal-

The "Relax" number in Body Double *cul-
minates in Melanie Griffith's seduction of
Craig Wasson (*Body Double, *Columbia,
1984). Copyright © 1984 Columbia Pictures
Industries, Inc.*

lucination) is not offered by De Palma. Indeed, the segment most re-
sembles a music video in its construction.

Beverle Houston, in "Music Video and the Spectator: Television, Ideology and Dream," defines music video as combining performance, a
subordinate narrative, and, most significantly, visual fragmentation dis-

rupting temporal and/or spatial unity.[25] The "Relax" sequence in *Body Double* clearly adheres to this formula. Given Holly Johnson's participation as host, the element of performance is important, while the seduction of Jake in the club forms the nominal narrative, and time/space in the sequence is certainly broken. While the "Relax" video that actually aired on MTV was not this particular clip, De Palma originally intended to use this sequence from the film as the promotional video. Perhaps this factor influenced the actual construction of the clip: the formal elements conspire to separate the video from the rest of the film. The viewer's recognition of the clip as music video represents the most significant form of distancing. Expectations from the sequence are clearly different due to its construction as music video.

In a fashion similar to the "Relax" clip, *Pretty in Pink* also utilizes music within the narrative. Andie's friend Duckie (Jon Cryer) attempts to impress Andie through lip-synching and dancing to "Try a Little Tenderness." Clearly, though, the song has a personal meaning to Duckie, since his "interpretation" involves feverish, hypnotic, and almost acrobatic dancing to the tune. However, the song is anchored in time and space, unlike the *Body Double* example. The intensity of Duckie's interpretation, along with the lack of motivation for the song within the developing story, leads to its separation from the rest of the film. John Hughes, the author of *Pretty in Pink*, clearly has a strong affinity for these sequences within his films: consider Ferris Bueller's lip-synching to "Danke Schoen" and "Twist and Shout" in *Ferris Bueller's Day Off* or John Candy's rendition of "The Flintstones Theme" in *Planes, Trains and Automobiles* (1987).

Excess in High Concept: The Promotional Music Video

If these high concept films are marked by a modularity in design created through an excess in the production, stars, and especially the soundtrack, this modularity is strengthened even further through the "flip side" of the music video sequences within the films: the promotional music videos. These music videos fulfill a double function: to promote the song for album sales (soundtrack or otherwise) and to promote the film which utilizes the song. In performing these functions, the music video usually, in fact, undermines the unity of the film through disintegrating the narrative in certain respects. As Barbara Klinger adroitly comments, the promotional apparati of a film tend to multiply the meanings from the text in order to increase the audience base: "Promotional categories will often tend to diversify the text by addressing several of its elements, including subject matter, stars, and style. But this particular type of inter-textual zone cannot be settled within the textual system; rather, it raids the text for features that can be accentuated and extended within its social appropriation."[26]

Part of this "raiding of the text" involves the fictional world of the high concept film expanding beyond the film and into the promotional music video. This type of cross-referencing is practiced often in television, where characters from one program appear in different programs, creating a "dense textual network," to use Mimi White's description.[27] With the music video, this referencing usually involves creating a space for the music artist through which the artist may "interact" with the fictional characters represented in clips from the film. Consider, for instance, the music video for "Danger Zone" from *Top Gun*. Wearing dark sunglasses, singer Kenny Loggins lies on a bed in a room dominated by the intense backlighting and minimal color scheme so strongly patterned within the film. Loggins acts both as a commentator on the action from the film, in effect "narrating" the flying sequences, and as a musical stand-in or double for star Tom Cruise. More specifically Loggins also encourages a reading of the song in sexual terms; whereas the film plays "Danger Zone" over the opening flying shots, the video connects these shots and other clips to Loggins languorously sprawled across the bed. The effect is to reposition the song, and the viewer's interpretation of the overall film, in sexual terms: the romance between Cruise and Kelly McGillis offers the real "danger zone" for the lead character Maverick.

This cross-referencing sometimes develops beyond merely integrating film clips and singer: Michael Douglas, Kathleen Turner, and Danny DeVito act as backup singers for Billy Ocean in the video "When the Goin' Gets Tough" from *The Jewel of the Nile* (1985); Madonna, the singer, gazes longingly at Madonna, the comedienne/actress, in clips from *Who's That Girl* (1987) in the promotional music video for the film. More elaborate examples of a fictional character's entering the world of the music video occur with the Aretha Franklin video for *Jumpin' Jack Flash* (1986) and the Guns N' Roses video "You Could Be Mine" for *Terminator 2* (1991). Unlike the *Top Gun* video, the fictional characters from both *Jumpin' Jack Flash* and *Terminator 2* actually enter the world of the video. Starting with a chase scene from *Jumpin' Jack Flash*, Whoopi Goldberg seeks refuge in an ominous building. As she enters, the space is revealed to be a studio where Aretha Franklin and Keith Richards are recording the song "Jumpin' Jack Flash." In an attempt to blend into the surroundings, Whoopi acts as one of the backup singers for Franklin. The Guns N' Roses video integrates action clips from the film, the band's performance of the song, and new footage, just for the video, of Arnold Schwarzenegger (as the Terminator) traversing the wild concertgoers to reach Guns N' Roses on the stage. The turn of events in both videos actually illuminates another aspect of the high concept style: the destruction of the diegetic unity through a reconfiguration of the film's narrative in media such as the promotional music video. If the excess within the film seeks to destroy the unity of the filmic system, then this process is strengthened by the extra-diegetic promotion, such as the music video, which reshapes and even reconceives the narrative.

This rewriting of the narrative in the promotional music video follows the economic orientation of the high concept style. Seeking to maximize the audience's points of contact with the film, the promotional material multiplies the possible meanings from the narrative. This multiplication is integral to the long-term maintenance of these films in the marketplace. Indeed, the music video functions not just as an emblem/icon of the film, but also as a method which complicates the narrative. This process seems very much connected to the pleasure associated with repeat viewing of the high concept films, a pleasure based on the play between familiarity (of story, characters, music in the original film) and discovery (of the story, characters, and music as refigured in the promotional music video). The plurality of the text encouraged by the disparity between the music video and the overall film centers this play and encourages a re-reading of the film. Roland Barthes's description of the joy from "re-reading" is especially applicable as an explanation of the method through which the promotional music video encourages a return to the original text: "Re-reading is no longer consumption, but play (that play is the return of the different). If then, a deliberate contradiction in terms, we *immediately* reread the text, it is in order to obtain, as though under the effect of a drug (that of recommencement, of difference), not the *real* text, but a plural text: the same and new." [28] This plurality is multiplied even further in the case of high concept through the contradictory nature of the relationship between the film and its supporting media, such as the promotional music video.

The contradictions in the construction of narrative between music video and film have been noted by, among others, Diane Shoos, Diana George, and Jon Lewis. As Shoos and George demonstrate, the music video for "Take My Breath Away" from *Top Gun* "misrepresents" the narrative through juxtaposing the scene of Charlie (Kelly McGillis) walking into the class to Maverick (Tom Cruise) turning his head, "apparently overcome by her beauty."[29] In fact, this gesture is motivated within the film by Maverick's surprise at Charlie's being his professor after he had attempted to seduce her during the previous night. Similarly, Lewis analyzes the two TV video versions of "When the Doves Cry" from *Purple Rain,* "both of which contain clips from the film and both of which are different from the 'video' of the song as depicted in the film."[30]

This process of rewriting the narrative through the promotional video is presented with the Bryan Ferry video "Kiss and Tell" from the film *Bright Lights, Big City* (1988). Derived from Ferry's solo album *Bete Noire,* the song was appropriated by director James Bridges as the embodiment of the sophisticated New York club scene which is central to both novel and film. Indeed, the music video is designed to stress the connection between song and film: at several points in the video, the lyrics directly represent or comment on clips from the film. Further, the connection of these clips with Ferry singing in an amorphous neon club/recording studio space presents Ferry as the figure of narrational authority, composing the song and, in effect, composing the film which accompanies the song. The connection between song and film is strengthened through several direct references in the lyrics: the opening "Ten cents a dance, it's the only price to pay" is matched to scenes of Jamie (Michael J. Fox) dancing at the New York club Odeon; "Flash photograph; it's the only light you see" is juxtaposed with Jamie's wife Amanda (Phoebe Cates) modeling high fashion clothes while photographers capture her image; "Dreamer–stealer of sighs" accompanies Jamie waking up and rubbing his eyes.

The music video moves forward through the alternation of three separate spaces: Ferry and his band in the ersatz neon studio, three female models dancing to the song in a similar, but separate, location, and the diegetic world of the film *Bright Lights,* which is selectively referenced by the video. The video's particular combination of image and music does, in fact, form a narrative. The lyrics describe a particularly jaded romanticism in which love is treated as an exchange akin to money ("Money talks — it never lies. Kiss and tell, give and take — eye for an eye"). Illustrating these lyrics, the clips from the film present the apparently fast-paced, nocturnal activities of the protagonist Jamie. We see the various women with whom he becomes romantically involved, shots of Jamie drinking, dancing, and roaming the "big city" of the film's title.

The second half of the video focuses on Jamie and Amanda, identified in the film, but not in the video, as his estranged wife. Amanda's

Filmic narrative vs. music video narrative
(Bright Lights, Big City, United Artists,
1988).

career as a model is mirrored in the video through cutting her scenes to
the anonymous models posing in the neon recording studio space. The
Jamie/Amanda scenes are derived from the few encounters between the
two in the film; in particular, the scenes of Jamie climbing onstage to
be near Amanda and of his subsequent rage in the bathroom are con-

nected in the video, suggesting cause and effect. Even further, the video includes in this section a scene from the film in which Amanda nonchalantly greets Jamie after he has spent weeks trying to see her. Jamie's reaction in the film is disbelief and outrage, he berates Amanda loudly. The video concludes with a playful amorous encounter between Jamie and Amanda, followed by a scene of Jamie hailing a cab — returning to the big city after his romantic liaison.

The narrative suggested by the music video — a series of romantic encounters dominated by the Jamie/Amanda coupling set against the New York club scene — offers a movement toward happiness and a romantic union. This movement is clearly a radical alteration of the filmic narrative, which concludes with the final separation of Jamie and Amanda and the suggestion that Jamie will leave the New York club world. This deviation is solidified not just through reordering the clips from the film, but also through joining shots within scenes which alter the entire meaning of the scenes. For example, the shot of Amanda greeting Jamie at the party is matched with a shot of Jamie raising his eyebrows and smiling impishly. The latter shot actually occurs in an earlier lunch scene; the music video elides Jamie's exasperated reaction with Amanda, which acts as a climax in the film. In effect, through the montage, the music video restructures the narrative of the film. For those viewers who have seen the film, this restructuring impacts the reading of the original narrative — multiplying the possible meanings and levels of interpretation — and thereby serves to further fracture the unity of the film. For those who have not yet seen the film, the restructuring suggests a "reading" of the film which is not in consonance with the actual filmic narrative.

Of course, other promotional media support for film, such as the soundtrack album and the tie-in novelizations, function to encourage multiple readings in a fashion similar to the promotional music video. The appropriation of the film clips within the promotional music video creates a potent force in destabilizing the unity of the film. A more recent tendency in some high concept films operates just as forcibly in rewriting the filmic narrative: soundtrack albums which include music not within the film, but rather "inspired" by the film. Consider the implications for the reception of two films definitely within the category of high concept: *Batman* and *Dick Tracy*. In both cases, separate soundtracks were issued: one including primarily the instrumental score, the other centered around a music artist associated with the project (Prince for *Batman*, Madonna for *Dick Tracy*).

With the Prince album for *Batman*, only two songs of nine were featured within the film ("Batdance" and "Partyman").[31] The remainder

Jack leads *"Partyman"* in Batman *(Batman, Warner Bros., 1989). © 1989 DC Comics Inc.*

of the songs on the album were inspired by characters and situations within the film. The tie between film and song is fostered by Prince's attributing each song to a particular character within the liner notes. For example, "Partyman" has "lead vocal by the Joker," while "Lemon Crush" has "lead vocal by Vicki Vale," although both are obviously sung by Prince. Prince creates a fresh narrative which operates in a fashion parallel to the basic narrative of the film (i.e., Batman saving Gotham City and Vicki Vale from the evil Joker). Just as the film opens with the decayed urban environment of Gotham City, the album opens with "The Future" detailing a similar bleak world ("I've seen the future/ And boy it's rough"). The album continues with songs describing the Joker's dementia ("Electric Chair"), the developing romance between Batman and Vicki ("Vicki Waiting," "Lemon Crush," "Scandalous"), and the Joker's attempts both to destroy Batman and gain control of Vicki ("Trust," "Partyman"). The effect of these songs is to resituate the original narrative of the film from the perspective of Prince's pop persona, emphasizing the style and sexuality of the characters, rather than focusing on the adventure and action in the filmic narrative. Similar to the promotional music video, this resituation possesses a strong economic motive based on multiplying possible points of connection with the film.

Similarly, the Madonna album for *Dick Tracy* includes only three songs from the film ("Sooner or Later," "More," and "What Can You Lose"). The remaining songs are predominantly novelty numbers matching the late-'30s period of the film; some of these songs relate to the characters within the film, others seem unconnected. For instance, "He's a Man," describing a tough guy in romance and crime-fighting, could easily be read as a description of Tracy himself, while "Cry Baby," with Madonna affecting a Betty Boop voice telling of her wimpish boyfriend, seems separate from the film. In songs like "Cry Baby," along with "Hanky Panky" and "I'm Going Bananas," Madonna creates cartoonlike characters which complement the characters within the strip and film *Dick Tracy*. While Madonna succinctly presents the romance between Breathless Mahoney (her character in the film) and Tracy in many of the songs, her Betty Boop and Carmen Miranda characterizations derail the narrative of the film, creating another set of female characters largely based on the concept of female desire. In this fashion, the

Madonna as Breathless Mahoney, and as many other characters on her album for Dick Tracy *(Dick Tracy, Disney, 1990).*

Dick Tracy soundtrack offers an even more radical shift than the Prince soundtrack in terms of destabilizing the reception of the original film.[32] In addition to this structure of parallel narratives, both soundtracks further undermine the diegetic narrative through sampling—i.e., the excerpting and rearranging of "found" sounds on records.[33] Indeed, Prince's "Batdance" is composed largely of samples from the film. The Joker's catch phrases—"Ever dance with the devil in the pale moonlight?" "Stop the press" "I got a live one here"—are "stolen" from the film by Prince, repeated throughout the song, and juxtaposed to phrases from Batman and Vicki Vale. Prince orchestrates the song, responding to the samples and interacting with the characters. For example, to the phrase "She is great, isn't she?", which Bruce Wayne says to his butler Alfred about Vicki Vale, Prince responds in "Batdance," "Ooh yeah, ooh yeah/I wanna bust that body." Similarly, in "Now I'm Following You" from the Madonna album, Madonna samples several distress calls for Tracy (e.g., "Come in, Tracy/Do you read me, Tracy"), to which the singer responds. To be expected, perhaps, given her persona, Madonna also offers endless samples on the word "dick" in the song. The samples in both songs clearly influence readings of the filmic narrative, with the words and phrases of the samples becoming overdetermined within the films. The stress on these words and the varied manipulations offered through the samples become another force encouraging excess within the narrative of the film.

The effect of these promotional forces on the structuring of the narrative extends beyond the "re-narrativizing" posited by Barbara Klinger, in which specific textual elements are placed within other narratives; indeed, the film and promotional music video are clearly interdependent in terms of narrative.[34] This interdependence derives from the modularity within the film, which allows the music video, functioning as excess, to be extracted and marketed. This modularity is bolstered even further in high concept by the restructuring of the narrative in the music video and related promotional material. The inclusion of these elements in a consideration of "reading" the high concept film text places this activity in territory much closer to theories governing the reception of television. Recall that terms such as distraction, interruption, and fragmentation have been utilized by, among others, Tania Modleski, John Fiske, and Raymond Williams to describe the act of watching television.[35] If the reception of these films encourages a distracted state of reception, the distraction is driven less by the social situation of the moviegoer than by the media structures creating contradictory sets of meanings within a text while working toward the same economic goal of maximizing profit.

The High Concept Image: Character Types and Genre

The perfection of the image and soundtrack within the high concept films is matched by characters presented strongly as "types": defined through a small number of characteristics, with physical appearance most significant to the definition of the characters. While Hollywood has always privileged the presentation of clearly definable, consistent characters, high concept relies even more strongly than previous Hollywood films upon character typing, rather than character exposition. This tendency also responds to the orientation of the high concept films in advertising terms: the characters within these films are offered frequently as models, selling the film and, more significantly, the lifestyle to which the film offers entry.

Consider, for example, the lead characters J. C. Wiatt (Diane Keaton) and Doc Cooper (Sam Shepard) in *Baby Boom*. The film opens with a voice-over narration by Linda Ellerbee concerning the plight of the high-powered working woman (dual commitments in home and workplace, new role models and new equality) which leads into a description of the fanatical schedule of investment banker J. C. Wiatt. In this way, the film's heroine is aligned clearly with the larger social category of "the working woman" who must sacrifice her personal life to her career. Of course, the film also constructs J. C. as the result of all the socially imposed constraints of the working woman. In an early scene in which she is given a promotion while being warned that a working woman "can't have it all" (meaning a successful marriage, family, and career), J. C. replies that she "doesn't want it all." This slippage continues throughout the film, with a social "type" being most significant as a way of defining the character. Secondarily, J. C. Wiatt is also aligned strongly with New York—the fast paced, big-city life which accompanies a leading business career. The movement of the plot is driven by this typing of the lead character: the trouble created for a driven urban working woman by a baby and a relocation to the country moves the plot forward. Similarly, the character of Doc Cooper is defined almost entirely by his country-style, small-town characteristics. Indeed, the contrast between the rural, rustic doctor and the curt, sophisticated urban business woman motivates the second half of the plot. The film, therefore, operates to construct its lead characters as types, embodying certain lifestyle choices which will be immediately obvious to the viewer.

Star persona reinforces this character typage by limiting the boundaries between which a character may be defined. Stars are, to some extent, predicated on style—a particular set of physical characteristics,

Character typing: Diane Keaton in Baby Boom *(Baby Boom, United Artists, 1987).*

demeanor, and attitude. This emphasis often overwhelms the character being portrayed so that the character is identified more strongly with the star than as an integral part of a unique story. Stardom, which has such a strong economic basis regardless, further encourages the movement to character typing. Consider, for instance, the brothers portrayed in *Twins* (1988). The film is centered around the difference between the two genetically engineered twins. The vast majority of the action, however, is centered solely around the *physical* difference between the twins, a factor reinforced by the casting of Danny DeVito and Arnold Schwarzenegger. The physical size and persona (DeVito: smart ass; Schwarzenegger: tough guy) of each actor and the stark difference between the two motivate the humor and narrative action in the film. The physical contrast between the two, especially given their fraternal relationship, dovetailed with the marketing for the film, with the ads featuring Schwarzenegger identified as DeVito and DeVito as Schwarzenegger with the tag line of two brothers so identical "even their mother can't tell them apart."[36] Again the lines between marketing, star persona, and character become blurred, with the economic motive driving this erosion of boundaries and the traditional development of character.

The movement toward character types has been fostered also through generic transformation. Considering that genre can be conceived as a pre-sold property and basis for the viewer's identification, high concept relies very heavily on a familiarity with genre. With the development of the genre film from classical to revisionist forms, generic iconography has been utilized increasingly as an "economical" means of transmitting information. While part of the result of this generic transformation is the placement of generic icons in altered contexts offering burlesque, as John Cawelti suggests, within the genre films themselves, characters and other icons can be telegraphed with broader and broader brush strokes. Walter Hill's *Streets of Fire* (1984) offers a clear example of this strategy. Hill's film places specific western and *film noir* genre conventions and characters in a purposely vague new wave world (the film opens with the title card, "Another time, another place").[37] The film constructs a veritable catalogue of generic characters: from the stoic western hero, his wild and free-spirited girl, the "good girl" back home, to the grizzled and jaded sidekick. Little motivation is offered for any of the characters, apart from their physical appearance and generic typology.

This tendency is replicated in several of the Sylvester Stallone films. Stallone is adept at locating specific generic icons and placing them in slightly altered contemporary contexts. Apart from the *Rocky* and *Rambo* series, the Stallone-directed high concept *Staying Alive* strongly functions through an increased reliance on intertextual motivation. In this sequel to *Saturday Night Fever*, Tony Manero (John Travolta) attempts to juggle two romantic relationships while pursuing his dream of being a Broadway dancer. Reworking the "understudy gets a big break" plotline from *42nd Street* (1933), Stallone recasts this theme in terms of the *Rocky* vision of redemption through physical perfection. The mixture of these two generic plotlines allows Stallone to utilize specific generic characters with little development: the hungry, naive dancer, his steadfast girl back home, and the exotic vamp who tempts him. While these types are instantly recognizable as derivative of standard musical-drama characters, Stallone then reformulates the characters through *Rocky*: Tony is equated with Rocky Balboa, Jackie (Cynthia Rhodes) follows Adrian, and the exotic otherness of villains Apollo Creed and Mr. T can be found in the British vamp Laura (Finola Hughes). The process is astutely described by Nick Roddick as "the latest stage in Sylvester Stallone's quest to remake American cinema in his own image."[38] Of course, the other textual level to *Staying Alive* is its status as a sequel so that, at the very least, Tony and his family are already developed as characters.

Similarly, *Reckless* (1984) operates as a teen rebellion film offering the misunderstood tough guy Rourke (Aidan Quinn) and the constrained middle class girl Tracey (Daryl Hannah) attracted to him. The character types are so familiar, from *Rebel without a Cause* (1955) and *The Wild One* (1954) down through *Saturday Night Fever* and *Grease*, that the film can present the lead characters with little explanation of motivation or desire. Indeed, in one of the only scenes devoted to character exposition, when questioned on "what he wants to get out of life," Rourke responds, "More." Given the strong generic roots of the character, such an explanation is enough for the audience. While both *Streets of Fire* and *Reckless* received little attention, either critically or at the boxoffice, many financially successful high concept films, such as *Top Gun, The Untouchables* (1987), and *Sixteen Candles* (1984), utilize a similar form of character typage.

The lack of character development in the high concept films leads to a greater investment in the physical aspects of the characters, including their appearance and demeanor. Indeed, many high concept films foreground the importance of style to the lead characters and their definition. *Flashdance* offers a strong example of this tendency. Indicative of this form of character (non)development is the scene of foreman Nick meeting Alex. Alex is listening to her Sony Walkman and reading French *Vogue*. When Nick questions her about reading the French fashion magazine, she replies, "I just look at the pictures." Similarly, the film constructs Alex primarily as a model, with a focus on her outward appearance and style. Indeed, Alex's wardrobe of baggy sweats and industrial fatigues became a fashion staple in the mid-1980s.[39] Alex is also defined through her dancing style: flashdancing. This dance style falls somewhere between stripping and breakdancing and was conceived originally as representative of a new dance craze. As screenwriter Joe Eszterhas recounts, though, the flashdance style actually had to be created for the film: "We tracked it [the dance style] to Toronto, and, in fact, flashdancing didn't exist. There was one girl in a Toronto club who did a stylized kind of stripping, but that was all. Paramount thought it was a phenomenon sweeping the country."[40]

Similarly, *American Gigolo* also offers a paradigm for this form of one-dimensional stylish characterization. A gigolo, whose livelihood depends upon his style and demeanor, would, of course, lend himself to this mode of character construction. Most striking, however, is how the major characters exist in a void, with little motivation or background. Director Paul Schrader severely limits an explanation of Julian's background; one learns only that he lived in Europe at one time and that he was previously employed by Madame Anne. Instead of character motivation or exposition, Schrader offers several scenes displaying the importance of style to Julian: Julian matching shirts, suits, and ties from his wardrobe; Julian appraising antiques at an auction; Julian charming women by speaking French; and Julian being groomed and manicured. Even within the film's ostensible "mystery" plot, the investigating police detective is defined in terms of style: a lengthy scene between Julian and Detective Sunday is centered on Sunday's lack of fashion sense, with Julian eventually giving him tips on style and fashion.

Consider how significant style is to the lead characters of such high concept films as *Cocktail* (Tom Cruise redefines style in bartending with his daring, spinning-in-the-air liquor bottles), *Planes, Trains and Automobiles* (based upon the difference in manner and demeanor between upscale executive Steve Martin and blue-collar salesman John Candy), *Less Than Zero* (1987; offering an image of the Beverly Hills teens years before *90210*), and *Pretty Woman* (with the plot centered on the physical transformation of Julia Roberts, supposedly also transforming the character from hooker to Beverly Hills companion). The characters in these films, as in the majority of high concept films, really function as (fashion) models — constituted through a look, an image, and a walk before the movie camera instead of before fashion photographers.

Another factor within high concept working against character development is the system of referencing which structures many high concept films. Foregrounding their existence as film, these high concept

*Style and character definition: Richard Gere
as the American gigolo (American Gigolo,
Paramount, 1980). Copyright © MCMLXXX
by Paramount Pictures Corporation.*

films offer a vast network of references to other films, television shows, and forms of mass media. This self-conscious referencing occurs in many contemporary films; this tendency, identified as intertextuality, has been associated frequently with postmodern texts.[41] While some of these works could be classified outside the boundaries of high concept (e.g., David Lynch's referencing in *Blue Velvet* [1986], the television series *Twin Peaks* [1990], and *Wild at Heart* [1990]), high concept relies more heavily on this intertextuality from an economic standpoint due to the audience's point of recognition. These references function as a "shorthand" method of transmitting information.[42] Since the core moviegoing public share a common body of media knowledge, filmmakers have been able to appropriate this knowledge in the construction of narrative and character.

Perhaps the most striking usage of this referencing system occurs in the John Hughes oeuvre, particularly with *Sixteen Candles, Ferris Bueller's Day Off, She's Having a Baby* (1988), and *Home Alone* (1990). Most significantly, Hughes constructs his characters as products of the mass media;

their lives and experiences are both formed and filtered through the mass media. A character such as Ferris Bueller offers the end point of this tendency, with the character defined almost entirely by his taste in music (Bryan Ferry, MTV, John Lennon and the Beatles, New Order, 10,000 Maniacs) and his references to television and movies (*Alien* [1979], *Dirty Harry* [1971], and *I Dream of Jeannie*). Hughes reinforces the media-oriented world through placing various popular movie theme songs in the film. For instance, a low-angle shot of a Ferrari speeding across Chicago is scored to the *Star Wars* theme, while "villain" Ed Rooney is set to the Inspector Clouseau *Pink Panther* theme during his investigation of Ferris. By using the media as reference points for the characters, Hughes is able to sketch the characters in very broad strokes. Characters' motivations are explained, at least partially, through this intertextual referencing. The result is a leveling of the psychology of the characters and diminishment of real-life motivational forces behind their actions.[43]

Director Etienne Chatiliez's comment — "To sell a car you have to sell

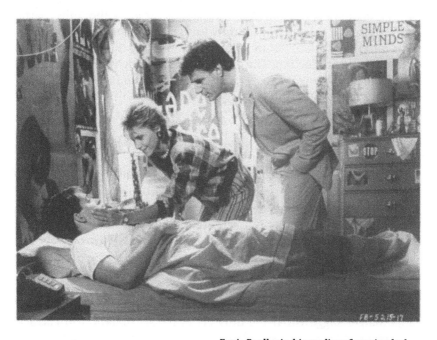

*Ferris Bueller in his media-referencing bedroom (*Ferris Bueller's Day Off, Paramount, 1986*). Copyright © 1986 by Paramount Pictures Corporation.*

a form of existence" — applies just as readily to high concept as to auto sales.⁴⁴ The cumulative effect of the films' physical look, stars, music, and devalued characters is to offer the viewer an entry point into a lifestyle, in much the same manner as lifestyles are suggested by advertising. Indeed, high concept's basis in advertising fosters this suggestion of a method of living for the viewer. In addition, the emphasis on style in the construction of the characters also frequently embodies a certain lifestyle advocated by the film. For instance, high concept films such as *St. Elmo's Fire*, *9½ Weeks*, and *Fatal Attraction*, through the style of the production and the characters within the narrative, offer visions of various lifestyles (e.g., prosperous East Coast college grads, high-tech New York banker, and upscale modern family life, respectively).

The particular configuration of "excess" on the one hand, and drained characters and genre on the other, suggests the manner in which high concept differs from other mainstream Hollywood films. Perhaps the most striking result of the high concept style is a weakening of identification with character and narrative. The modularity of the films' units, added to the one-dimensional quality of the characters, distances the viewer from the traditional task of reading the films' narrative. In place of this identification with narrative, the viewer becomes sewn into the "surface" of the film, contemplating the style of the narrative and the production. The excess created through such channels as the production design, stars, music, and promotional apparati, all of which are so important to high concept, enhances this appreciation of the films' surface qualities.

Style, Classical Hollywood, and the Art Cinema

From an economic perspective, the high concept style is a form of product differentiation connected to the rise of industry conglomeration. Indeed, the many connections in high concept between style and marketing no doubt, on some level, appeal to the conglomerates eager to maximize the marketability of every media product. A film with marketing assets sewn into its aesthetic construction lowers the inherent financial risk of commercial filmmaking. From an aesthetic perspective, the high concept style has ties with both the classical Hollywood cinema and the art cinema. David Bordwell and Janet Staiger suggest that the only claim for an alteration in classical Hollywood style in the "post-classical" era is inspired by the art cinema: "The strongest argument for a New Hollywood rests upon the claim that the directors' works constitute a non-classical approach to narrative and technique. . . . As the 'old' Hollywood had incorporated and refunction-alized devices from German Expressionism and Soviet montage, the 'New' Hollywood has selectively borrowed from the international art cinema."[45] I would posit not only that the art cinema has altered the auteur-driven "New Hollywood," as Bordwell and Staiger suggest, but that some traits of the art cinema have been assimilated into mainstream Hollywood cinema in the form of high concept.

In contrast to the norms of classical Hollywood, the art cinema foregrounds realism and authorial expressivity in the system of the film.[46] The self-consciousness of high concept suggests that some force ("the author"?) is constructing the style — the configuration of perfect images, stars, music, narrative, and genre — which has become coded across these films. "Authorial expressivity" is inadequate as an explanation, though, since, as I have suggested, the style exists separate from, and excessive to, the apparent narrative. Rather than being motivated by the vision of a single author, the strong commercial orientation of the style suggests a designation of "industrial expressivity" as a mark of high concept.

The movement between the art cinema and high concept can be charted through Jim McBride's *Breathless*, a 1983 American remake of the art house classic, Jean-Luc Godard's *A bout de souffle* (1959). In telling of a slick hustler's doomed romance while fleeing the police, Mc-Bride foregrounds the importance of style in and of itself; as one *Breathless* character comments, "How many times have I told you that style counts." Illustrating its allegiance to high concept, *Breathless* juxtaposes music, pop culture, and the star performance of Richard Gere to create moments that are excessive: the patently artificial driving scenes, in the desert, with Gere crooning "Great Balls of Fire" against a red "movie" sunset; on the run from the law, Gere and Valerie Kaprisky make love in a movie theater balcony against the *film noir* classic *Gun Crazy* (1949); the finale in which a supposedly tense standoff between Gere and the police is broken by Gere dancing to Jerry Lee Lewis's "Breathless" playing on the soundtrack. These moments exceed their narrative significance, self-consciously privileging style, and the overtness of these moments echoes the narration of the Godard film. In terms of referencing, though, the commercial ties between high concept and the art cinema are minimal. The audiences drawn to *Breathless* were motivated by Gere, directly after his romantic blockbuster *An Officer and a Gentleman* (1982), rather than by the American reworking of a French classic.

The Godard/McBride match also illustrates the complexity of isolating and identifying narrational styles, whether in the art cinema or in

*The high concept remake of an art cinema
classic (*Breathless, *Orion, 1983). Photo
by Herb Ritts, © 1982 Orion Pictures
Corporation.*

high concept. *Breathless* (high concept) is based on *A bout de souffle* (Godard→ French New Wave→ art cinema), which in turn draws heavily from *film noir* and the American B-movies. Godard even dedicated his film to a B-movie studio, Monogram Pictures. In preparing for the American remake, McBride and writer L. M. Kit Carson sought to emulate not only Godard, but Godard's source material. As Carson describes the film's preproduction, "We're writing and screening movies: *Gun Crazy*, Kubrick's first movie, *Killer's Kiss*. [Mike] Medavoy [head of Orion at the time] runs *High Sierra*, the ending of which Godard lifted whole to make the ending of *A bout de souffle*."[47] In this manner, high concept is joined not only to the art cinema, but also, in a very direct way, right back to classical Hollywood.[48]

If the art cinema is an influence, the self-consciousness of the high concept style also extends from those moments of excess within classical Hollywood cinema. Indeed, as a style of filmmaking, high concept can be defined by its very overt narrational qualities. The connection of these techniques to the art cinema does explain the aesthetics of the style; high concept filmmakers such as Adrian Lyne and Paul Schrader even explicitly acknowledge the connection. Schrader utilized Ferdinando Scarfiotti, designer for many Bernardo Bertolucci films, as "visual consultant" on both *American Gigolo* and *Cat People* (1982).[49] Schrader's choice of Scarfiotti was motivated by the self-conscious style of Bertolucci's *The Conformist* (1970): "*The Conformist* was a very important film for my generation, because it was a film that reintroduced the concept of high style. Movies used to have high style in the thirties and forties and then gradually, through the fifties and sixties, they became more realistic, less production-designed, and *The Conformist* became a real sort of rallying cry."[50] Similarly, *Flashdance* cinematographer Don Peterman links Adrian Lyne with Bertolucci's "high style": "The director and cinematographer also viewed Bertolucci's *The Conformist* twice and *Last Tango in Paris*. 'He [Lyne] called Bertolucci "the man,"' says Peterman. 'Whenever we got into a difficult shooting situation, he would say, "How would the man handle this? He wouldn't play it safe. He would go for it." And then *we* would go for it.'"[51] The huge aesthetic difference between *The Conformist* and *Flashdance* illustrates the economic basis of Lyne's film and of the high concept style in general: the inherent goal is to appropriate the (art cinema) style and apply it to a marketable and highly exploitable premise. In this manner, high concept fuses marketing and style together yet again.

Regardless of the connection to classical Hollywood or the art cinema, the most significant aspect of the high concept style in the marketplace is its commercial orientation. This orientation derives from the manner in which the elements join together to form an image (or images) which are extracted for the marketing and merchandising of the film. Ultimately it is the process — the coherent and repeated structuring of a film and its elements around the marketing possibilities in the project — that distinguishes high concept from other forms of production within both the American and foreign film industries.

3 High Concept and Changes in the Market for Entertainment

With strong ties to marketing, the high concept picture can be considered the most direct response to the demands of the marketplace, with such films configured to be highly commercial. High concept has its roots in the economic history of the American film industry. This style of filmmaking has been molded by several major structural and economic shifts which have occurred in the post–World War II market for film. These shifts — both within the structure of the film industry and within the market for film as an entertainment product — have served increasingly to privilege high concept as a focus for the mainstream Hollywood industry. As this marketplace is intimately connected to the development of the film industry in previous decades, I will sketch the major historical changes which established, and serve to maintain, this period of industrial and aesthetic film history. These institutional changes include the breakdown of the studio system, the rise of television, and, especially relevant for an understanding of high concept, the conglomeration of the film industry. As a background to these changes, I will characterize the overall marketplace for film in which high concept operates, and, more significantly, the ways through which industrial changes in this market influence film content.

The Marketplace and Traditional Definitions

An analysis of the film marketplace depends on several central assumptions of economic theory, many of which fall under the field of industrial organization. Industrial organization analyzes the structure of each marketplace and the effects of various markets upon economic agents (i.e., buyers and sellers). Generally a market is defined as any area in which buyers and sellers negotiate the exchange of a well-defined commodity. The central hypothesis of industrial organization economics is that company behavior will be affected by the structure of the market. In other words, the structure of the marketplace for a product will influence the behavior of the buyers and sellers within that marketplace. Therefore, the price and quantity established for a product within the market are determined, in large part, by the market structure. Market structure is a fairly loose term used to describe all those attributes of the market that influence the nature of the competitive process: the size distribution of firms, barriers to and conditions for entry, product differentiation, firm cost structure, and the degree of government regulation. Many analyses consider the effect of market structure on the conduct and performance of firms: an approach which attempts to explain how decisions within a market are shaped by the major characteristics of that market. My analysis of the contemporary film industry will draw upon the study of market structure, and, in particular, will focus on the ways in which both the market for film and the "product" film can be conceptualized.

In terms of market structure, the motion picture industry in the "Golden Age" of the studio system has been described as a mature oligopoly: a market controlled by a small number of firms, each with a fairly large market share. By 1930, those studios referred to as "The Big Five" (Warner Bros., Loews/MGM, Paramount, RKO, and Twentieth Century–Fox) were vertically integrated, responsible for all facets of production, distribution, and exhibition. This arrangement possessed a clear economic rationale, since the ownership of theaters acted as an insurance policy for the majors: the companies were always assured of a minimum market for their product due to their ownership of the upscale first-run houses. This relationship frustrated, among others, the independent theater owners, who accused the majors of preferential treatment for their own movie theaters, as well as discriminatory practices, such as blind bidding and block booking. Eventually the government responded to these charges, via an antitrust suit filed in Manhattan on July 20, 1938, against the eight major producers (the Big Five and the Little Three — Columbia, Universal, and United Artists — who, unlike the Big Five, did not own theaters), twenty-five affiliated companies, and 133 officers and directors, charging price fixing and attempts to monopolize trade in film through theater ownership.[1] Ten years later, the Justice Department ruled for an "arm's length transaction" between the majors and the theater chains. The majors were given five years to divorce themselves from their theater chains.

The so-called "Paramount Case" drew attention to the oligopolistic structure of the industry, with the landmark victory for antitrust specifying the termination of all pooling agreements among the Big Five and the divestiture of all theaters operated in pools. Although this decision was formulated to encourage renewed competition within the industry, the majority of industry analysts believe that, since the Paramount consent decree, the industry has remained a "bilateral monopoly": a two-sided market in which the sellers (the distributors) and the buyers (the large theater chains) are each part of close-knit monopolies.[2]

The structural changes introduced by the Paramount Case occurred at the same time as several other major factors — particularly the rise of television and postwar consumerism — were refiguring the studio system. All these influences have been cited as depressing domestic box-office revenues for the Hollywood studios, although their relative influence is difficult to assess. After an initial decrease during the early Depression, boxoffice receipts in the U.S. increased steadily, reaching an apex of $1,692 million in 1946. During the fifties and sixties, however, boxoffice receipts spiraled downward, so that in 1961, fifteen years after the peak, receipts had dropped over 43 percent to $955 million.[3]

The commercial expansion of television, which began in 1948, reached the 90 percent penetration level by the end of the next decade.[4] After an initial period of treating television as a bothersome novelty, the major studios began to respond to the development of television as a possible means of regaining their lost revenues. This response transpired in three different forms. First, the studios attempted to differentiate their product from television. Techniques such as 3-D, increased color production, and the institution of the various widescreen techniques (Cinerama, Cinemascope, VistaVision) represented methods in the mid-1950s to offer viewers an experience unlike television. With the exception of the move to widescreen and color, which became the norm for virtually all feature films by the mid-1960s, these experiments held little lasting appeal to motion picture viewers. Second, the studios actually entered into the market for television by producing filmed programming for the home viewer: in 1955, the majors began "producing series with their names in the titles such as 'The MGM Parade,' 'The Twentieth Century–Fox Theater,' and 'Warner Brothers Presents.'"[5] The advantages to collaboration were many: the studios could use their own largely idle lots and facilities to produce the shows, television possessed a voracious appetite for programming in the early days, and the studios could advertise their forthcoming theatrical pictures on television. Third, the studios realized the value of their film libraries as a source of programming for television. Since pre-1948 films could be offered for sale in perpetuity, these features became the initial focus for the studios. Contracts with actors and directors after 1949 contained clauses for residual payments, thereby reducing potential revenues to the studios. By the '60s, films would become a staple for prime-time television scheduling, with all three networks devoting at least one night per week to "at the movies." The three strategies of involvement with television anticipated the ways in which the two media would become increasingly interdependent.[6]

Another possible explanation for the fall in attendance and revenue is the rise in postwar consumerism. During the years 1947–1961, families increased by 28 percent, disposable income increased by 60 percent, as did the purchasing power of the consumer.[7] The changes in income represent a shift or redistribution of wealth: while the top income bracket remained relatively stable, the middle and upper-middle brackets increased substantially. With more goods available in the postwar period, the substitution of other goods and activities for motion pictures simply illustrated a readjustment in light of the greater array of goods. This substitution away from motion picture attendance might have been augmented by the issue of public taste. There is some evidence that postwar feature films failed to appeal to the public as strongly as earlier films. For example, a March 1949 *Fortune* survey found that 38 percent of moviegoers felt that there had been a decline in the quality of movies in the past two years.[8]

The lowered demand for motion pictures, added to the Paramount Case, aided the dissolution of the mature studio system and the movement toward "the package-unit system" of production. Janet Staiger describes the package-unit mode as follows: "Rather than an individual company containing the source of the labor and materials, the entire industry became the pool for these. A producer organized a film project: he or she secured financing and combined the necessary laborers (whose roles had previously been defined by the standardized production structures and subdivision of work categories) and the means of production (the narrative 'property,' the equipment, and the physical sites of production)."[9] With projects existing on a film-by-film basis, the economic "cushion" of the studio could no longer offset the downfall created by a risky commercial project. Accordingly, films with the greatest inherent chance of returning their investment became more significant in this era. This attempt to foreground projects with inherent marketability can be viewed as the beginnings of high concept films, which depend entirely on their marketing assets.

Conglomeration and Film Content: The Roadshow, The Youth Picture, The Blockbuster

After the move to the package-unit system, the studios were no longer vertically integrated; in fact, the studios became primarily distributors of film after this time. The studios' loss of power as autonomous economic agents was illustrated through several mergers with larger conglomerates. The 1960s are often referred to as "The Go-Go Years" — a coy reference to the extreme upheaval within the industry in terms of company ownership, as well as to popular dancers of the era. Weakened by the fall in revenue and the largely unsuccessful attempts to regain their market, four of the major distributors (Universal, Paramount, Warner Bros., United Artists) merged with or were shadowed by conglomerates, most of which had little direct connection with the film industry. As Tino Balio suggests, the studios were attractive to the conglomerates primarily due to their film libraries, which could be exploited in television, their real estate, and their capital assets, and due to the suspicion that their stocks were undervalued because of a sluggish boxoffice in the early 1960s.[10] These mergers were characterized not as hostile takeovers, but rather as diversification of risk for the conglomerates through an increased capital base. While the autonomy of the studios might have been threatened by these takeovers, the conglomeration of the studios actually benefited some studios, particularly Paramount and Warner Bros.; in these cases, the takeovers served to strengthen substantially the market position of the film companies.

Since the media mergers in the 1980s shaping high concept were caused partially by the mixed assets available in the film conglomerates established during the first "wave" of mergers two decades previously, I will briefly outline these earlier ownership changes in the major companies. Universal became the first company to undergo conglomeration, merging to form MCA/Revue Productions in 1952. MCA, developed by Lew Wasserman, initially began as a music talent agency. Given the advent of television, Wasserman combined his company with Revue Productions: the premise was to place MCA clients into television packages, which Revue would then produce. When the Justice Department opposed the integrated agency and production unit, MCA divorced itself from the talent agency business in 1962.[11] Deciding to expand into motion picture production as a compensation, MCA bought Universal Pictures. MCA already had ties with the film company — indeed, MCA had purchased Universal City, the studio facility, several years before buying the film company.[12] As a conglomerate, MCA has been extremely active in television programming, and this success has been difficult for MCA to duplicate with its theatrical features.[13] Unlike other conglomerated film companies, such as Paramount or United Artists, Universal's film and television operations have contributed a large share of MCA's revenue (59 percent in 1980). In this manner, MCA can be seen as a paradigm for those conglomerates focused on media during the '80s. Indeed, Wasserman may well be the earliest proponent within the film industry of "synergy," a term popularized by the media to describe the commercial possibilities of mutually interlocking commercial ventures. MCA also engages in recorded music and music publishing, book publishing, retail and mail order sales, recreation services, financial services, and data processing.[14]

Paramount Pictures merged with Charles Bludhorn's Gulf & Western Industries in 1966. The conglomerate, developed almost singlehandedly by Bludhorn, had a diverse portfolio including over three hundred subsidiaries in manufacturing, consumer and agricultural products, natural resources, apparel products, paper and building products, automotive replacement parts, and financial services divisions.[15] While Paramount's films had been performing dismally at the boxoffice, Gulf & Western was attracted to the extensive library of films owned by Paramount: even considering only the more recent titles, their estimated worth was placed at $200 million. The next years saw two important structural changes within Paramount. Through supplying its features to television (via MCA) and through developing original television programming, Paramount diversified heavily into television production, eventually becoming a major supplier of programming. Its position within the television market was strengthened through acquiring Desilu Productions for $17 million in 1967.[16] The other major structural change was the appointment of Robert Evans as production head in 1967. Evans, in the next several years, would be responsible for developing and supervising such Paramount blockbusters as *Love Story* (1970), *The Godfather* (1972), and *Death Wish* (1974), as well as the critically acclaimed *Serpico* (1973), *The Conversation* (1974), *The Godfather, Part II* (1974), and *Chinatown* (1974).[17] More importantly, offering a means of long-term stability, Paramount became part of Gulf & Western's Leisure Time Group, which included Famous Music Corporation, Simon and Schuster Publishing House, a sports arena, and Famous Players Limited (the second largest theater chain in Canada). The entire Leisure Time Group garnered only between 11 and 15 percent of Gulf & Western's revenue; therefore, minuses in Paramount's yearly balance sheet could easily be offset by pluses from numerous other companies within Gulf & Western.[18]

Unlike Paramount, which became a small part of Gulf & Western, Warner Bros. became a large component of a conglomerate. In March 1967, Warner Bros. merged with Seven Arts productions, a Canadian distributor of films to television, becoming Warner Bros./Seven Arts productions. Despite concern within the industry that Warner Bros. would move completely into the domain of television production, the studio continued producing films. Two years later, the company merged with the conglomerate Kinney National Service, under the direction of Steven Ross. Ross eventually formed Warner Communications, Inc., a large entertainment conglomerate with an emphasis in the music business, television and film entertainment, consumer electronics and toys, and publishing.

In the same year as Warner's second merger, United Artists was sold to Transamerica Inc., known primarily as a major insurance company. As Steven Bach describes in his book *Final Cut: Dreams and Disaster in the Making of Heaven's Gate*, United Artists seemed to be an attractive subsidiary for Transamerica, since the sluggish Transamerica stock, in theory, would be revitalized by a glamorous subsidiary in the movie business.[19] UA's Arthur Krim and Robert Benjamin were attracted by both the stability of Transamerica and the opportunity to expand production, helped by the large financial cushion of the parent company.

The remaining three majors (MGM, Twentieth Century–Fox, Columbia) remained unaffiliated with conglomerates through the mid-1970s. With these ownership changes in place by the end of the 1960s, structurally the industry remained fairly stable through the next decade. As expected, the companies affiliated with conglomerates generally had a larger market share than the other distributors. This result can be gauged through the average of the market shares for 1970–1980 for the majors: Warner Bros. 14.5 percent; Paramount 14.0 percent; Fox 14.0 percent; Universal 13.9 percent; United Artists 11.5 percent; Columbia 10.6 percent; MGM 5.8 percent.[20] Of the unaffiliated companies, only Twentieth Century–Fox showed strength (partly due to the phenomenal success of *Star Wars* in 1977, which boosted Fox to a first-place 19.5 percent market share in that year). The structure of the industry resulting from the first wave of mergers established the importance of both conglomerate control as a method of long-term stability and an emphasis on the market opportunities of exploiting films in affiliated media in the conglomerate. Both strategies served to develop high concept as a style of filmmaking in the subsequent decades.

The conglomeration of the industry was accompanied by changes within the "product" of the industry. After the success of an increasing number of large-scale films during the 1950s, in the early '60s, the studios began to focus on the large-scale, roadshow picture as the anchor of their distribution schedules. In many respects, the roadshow picture can be seen as another attempt to present film as different from television — or, to be more precise, as bigger, grander, and more spectacular than television. Roadshowing, with the advance, reserved seating, limited showings, and "epic" film subjects, attempted to shift the act of moviegoing into a special occasion: an event. Frequently these films were musicals (*Camelot* [1967], *Funny Girl* [1968], *Star!* [1968], *Hello, Dolly!* [1969], *Darling Lili* [1970]), or epics (*Spartacus* [1960], *Lawrence of Arabia* [1962], *Doctor Zhivago* [1965], *Battle of Britain* [1969], *Ryan's Daughter* [1970]). While the emphasis on spectacle produced some large-scale hits such as *The Sound of Music* and *Doctor Zhivago*, by the end of the decade, this type of production became increasingly problematic. As Darryl Zanuck, then head of Twentieth Century–Fox, commented in 1968: "We've got $50 million tied up in these three musicals, *Dr. Dolittle, Star!, Hello, Dolly!*, and quite frankly if we hadn't had such an enormous success with *The Sound of Music*, I'd be petrified."[21] Zanuck's fears were justified as Fox, along with the other majors, suffered large losses from expensive projects which failed at the boxoffice.[22]

As Hollywood was bemoaning the death of the roadshow picture, the youth film was gaining popularity: the trend can be traced back to such films as *The Graduate* and *Bonnie & Clyde* in 1967, *Easy Rider* and *Midnight Cowboy* in 1969. This movement was driven by the yet-to-be-named "baby boom" generation, at that time in their teens and early twenties, who were eager to respond to media which mirrored their disenfranchised state. Studios began to rethink their production slates and distribution practices, and by the end of the decade, the large-scale and roadshow picture had become the exception, rather than the rule, for the major distributors. From an economic perspective, as an established method for attempting to maximize boxoffice revenue proved faulty, the majors began to investigate other possibilities. This investigation created an incredibly rich period of American film history; in many ways, the years 1969–1975 can be characterized as a period of extensive experimentation in industrial practice, film form, and content.[23] As producer Peter Guber, who in the first half of the 1970s was head of worldwide production at Columbia Pictures, commented in an interview, "The early 70s [were] when young filmmakers made their inroads, where you saw Peter Bogdanovich's *The Last Picture Show*, Marty Scorsese's *Taxi Driver*, Hal Ashby's *The Last Detail*, Bob Rafelson's *Five Easy Pieces* . . . where you saw all the young filmmakers begin to emerge with smaller films and more daring subjects."[24] Interestingly, all the films mentioned by Guber were made at Columbia, recognized as one of the first studios during this era to finance movies targeted specifically at the youth market.[25] Apart from the films already mentioned, other noteworthy films during this period of targeting the youth market through narrative and formal experimentation include *Alice's Restaurant* (1969), *Medium Cool* (1969), *M.A.S.H.* (1970), *Carnal Knowledge* (1971), *Slaughterhouse-Five* (1972), *American Graffiti* (1973), *Blume in Love* (1973), and *Phantom of the Paradise* (1974).

An emphasis on the auteur filmmaker is another unifying characteristic of the product in this era. During the period of formal experimentation, directors such as Robert Altman, Paul Mazursky, and Hal Ashby, while still being funded by the majors, were given extreme latitude in the composition of their films. This liberating period of experimentation is especially striking in the case of Altman. Even though his films made little or no profit since *M.A.S.H.* in 1970, Altman continued to work continuously through the decade, even signing an exclusive contract with Twentieth Century–Fox in 1977.[26] After freedom in the early seventies, one can see how the mainstream film industry closed its doors to the auteur. By the end of the decade, the period of auteurism and formal experimentation had ended. Altman's demise was also evident: amazingly, after *Popeye* in 1980, Altman has been unable to work for a major distributor. His only film for a major studio since that time (*O.C. & Stiggs*) was made in 1983 for MGM, released in a handful of theaters four years later, and then released directly to home video.[27] Since his estrangement from the majors after the experimentation period, Altman has been forced to work in other media (cable for *The Laundromat* [1985] and *Tanner '88* [1988], network television for *The Room* [1987], *The Dumb Waiter* [1987], *The Caine Mutiny Court-Martial* [1988]) and for independent studios (Cinecom for *Come Back to the Five and Dime, Jimmy Dean, Jimmy Dean* [1982], United Artists Classics for *Streamers* [1983], Cannon for *Fool For Love* [1986], New World for *Beyond Therapy* [1987], Hemdale for *Vincent and Theo* [1990], Fine Line for *The Player* [1992] and *Short Cuts* [1993]).

This period seems to have grown, in part, from a gradual recognition of the younger audience segment on the part of the industry. This recognition, though, was accompanied by a confusion regarding how this audience segment might be reached. The confusion allowed for an incredibly rich period of filmmaking which, while still responding to the economic imperative of the film industry (i.e., to maximize boxoffice revenue), failed to constrain the filmmakers substantially. As Gerald Mast points out, "The iconoclastic, antimyth films, which cost near or less than the 1970 industry average of $3 million, made consistent, if modest profits."[28] Typically, these films are considered, after the fact, as

Nashville: *critical sensation, modest profits*
*(*Nashville, Paramount, 1975*).*

being more financially successful than they actually were. Industry analyst Stuart Byron describes this situation with Robert Altman's *Nashville*.
Byron admits that the film made a small profit, but warns about the
perception that the film was a boxoffice success: "[I]t is still amazing to
me that the impression was so prevalent in the cultural reaches of Manhattan that *Nashville* was one of the year's commercial blockbusters
rather than, as it was, the twenty-seventh highest-grossing film of the
year. . . . It should be stated again and again that New York is a unique

market, one in which a handful of sophisticated movies get the crowds which don't go to, say, *W. W. and the Dixie Dance-Kings* or *The Other Side of the Mountain.*"[29]

J. Hoberman states that the period of experimentation concludes in 1976 with *One Flew over the Cuckoo's Nest*, the year's biggest commercial and critical hit.[30] On one level, the period's demise responded to a real economic incentive: *One Flew over the Cuckoo's Nest* notwithstanding, the experimental films became less and less able to recoup their costs, and the negative costs were also greatly expanding in the inflationary era. Several films heralded the end of the era and the accompanying disillusionment in the film industry with the auteurs: Peter Bogdanovich's *Daisy Miller* in 1974, *At Long Last Love* in 1975, and *Nickelodeon* in 1976; Hal Ashby's *Bound for Glory* in 1976; and particularly William Friedkin's *Sorcerer* and Scorsese's *New York, New York*, both in 1977. The greatest — or, at least, the most widely publicized — auteurist debacle, however, was Michael Cimino's *Heaven's Gate*, several years in the making, and finally released in 1980.[31]

James Monaco aptly describes the case of *Sorcerer*, which could apply, to a lesser extent, to the other films listed above: "*Sorcerer* (1977), the gift he [Friedkin] convinced two major studios [Paramount and Universal] to give him for hitting the bell with *The Exorcist*, cost upwards of $18 million [n.b.: *Variety* estimates the cost at $22 million], but it is more restrained than Billy's earlier films, even if the sum effect is a grandly naive gesture of self-indulgence. The kid, growing old, wanted to remake his hero Clouzot's *Wages of Fear*. It took him years; he shot on four continents (the trips are becoming a Friedkin trademark); and the film when released was a total writeoff."[32] Similarly, *New York, New York* (1977), a pastiche of classic musicals starring Liza Minnelli and Robert De Niro, could be viewed as another nail in the coffin for the experimental era. With three well received and financially mediocre studio films (*Mean Streets* [1973], *Alice Doesn't Live Here Anymore* [1974], *Taxi Driver* [1976]) under his belt, Scorsese was given free rein by United Artists to direct a $14 million musical which reflected the already established Scorsese themes and obsessions, albeit filtered through a loose musical framework. The film earned domestic (U.S.-Canada) rentals of only $6 million and was widely attacked by the critics for its over-indulgence.[33]

Unfortunately, this lesson was not sufficient for United Artists; three years after the Scorsese film, the studio experienced an even greater disaster with Michael Cimino's *Heaven's Gate*. United Artists announced Cimino's epic western as a project in November 1978. Based on the success of his Oscar-winning *The Deerhunter*, United Artists budgeted

New York, New York: *the mix of Scorsese
and musical revisionism proved commercially unappealing (*New York, New York,
United Artists, 1977). Copyright © 1977,
United Artists Corporation.*

$7.5 million for the film, and production began in April 1979. In Au-
gust, UA seized fiscal control of the film, which was still in production;
the cost had risen to $21 million, with $30 million projected as the final
cost figure.[34] United Artists justified the extra expenditure given the history of *The Deerhunter*. Cimino had exceeded the budget on that film,
EMI had considered replacing him as director, but the film eventually
won five Academy Awards and grossed over $55 million domestically. A
year after filming began on *Heaven's Gate*, Cimino completed principal
photography — the cost had reached almost $35 million.[35] On Novem-
ber 18, 1980, the film opened in New York to unanimously vitriolic
reviews. The Los Angeles and Toronto premieres were canceled, and
Cimino returned to the editing room to cut a shorter version of the
picture. The revised version opened in April 1981 to damning reviews
and dismal boxoffice returns. After six months in general release, the
film garnered only $1.5 million in domestic rentals on a cost which
eventually expanded to $43 million.[36] Cimino's film can be seen as an

addendum to the experimental era. More generally, though, while directors like Ashby, Bogdanovich, Friedkin, and Arthur Penn continued working, one could argue that their most interesting and provocative works were produced during this period of aesthetic and accompanying financial experimentation.

The end of the experimental period was heralded by a return to the large-scale, grand filmmaking, which had been Hollywood's modus operandi in the mid-to-late 1960s. Unlike the roadshow era, however, Hollywood did not fixate primarily on musicals and epics; by the mid-1970s, the roadshow had transmuted into the blockbuster. The blockbuster can be appreciated through Peter Guber's description of this period of filmmaking: "[The banks] wanted pictures with an 'upside potential' which meant roughly, Robert Redford and Paul Newman together, with Barbra Streisand singing, Steve McQueen punching, Clint Eastwood jumping, music by Marvin Hamlisch, all in stereo, on the wide screen, going out as a hard-ticketed road show where you have to book your seats, based on a #1 bestseller which was #1 for sixty weeks and a television show which was #1 for at least a season."[37] Guber's

An opulent set piece from Cimino's film: the Heaven's Gate *roller rink (*Heaven's Gate, United Artists, 1980). Copyright © 1981 by United Artists Corporation.

rather hyperbolic definition is useful, since it inventories the components of the blockbuster: a pre-sold property (such as a best-selling novel or play), within a traditional film genre, usually supported by bankable stars (operating within their particular genre) and director.

Paramount fostered this trend with the phenomenally successful *Love Story* (total rentals: $50.0 million) and *The Godfather* (total rentals: $85.7 million).[38] Both of these films were marketable, connected to bestsellers, and supported by catch phrases which became part of popular American culture.[39] In addition, the following films also solidified the blockbuster era: *Airport* (an adaptation of Arthur Hailey's bestseller, featuring an all-star cast; 1970; rentals: $45.3 million), *The Exorcist* (William Peter Blatty's horror novel directed by William Friedkin, who had won an Academy Award for *The French Connection*; 1973; rentals: $89.0 million), *Papillon* (Steve McQueen and Dustin Hoffman in epic adventure tale; 1973; rentals: $22.5 million), *The Towering Inferno* (all-star cast, including McQueen and Paul Newman, in an adventure/disaster film which was financed by both Twentieth Century–Fox and Warner Bros.; 1974; rentals: $52.0 million), and *Jaws* (Steven Spielberg's breakthrough film based on Peter Benchley's pulp bestseller; 1975; rentals: $129.5 million). Of course, the pre-sold elements of the blockbuster do not always attract strong boxoffice. Paramount's *The Great Gatsby* (1974; rentals: $14.2 million) and *King Kong* (1976; rentals: $35.8 million) both received an extraordinary amount of pre-release publicity and yet, while viewer awareness was obviously high for both films, neither performed according to expectations.

Why did Hollywood turn toward the blockbuster as a means of economic salvation? On one level, the decision was extremely conservative economically. Films which are packaged and composed of financially "proven" components would seem to have a greater chance of attracting an audience.[40] This argument is also fueled by the increasing cost of production. In 1975, the average cost to produce and market a film was $3.1 million. This figure rose steadily to $14.4 million by 1984.[41] Increasingly, the rise in production costs marked a decline for the small, experimental picture. As the break-even point moved upward, the majors became interested only in the large revenues possible through the blockbuster films. Occasionally a schedule would be balanced by some "prestige" films, which, while possessing limited boxoffice potential, fostered the reputation of film as art and solidified relationships with the critics and exhibitors. For instance, in 1976, Paramount's release schedule was anchored by such potential blockbusters as *King Kong, Marathon Man,* and *The Last Tycoon.* The studio completed its release schedule with some films which obviously would have limited appeal

Table 2. Number of Releases by Major Distributors, 1970–1978

	1970	1971	1972	1973	1974	1975	1976	1977	1978
Columbia	28	37	27	16	21	15	15	10	14
MGM	21	20	22	16	*	*	*	*	*
Paramount	16	21	22	26	23	11	18	15	14
Twentieth Century–Fox	14	16	25	14	18	19	18	14	7
United Artists	40	26	20	18	21	21	22	14	19
Universal	17	16	16	19	11	10	13	17	21
Warner Bros.	15	17	18	22	15	19	11	14	18
Total	151	153	150	131	109	95	97	84	93

*After 1974, films released through United Artists.
Source: Motion Picture Association of America.

at the boxoffice, yet which might attract critical attention for the studio: Ingmar Bergman's intense psychological drama *Face to Face*, Elaine May's quirky crime drama *Mikey and Nicky*, and Roman Polanski's bizarre tale of paranoia, *The Tenant*. Nevertheless, the emphasis shifted to the more marketable, easily packaged film, so that studios actually cut their release schedules to divert money into the more extravagant productions. This trend toward more limited release schedules can be seen in Table 2, which shows the number of new releases from the majors for 1970 to 1978. From a peak of 153 films in 1971, the total drops to only 84 films in 1977. The brunt of these cutbacks occurred with the small, personal films which had thrived earlier in the decade. As James Monaco remarked in 1979, "Increasingly we are all going to see the same ten movies."[42]

Furthering the limited number of releases were two other factors: the effect of diversified risk upon the studio and the growing importance of foreign markets. As each studio was sold to a conglomerate, the studio's identity as an entity separate from the other subsidiaries within the conglomerate became more muted. For example, in 1970, United Artists suffered a large pre-tax loss which was not written off across a three-year period, as had been customary, since the sum was offset by a surplus from Occidental Life Insurance, another Transamerica company.[43] In this manner, the growth of the entire conglomerate is favored over extraordinary growth in any one subsidiary. Consequently, although companies such as Transamerica wanted their film subsidiaries to show a profit, most of the conglomerates discouraged aesthetic experimentation and expansion of production. In fact, cost minimization almost dictated that the studios should lower the number of releases to maximize profits.

Traditionally the foreign markets supplied a small percentage of total boxoffice revenue, yet with the postwar decline in domestic boxoffice, these markets became increasingly important to total revenue. By the late 1960s, export rental income accounted for about one-half of total rental revenue.[44] Perhaps due to cultural difference, the "personal" American projects of the early-to-mid 1970s did not sell as well overseas. As industry analyst Joseph Phillips notes, foreign audiences seem to prefer adventure films and blockbusters to personal dramas: "One formula that seems to possess a high probability of market success is the adventure story, often involving a disaster of enormous proportions. This formula appears to have great international audience potential. It calls for 'blockbuster' treatment involving investment of great lumps of capital, which, of course, the major U.S. film companies are best able to provide."[45] This factor has added to the increasing emphasis upon the big-budget, packaged film.

The sum of these institutional changes — principally the Paramount Case, the rise of television, and the conglomeration of the industry — led to a tightening or contraction within the motion picture industry. This contraction involved not only the number of releases from the majors, but also a tightening of the economic risks involved with filmmaking. Conglomerates entering the field, often with no prior experience with entertainment or film, sought to minimize the risks of motion picture production through making those films with built-in audience appeal (i.e., the roadshow and later the blockbuster) and through an attempt to tap the youth audience during Hollywood's auteur period. The mid-1970s can be seen, therefore, as a period of consolidation for the film industry. The conglomeration during the previous decade at first permitted, then extinguished, diversity in American filmmaking. The solution to the conglomerates' concern over their marketplace was the blockbuster, which represented an attempt to differentiate one film from others by virtue of components which were pre-sold. With the rise of the blockbuster era, the films which became more and more typical fell back upon traditional genres and modes, with an emphasis upon the spectacular (for instance, the disaster films such as *The Poseidon Adventure* [1972] or *Earthquake* [1974]). The aesthetics of the blockbuster, along with the accompanying economic forces which served to produce this form, create the genesis for high concept. Indeed, high concept can be viewed as a progression from the blockbuster. High concept shares the emphasis on pre-sold components, yet modifies the style and narrative of the blockbuster. These variations on the blockbuster grew, in part, from major structural changes in the industry during the late 1970s.

Uncertainty in the Marketplace: The Development of the Contemporary Industry Structure

The changes within Hollywood and in its product created through the conglomeration of the industry during the 1960s were still being worked through when a potentially much greater force was recognized by the industry. By the mid-1970s, the "new" television technologies — cable television, pay TV, and home video — were on the horizon. The film industry responded to these technologies with an attempt to enter and control these new markets. This strategy was not without precedent. Just as Hollywood tried to enter the burgeoning television market through investing in television technology, theater television, subscription television, and television station ownership nearly four decades earlier, the consistent response to the new technologies seemed to be movement into these markets.[46] As Douglas Gomery comments, "A party (or parties) has reasoned that great profits lie in the future for a major movie production company which can properly be maneuvered into supplying the 'new' television technologies."[47] The primary economic rationale for this strategy was the reduction of risk which could be obtained through control of the affiliated (and connected) markets. Through the control of these markets, the film industry hoped to conquer any fall in demand at the theatrical "window" (the industry term for the different venues in which a product might be shown) through an investment in the subsequent windows of a film's release.[48] High concept, as a focus for the mainstream industry, was strengthened by these new markets. The style and marketing hooks of high concept, designed to establish the image of the film clearly, allowed the film to "play" across all the different release windows.

After the introduction of Sony's Betamax in the mid-'70s, the majors attempted to secure a market position within home video. Long-term success in this market for the majors was dependent heavily upon two factors: ownership of a distribution system, and a correct estimation of the elasticity of demand for their product. The most powerful majors possessed an in-house home video operation, thereby coordinating the marketing, sales, and distribution of the video within their own company.[49] On the other hand, the weaker studios and mini-majors had to license their films to outside video distributors at a much lower profit rate: for example, Tri-Star signed deals for home video rights with both RCA and CBS in 1984, while Orion has released many videos through HBO/Cannon video.[50] Until the development of Orion Home Video in 1986, Orion, in particular, suffered from this strategy, having to release blockbusters, such as *Platoon* (1986), through other labels.

A more important key to long-term financial success for the majors' involvement with home video concerned the pricing of videos. Initially, movies on tape sold for well over $50, and the ratio of sales to rentals was dismal: "For every videocassette sale, there are about 10 tape rentals, bringing the total for 1983 to 100 million."[51] The minimal sales to the home market were broken by Paramount Home Video through a series of pricing experiments which served to refigure the home video market. Completely against the traditional pricing scheme of $50–$70, Paramount released *Star Trek II: The Wrath of Khan* on video at a retail price of $39.95 in late 1982. Sales volume doubled at this lower price.[52] Following within the next year were the extraordinary video successes of *An Officer and a Gentleman, Flashdance,* and *Raiders of the Lost Ark;* all were priced at $39.95, and all shipped record numbers of units.[53] At the end of the first full year of low pricing, Paramount also instituted a Christmas promotion dubbed "25 Great Gifts Under $25." This move further reduced prices and sold units to capacity through the entire promotion.[54] The Paramount Christmas promotion clarified that the maximum revenue would come from "the sell-through potential" of a particular video (i.e., the purchase of the video directly by the consumer, rather than by the video store owner).

Other companies soon followed Paramount's lead: MCA cut 50 percent off selected prices, Disney instituted "7 Limited Golden Edition" video volumes at the price of $29.95, and Media Home Entertainment started its price list at $19.95.[55] Given the strong interest generated by boxoffice hits, the sell-through pricing can generate a great deal more revenue than the steeper price. Allan Caplan, chairman of the Applause video retail chain, explains the arithmetics of the sell-through pricing in these terms: "An 'A' film capable of selling 400,000 units at the usual retail price, $89.95, generates $22-million wholesale to its supplier . . . but at a $24.95 suggested retail, and selling 3–4 million units, the total skyrockets to $42–58 million."[56] Even with unsuccessful films, though, profit still may be forthcoming: Disney received over $1 million each from the video sales of *Tex* (1982), *Running Brave* (1983), and *Something Wicked This Way Comes* (1983), all of which performed dismally at the theatrical boxoffice. By the mid-1980s, therefore, home video revenues were becoming increasingly important as a window in the industry.

Whereas in 1980, only 3.0 million pre-recorded tapes were sold to either the home market or rental firms, 57.7 million were sold in 1985, and this figure tripled to 161.4 million in 1988.[57]

The story of the majors' involvement with pay cable virtually collapses into a story of their interaction with Home Box Office (HBO), America's largest pay-cable television service, started as a local pay-television service in 1972 by Chuck Dolan.[58] By being the first cable supplier, HBO was able to extract preferential licenses from the studios. Rather than fight the development of the technology, Columbia benefited from an exclusive distribution arrangement with HBO, signing a deal in 1981 for five years of movies on an exclusive basis.[59] To reward this commitment, and in consideration of the fact that most studio deals were only for one year rather than five, HBO paid Columbia premium rates for its product. Two years later, Paramount gave Showtime an exclusive deal on its next eleven films — a decision made in large part by Barry Diller to dilute the strength of HBO by supporting its major rival.[60] Subsequently, Universal and Warner Bros. both signed multi-year exclusive deals with HBO.[61] Meanwhile, HBO also gained a large advantage over its competitors by receiving a ten-year access to the entire 4,700-title MGM/UA library, the largest and most lucrative movie vault.[62]

The strategy utilized by the studios in response to the power of HBO and the possible profits of cable extends beyond exclusive contracts. In 1979, Columbia, Paramount, MCA/Universal, Twentieth Century–Fox, and Getty Oil developed a cable network named "Premiere" which would have exclusive rights to the partners' films.[63] This venture was met with hostility by both HBO and Showtime. The Justice Department filed an antitrust suit in August 1980, describing Premiere as an "illegal conspiracy" which would, in effect, monopolize the cable market.[64] Premiere was successfully blocked by HBO only two days before its airdate. Basing its objections upon the size of the theatrical film industry controlled by the partners, HBO won the suit on antitrust grounds, and Premiere never aired.[65]

The only major to have an interest in a cable company prior to the abortive Premiere venture was Warner Communications. Warner invested early in cable, and has controlled a large percentage of Showtime/The Movie Channel (American Express is the other major partner).[66] This structure changed in January 1983 when Warner joined with Paramount and MCA Incorporated to become equal partners in the Movie Channel. The majors stressed that exclusivity would not be part of the arrangement and that access to the partners' films would not be denied to competitors, including HBO. Again this move was designed to lessen the power of HBO, whose subscriber base represented a virtual monopoly over the cable market (in 1982, HBO had 11 million subscribers, followed by Showtime with only 3.5 million).[67] By that time, HBO's control was credited with securing films for less than their market value. The Movie Channel agreement marked the first major collusive activity by the majors to secure a piece of the pay cable pie and to protect the value of their film libraries.[68]

Analysis of the majors' institutional development since the advent of the new media leads to several conclusions. In general, the companies which have been consistently strong throughout the 1980s are distinguished by the following characteristics: (1) control since the 1960s by one of the conglomerates focused on media, (2) a stability of management, and (3) diversification and innovation into other delivery systems. These three characteristics coalesce, with the strongest conglomerates (Gulf & Western, Time Warner) focusing on the synergy between film, the new delivery systems, and their related media companies.

One measure of success is the market share garnered by the company. As Dennis Mueller points out, "Several recent studies have found that market shares are positively related to profitability, and market share is a frequently cited objective of corporate management."[69] Considering market shares during the 1970s and '80s, one can see that Paramount consistently has dominated the marketplace. Figures 1 through 3 show average market shares for feature film rentals from U.S. and Canadian theaters for the majors during different time periods. Figure 1 considers the average market share for the 1970s. Although Paramount (15 percent) leads the studios, Warner Bros., Fox, and Universal are each within 2 percent of Paramount's figure. The adage of "sharing the market" does seem apt to describe this period. Figures 2 and 3 show the development of the market shares in the 1980s. Figure 2 covers the entire decade (1980 to 1989), while Figure 3 shows only the last four years (1986–1989).[70] Figure 2 shows the beginning of a more differentiated pattern of shares. Apart from the introduction of Tri-Star and Orion, the only drastic change in individual share is with MGM(/UA), which falls from 12.3 percent to 7.7 percent of the market.[71] In Figure 3, however, the pattern becomes much more pronounced: Paramount clearly stands above the other studios, garnering 18 percent of the total market, followed by Disney (14.5 percent) and Warner Bros. (13.7 percent). The remarkable performance of Disney in the latter part of the 1980s contrasts with its lackluster revenue in the 1970s. After Disney and Warner Bros., the next closest competitor is Universal (11.5 percent), while the remaining studios each controlled less than 10 percent of the rental market. How can one explain this marked shift in the market—par-

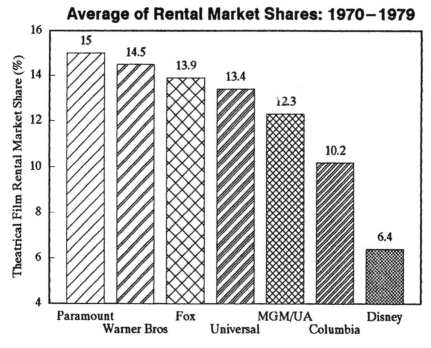

Figure 1. *Average of rental market shares: 1970–1979.*

ticularly the rise of Paramount, Warner Bros., and Disney—within the past two decades? Paramount, Disney, and Warner Bros. are the studios most often associated with high concept. Part of their strategy has been to focus on diversifying not just into different media, but also in the film marketplace through high concept.

Paramount's position within the contemporary industry grew under the supervision of Gulf & Western's Charles Bludhorn, who appointed Barry Diller as the chairman of Paramount in 1974. Diller, whose background was in television at ABC, reorganized the studio and made a relentless effort to focus on story in the Paramount films.[72] Along with Michael Eisner, Diller supervised a long list of hit films, including *Ordinary People* (1980), *Raiders of the Lost Ark* (1981), and *Flashdance*.[73] Paramount's salient trait might well be its need to maintain close control over and attention to every project. The desire to treat each project on an individual basis, rather than as merely part of a large release schedule, separates Paramount from the other studios. Tony Schwartz's investigation of the Diller regime at Paramount includes a quote from an independent (anonymous) producer: "Are they smarter than the execu-

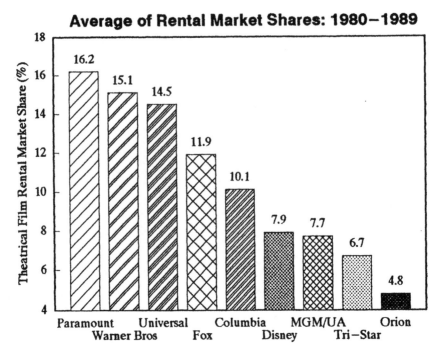

Figure 2. Average of rental market shares: 1980–1989.

tives at other studios? The answer is yes. Are the movies better for their input? Probably. But who wants to work all the time in a bunker atmosphere, under the constant threat of the guillotine?"[74] Interviews with many of the key marketing and distribution executives produce a completely different perspective. Mardi Marans, former Senior Vice-President of Marketing, whose experience at Paramount followed a thirteen-year tenure at Warner Bros., discussed Paramount's management style in the following terms, distancing herself from the assertion that Paramount requires extremely close control over every project: "It's like a family environment. The filmmaker goes out and makes his movie, and he's out there on his own. More than anything, it's [Paramount's interest] not the need to have hands-on involvement, as much as it is to be a support system. He has to have his creative right, and we do whatever we can to make the environment so that he makes the best movie possible. When they come back with it, we ask what can be done if he needs help to make it better and then to bring it to market."[75]

Gulf & Western's founder and chairman, Charles Bludhorn, died suddenly of a heart attack in 1983. His replacement, Martin S. Davis,

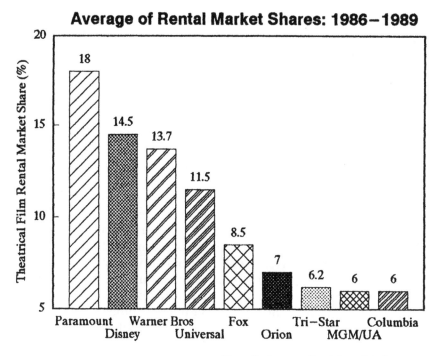

Average of Rental Market Shares: 1986-1989

Figure 3. Average of rental market shares: 1986-1989.

desired a closer hand in the management of Paramount, and clashed strongly with Diller.[76] Lured by an attractive financial offer by Twentieth Century–Fox owner Marvin Davis, Diller left Paramount in 1984.[77] Almost simultaneously, Eisner left for Walt Disney Productions, as did many of the key production executives.[78] Nevertheless, after an initially rough start, Paramount's winning streak continued under the direction of a new chairman, twenty-four-year Paramount veteran Frank Mancuso.[79] Paramount also has developed in the past years into other media, in particular, a 50 percent interest in the USA Network and exclusive rights to Showtime/The Movie Channel.[80] Gulf & Western also operates 470 U.S. movie theaters (Festival, Trans-Lux, and Mann), and still maintains its ownership of Famous Players Theaters in Canada.[81]

Paramount also has benefited from the cross-fertilization possible from its television and movie divisions: successful television series have been developed from the *Star Trek* and *Friday the 13th* series, and lucrative licensing campaigns have also been developed from these telefilms.[82] Financial analyst Christopher Dixon, of Kidder, Peabody & Co., compares this strategy to the establishment of brand names which can

identify a company across a range of different products: "They're looking to create brand names with products that have a long shelf-life."[83]
Indeed, the synergy between the different divisions at Paramount also
is credited as one difference between Paramount and other studios. For
example, Diana Widom, former Senior Vice-President of Publicity, comments, "There is a tremendous interaction between the marketing department, production and distribution. All these key departments are
working together. There's a flow of information, of ideas, and exchange
of ideas—that's what makes Paramount unique."[84] Perhaps this open-
ness was one component of Paramount's creative and professional success story over the past two decades.

Like Paramount, Warner Bros. has been able to maintain a solid market share during the past two decades, even increasing slightly from the
1970s (14.5 percent) to the 1980s (15.1 percent). Steven J. Ross has
guided the company through several difficult events in the past decade,
including the huge losses ($536 million) from the video game/computer
division Atari and the attempted (and unsuccessful) takeover by Rupert
Murdoch in 1983.[85] Still, as Robert Gustafson notes in his analysis of the
Warner conglomerate, "the principle of multiple profit centers which
reinforce each other" has served the company well.[86] Warner films
generate revenues from their theatrical release, through home video
(Warner Home Video), cable (Warner Amex Cable, the Movie Channel),
television (Warner Television Distribution), and the affiliated product
tie-ins (perhaps Warner Records, Warner Books, Atari). The early integration with pay cable and the stability of Ross's chairmanship have
produced a company which appears very progressive in its approach to
the changing dictates of the marketplace. The cross between the different media is blurred at Warner Bros., although not as extensively as at
Paramount. For instance, Warner's *Superman* series produced three successful films on the level of Paramount's *Star Trek* series. Of course, the
marketing and product tie-ins were mounted on a phenomenal scale for
these films. These large-scale projects are interspersed with more personal, artistically oriented projects; for example, Warner Bros. has produced all the Stanley Kubrick films since 1971.

Warner's stability and the numerous associated media firms under
WCI (Warner Communications Inc.) were responsible for the largest
conglomerate takeover, the marriage between WCI and Time Inc. in
July 1989. The Time/Warner alliance reflects the desire of two large conglomerates to create an integrated worldwide corporation specializing
in media and the entertainment business: a company with a theatrical
film business, record business, publishing, cable operations, television
syndication, and extensive international media ownership.[87] More spe-

cifically, the deal enabled Warner to place its product into Home Box Office, owned by Time and operating both HBO and Cinemax.[88] The merger was presented in the media as a strike against the takeover of the media by foreign operations, such as Bertelsmann of West Germany, Robert Maxwell of England, Rupert Murdoch of Australia, Giancarlo Parretti of Italy, and the conglomerates of Japan.[89] Financial analysts were advising that, in order to compete with large foreign corporations, the American media companies should band together; Gordon Crawford, of the Capital Group, commented, "I think the [Time/Warner] merger is brilliant because it creates the biggest, best-positioned, most powerful entertainment media company in the world. The way the industry is tending is toward large, global, vertically integrated companies."[90]

The merger was prolonged by a battle with Paramount Communications Inc., which made a hostile $12.2-billion, $200-per-share bid for Time, basically hoping to create a similar integrated media giant.[91] This move by Paramount received a strongly negative reaction within the press and the entertainment industry. Even reclusive media mogul George Lucas addressed the issue in a letter to the *Wall Street Journal*, "Paramount's hostile attack on the union of Time and Warner disrupted a strategic combination of potentially enormous and lasting significance for the U.S. entertainment industry. . . . It has surely contributed to losing America's war in the global marketplace."[92]

Although Walt Disney Productions basically was not a threat to the majors during the 1970s, the company made great strides in the latter half of the 1980s. Growing from a dismal 3 percent of the market at the beginning of the decade, Disney rose to 14 percent in 1989 and to 14.5 percent for the period 1986 through 1989, placing it second only to Paramount.[93] Disney's success seems due to three principal components: the formation of Touchstone Pictures in 1984, the arrival of the Paramount team Eisner–Jeffrey Katzenberg in the same year, and the entry of Disney into other entertainment ventures.[94] Touchstone was formed primarily to supply more adult-oriented films without losing the family stamp of the Disney name.[95] In its first year, Touchstone produced *Splash* (revenues: $62.1 million) and the less successful *Country* ($8.3 million). The new team's influence was not felt until two years later with the 1986 releases of *Down and Out in Beverly Hills, Ruthless People, The Color of Money,* and *Tough Guys.*

By the time Disney had begun to make a real dent in the marketplace, several traits became clear within its films and, indeed, within the Disney operation. One cannot overestimate the importance of Eisner and Katzenberg to the development. Especially significant is their emphasis upon story, medium-budget projects, and the desire for close control

and interaction with the filmmakers. While these traits have been inter-
nalized within Paramount, the originators (Diller, Eisner, and Katzenberg) have proceeded to spread their philosophy to other companies.
Following Diller's move to Fox, Eisner and Katzenberg left Paramount
for Disney. Since Disney was not beset by the grave structural problems
of Fox, the company has been able to adapt the Paramount strategy to
the configuration of the new company. While Disney has been most
successful with upscale comedies, its production schedule has become
more varied, with forays into action/adventure (*Shoot to Kill* [1988], *An
Innocent Man* [1989]) and domestic drama (*The Good Mother* [1988],
Blaze [1989]). With a couple of important exceptions (*Beaches* [1988]
and *Dead Poets Society* [1989]), though, Disney has been unable to extend its successes beyond the formulaic comedies. Whether Disney will
be able to compete on a long-term basis with majors such as Paramount
is open to debate, although the substantial assets of the Disney Channel, Disney Home Video, and, especially, the Disneyland/Disney World
theme parks offer room for experimentation.[96] Indeed, the theme parks
and resorts represent a large percentage of Disney's annual income, garnering $785.4 million in 1989, 64 percent of the company's total oper-
ating profits.[97]

Apart from Paramount and Warner Bros., the other film conglomerates of the '60s—MCA and United Artists—fared less well, with MCA
substantially more successful than United Artists. MCA continued to develop throughout the 1970s and '80s, although its growth and diversification did not rival either Paramount's or Warner's. Its film division
was helped by an association with Steven Spielberg, responsible for
Universal's *Jaws* (1975) and *E.T. the Extra-Terrestrial* (1982). Seeking the
security of Time Warner, Lew Wasserman sold MCA to leading consumer electronics firm Matsushita in 1990 for $6.6 billion.[98] Although
the deal was motivated by the desire to link the hardware producer
(Matsushita) with the software producer (MCA), the benefits from such
an association may be limited. As investment banker Herb Schlosser
comments, "The synergies are overrated. For $500 million you could
license all the software in the world for a new system."[99]

In many ways, the history of United Artists in the past twenty years
underlines the potential problems of continual mergers and management changes. After Transamerica acquired the profitable company
in 1968, UA became one of the most successful distributors of the mid-
1970s, posting a 16 percent market share in 1976 and 18 percent in
1977. Soon after the takeover, a feud erupted between the Transamerica
executives and UA's long-time chief executives Arthur Krim and Robert

Benjamin. Apparently, Transamerica substantially reduced expenditures for the white collar workers at UA and installed a computerized information system for projecting profits and tracking budgets.[100] This change in management style offended the old UA regime, and pressure from the situation caused the team of Arthur Krim, Eric Pleskow, Robert Benjamin, William Bernstein, and Mike Medavoy to offer to buy UA from Transamerica. After the conglomerate's refusal to sell, the executives quit and formed Orion Pictures in January 1978.

Since that time, United Artists has passed through several different owners, with Kirk Kerkorian and Ted Turner playing a major role in these transformations. Since 1982, there have been many changes in top management; among those well-known executives who have controlled either MGM or UA since that time are Frank Yablans, Freddie Fields, Jerry Weintraub, Lee Rich, Alan Ladd, Jr., and Tony Thomopolous.[101] Numerous MGM/UA films in the late '80s were relegated to regional or extremely limited releases: *Illegally Yours* (1987), *Some Girls* (1988), *The Rachel Papers* (1989), *True Love* (1989), and *A Dry White Season* (1989). Most significantly, though, the internal problems within the company have severely weakened its position within the marketplace: MGM/UA's market share dropped from 11 percent in 1982 to 6 percent in 1989. In addition, the company has invested little in the new technologies in terms of cable, home video, or theater ownership. The case of MGM/UA represents the dangers of media mergers for the overall growth and diversification of a company which is dealing constantly with takeover bids and management shifts, and thus fails to adapt to the rapidly changing industry.

Those companies which did not undergo conglomeration in the 1960s have been unable to withstand the development and diversification of the current industry. Due to their narrow portfolio of assets, both Columbia and Twentieth Century–Fox were perfect targets for takeover bids. At the beginning of the 1980s, both companies acquiesced to ownership changes which, in the long run, have been detrimental to the growth of the film companies.[102] In June 1981, Denver oil baron Marvin Davis acquired Twentieth Century–Fox, one of the few times an individual has actually been able to buy a film company.[103] Davis replaced head of production Sherry Lansing with Joe Wizan, and promptly began to spin off some Fox assets to ameliorate debt. In September 1984, Davis placed Barry Diller (from Paramount) as chairman of Fox. In the same month Davis sold the company to the News Corporation, 46 percent controlled by Rupert Murdoch. Murdoch's plan with Fox was to create a new television network to provide programming to non-network stations and to the seven Metromedia stations acquired by Murdoch for $1.6 billion.[104] Part of Fox's problem was this goal: instead of moving aggressively into home video, cable, and theater purchases, Fox expended a great deal of energy and finance on the development of the fourth network.

Unlike Fox's, Columbia's merger history can be interpreted as an attempt to deal with the new delivery systems. In January 1982, Coca-Cola purchased Columbia Pictures for $820 million.[105] This move seems reminiscent of Transamerica's involvement with United Artists. Both companies sought to enter the film business to stimulate their stock and to acquire access to a valuable library of film and television programming. Coca-Cola's own experience with its soft drink(s) has shown that diversification can lead to an increased share of the market. Consider Coca-Cola's experience with the various Coke spin-offs: Diet Coke, Cherry Coke, Diet Cherry, No Caffeine Coke, No Caffeine Diet Coke, etc. Coke chose to diversify the product from Columbia via the provocative move of creating an entirely "new" line of product. As Gomery describes, Coke knew that theater owners would not want to grant Columbia's bookers twice the number of valuable Christmas and summer booking slots.[106] Therefore, as a solution, Columbia chose to become partners in a new studio, Tri-Star. As Columbia executive vice-president Victor Kaufman commented at the time, the move was made since "Columbia [i.e., Coca-Cola] wants to participate in the ownership of as many films as possible."[107]

In its original conception, Tri-Star, founded in December 1982, was the ultimate consequence of the new media developments. The studio was initially a co-venture involving Columbia, CBS Inc., and HBO. The rationale behind Tri-Star makes complete economic sense: Tri-Star produces the films; Columbia, for a fee, handles the distribution; HBO is granted the pay-TV run, and CBS receives the network and syndicated television runs. As well as assuring two additional video windows for Columbia's product, the enterprise strengthened HBO's involvement with the film industry. A major provision of the deal was that HBO would invest in all of Columbia's theatricals and would gain an equity interest in excess of 25 percent.[108] HBO wanted to position itself as a player within both the film and cable industries. Similarly, CBS was attempting to establish a strong place for itself in the increasingly integrated media marketplace.[109] In its first years of operation, Tri-Star managed to produce several successful films, including *The Natural* (1984), *Rambo: First Blood Part II* (1985), *Short Circuit* (1986), and *Blind Date* (1987).

After the extreme upheaval of the mid-1980s, and four production heads (Frank Price, 1978–1983; Guy McElwaine, 1983–1986; David Putt-nam, 1986–1987; Dawn Steel, 1988–1990), Columbia became part of a second conglomerate — the Sony Corp. — at the end of the decade. Sony had been expanding into the media market primarily as a means of supplying software to match its strong consumer electronics division; following this rationale, the Sony/Columbia merger made more eco-nomic sense than the Coke/Columbia match, since Coke's soft-drink operation would not benefit substantially from the entertainment com-pany. Sony's first move into the North American market was to acquire CBS Records for $2 billion in January 1988.[110] However, the benefits of the Columbia acquisition offered even more synergy for Sony: in par-ticular, television and film production and distribution, or, in other words, the software to drive hardware sales. Having paid nearly $5 bil-lion for the studio, Sony placed Peter Guber and Jon Peters at the head of Columbia. This management decision proved to be costly, to the tune of nearly $1 billion, since Sony had to buy both the Guber-Peters company, as well as appease Warner Bros., which had just signed a de-velopment deal with the producers.[111]

The movement of the film industry through the past decade reveals the increasing polarization in the marketplace. Figure 3 (covering 1986 to 1989) presents this polarization clearly in comparison with the mar-ket share tables for the two prior periods. The most successful compa-nies (Paramount and Time Warner) have diversified (especially into the new delivery systems) and have actually increased their market power through consistent and unified growth in their companies. These con-glomerates, along with Disney, have practiced diversification within their entertainment products, through high concept, to parallel their diversification into allied media. The attempts to maximize the synergy between different media were matched in these conglomerates by the drive to focus and target moviegoers through the differentiated product of high concept. Other majors (particularly Columbia and United Art-ists), without such a focus, have simply lost their former stature within the industry.

The narrowing of the marketplace indicates that the economic power within the industry has become concentrated among very few firms, with the previously strongest firms (Paramount and Warner Bros.) simply bolstering their position within the industry. Have the largest firms been able to gain market power on the basis of structural factors alone, such as the benefits of conglomeration for the studios, or have these companies utilized their products to gain power? One could argue that, implicitly, part of their strategy has been to differentiate their prin-cipal product (i.e., film) from the majority of films released in the market. This differentiation has often taken an aesthetic form, so that the actual components of film are altered during development and production. High concept is basically an extreme form of differentiation for the majors.

Differentiation of Product

In many ways, studios have always responded to the opportunities offered through product differentiation. The blockbuster era can be explained in terms of differentiation; a blockbuster is separated from the majority of other releases by the size (budget, reputation, bankable source material) and scope of the project. Given that film can be considered as a product with certain characteristics, a film which differs from the norm potentially can increase its share of the pie. Therefore, a blockbuster could be differentiated through such qualities as *more* stars, *higher* budget, *more* exciting story. For instance, in 1976, *King Kong* was marketed with the line "The most exciting original motion picture event of all time" set against a shot of Kong straddling the World Trade Center. The rhetoric of the ad — "event," "most exciting," "original," "of all time" — joined to the towering ape clearly positions the film as bigger and grander than any other film in the marketplace. While studios attempt to distinguish films through their own marketing, films *are* different: films are produced, distributed, and exhibited through different routes (e.g., limited, tiered, and saturation release schedules) and appeal to different audiences. Characterizing film as a single product with perfect substitution amongst the different competing properties is a clear misrepresentation of the economic market for film.

Clearly evident as forms of differentiation are such enterprises as 3-D film and the development of "boutique" or independent studios. Perhaps as a reaction to the introduction of the new delivery systems, the spring and summer of 1983 saw the largest output of commercial 3-D films since the 3-D boom of the 1950s. Films such as *Comin' at Ya!* (1981; boxoffice gross: $12 million) and *Friday the 13th Part 3 — 3-D* (1982; boxoffice gross: $36 million) helped to revive the cycle.[112] 3-D, which expands the viewer's depth perception of film to three-dimensional space, is the most obvious method to differentiate the product of film. As was the case with the advent of television three decades earlier, the differentiation involved offering an "experience" which contrasted with the other media forms. The resurgence was short-lived, however, primarily due to the large exhibition costs associated with the presentations.

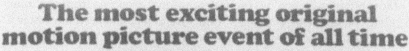

The rhetoric of marketing King Kong *(King Kong, Paramount, 1976).*

More significant as a differentiated product are films from the independent studios. Unlike the 3-D film, the independent studio offers a product situated somewhere between the traditional "art-house" and the mainstream studio fare.[113] Realizing the potential from targeting an upscale, educated audience aged twenty-five to forty-five (in other words, a segment of the baby boom market), companies have been producing films which represent a viable alternative for the older audience. Among the more prominent of the independent studios have been New Line Cinema, Miramax, Hemdale Film Corporation, Cinecom Entertainment Group, Alive Films, Island Pictures, and Atlantic Releasing.[114] The unifying elements among these films are an attention to theme, character relationships, and social relevance. While these traits have long been associated with the European art film movement, the commercial American studio film is still driven by plot and causation. The more prominent "boutique" films of recent years include *Kiss of the Spiderwoman* (1985), *A Room with a View* (1986), *The Whales of August* (1987), *sex, lies, and videotape* (1989), *My Left Foot* (1989), *Howards End* (1992), and *The Crying Game* (1992). These films fall outside the domain of the majors by being too small/personal (e.g., *Choose Me* [1984], *The Whales of August*), controversial (e.g., *Kiss of the Spiderwoman, River's Edge* [1987]), or unmarketable. Even though Miramax's *sex, lies, and videotape*, with rentals of $10 million, outgrossed such mainstream studio dramas as Fox's *The Fabulous Baker Boys*, Disney's *Blaze*, and Columbia's *Casualties of War* in 1989, the film's subject matter immediately placed it outside consideration by the major studios.[115] (Just imagine the marketing team at Paramount trying to develop ad lines and thirty-second television commercials for a movie about a man whose only form of social interaction and sexual stimulation is taping women discussing their sex lives in explicit detail.)

Leon Falk, director of product acquisition at Cinecom, offers the following illuminating explanation for his company's decisions: "There's a belief [at Cinecom] that film is not simply a marketable commodity or a form of entertainment, but that it has tremendous values in terms of communication and tremendous possibilities for art."[116] The aesthetic difference of the films is augmented by a difference in finance and funding. Due to the lower cost (usually under $7–8 million), the producing costs are almost completely covered by pre-financing and the pre-sale of home video and other rights before production begins.[117] The result is a product quite strikingly different from the (still) largely genre-oriented films from the majors. The films are also differentiated by their quite specific appeal to segments of the audience largely untouched by the major studios. To use an extreme example, *The Whales of August,* featuring a cast of veteran actors and dealing with the problems of mental illness, death, and family relationships among the elderly, hardly had the ability to cross over into a more broad-based audience as did Universal's *On Golden Pond* (1981), which dealt with many of the same issues and concerns in a more accessible manner (partly through the resonance offered by the real-life conflicts between stars Henry and Jane Fonda).[118]

Considering film as a commodity following the laws of economics, the demand depends upon the price of admission and a large number of product characteristics. To be more specific, the demand for film is a function of the individual consumer's tastes, the competing entertainment offerings (such as television, cable, home video), the level of disposable income, and many other factors. The importance of the consumer's tastes as a factor influencing demand introduces the very important facet of market segmentation. Market segmentation, or the division of the whole market by demographic segments, is realized by the film industry through targeting films at certain well-defined audience demographics. For example, a film such as Paramount's *Flashdance* obviously has primary appeal to a young, female audience, and its story, concept, development, and marketing were initially designed to appeal to this audience.[119] In contrast, Paramount's *A New Life* (1988; an Alan Alda film dealing with post-marital problems) was designed to target an older, predominantly female audience.[120] How much overlap would there really be between the two audiences for these films? The unique demand shown by each group allows the entire market of filmgoers to be divided into segments with distinct demand functions.[121] In this way, market segmentation appears to be a useful method to discuss the film audience in a more specific and directed fashion.

The difficulty with considering market segmentation alone is that it interacts with product differentiation as a market condition. The marketplace for film is divided not just by the different demand functions (or preferences) of the viewers, but also by the differences between the many films which appear simultaneously in the market. For instance, in February 1984 the market for film could be divided along the lines of films with appeal to certain demographics (e.g., *Footloose* would appeal to a young female crowd, while *Terms of Endearment* appealed to an older female demographic), along with films which differ from each other by such product characteristics as genre, stars, and visual style (e.g., *Footloose* is a teen musical-drama, while *Terms of Endearment* is a personal/family drama). Clearly these two methods of defining the market are intimately connected. *Footloose* was certainly designed as a "product" to appeal to a teen crowd. Consider the rock soundtrack, fea-

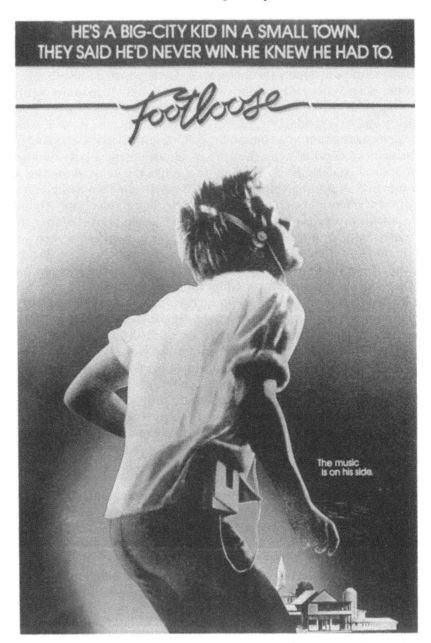

Footloose: *designed to attract a young, teen audience* (Footloose, *Paramount, 1984).*

turing Kenny Loggins, Bonnie Tyler, and Shalamar; the story centering around an alienated youth bucking the system by organizing a school dance; and the attractive young stars (Lori Singer and Kevin Bacon) trying to deal with first love. The film was designed to attract a young teen audience, while its appeal to a middle-aged male would be nonexistent. In other words, the differences shown between each film in the market ("product differentiation") are orchestrated to further segment the market ("market segmentation"). Therefore, product differentiation can be seen as a means of implementing market segmentation.[122]

Through what methods can products be differentiated within the market? Product differentiation can be implemented through two different routes: in terms of *variety* and *quality*.[123] Differentiation due to product variety relates to the characteristics of the commodity. Consumer preferences are distributed over a range of some characteristic of the product. As the number of differentiated versions of the product increases, so does consumer satisfaction, since the individual tastes of each consumer may be met through the differentiated products. In this manner, firms are able to gain certain segments of the market through their slightly differentiated products. Considering film, product characteristics could include such factors as plotline, stars, production value, genre, social relevance, and difference/similarity to other films (originality). Additionally, factors related to the exhibition of the film clearly are attributes important to some audience members: geographic location, convenience, theater maintenance, staff courtesy and service, and projection/sound quality. Therefore, an example of an increase in product variety to achieve a larger share of the market might be offered by a film such as *Batman*, which differentiates itself from both the television series and other comic strip adventures movies (such as *Flash Gordon* [1980], *Superman* [1978], and *Dick Tracy*) through its stars (particularly the close fit between Jack Nicholson and the role of the Joker), music (by Prince), production design (by Anton Furst), and somber approach to the comic book legend. These unique elements could be interpreted as product differentiation, making *Batman* different from both the other comic-book movies and competing films in the marketplace. If consumers are perceived as valuing each of these attributes more or less equally, then the model of product differentiation collapses into variations of product quality. Otherwise, differentiation depends upon the varied attributes inherent in the moviegoing experience.[124]

Variations in product quality assume that consumers value some underlying attribute contained within the product. The larger the amount of the attribute contained within the product, the greater the satisfaction of the consumer. The evaluation of the film by the consumer as "good" or "worth seeing" relates to the perceived quality of the film. Of course, variations in the product quality are also established *before* the viewer purchases a ticket, since reviews, publicity, and word of mouth all create an expectation of a certain level of quality. Films which are perceived as being of a higher quality ("better entertainment value") will garner a larger market share, other things remaining equal. Since each viewer has a different demand and utility function, the evaluation of quality will differ from consumer to consumer; otherwise, in the extreme case, one film would corner the entire audience of filmgoers.

The studios' implicit understanding of variations in product quality and product variety as marketplace strategies can be gauged through a film's marketing campaign. Consider, for example, the function of critics' quotes in print ads for a film. The critics' opinions substitute for the possible reaction of the patron; therefore, a rave from a certain critic indicates higher quality before actual attendance of the film. In fact, certain films—particularly art-house films—depend upon a variation in product quality as a method to gain audience interest and patronage. Consider three ads from Paramount movies in 1978 as representative of how studios differentiate and market movies through product variety and quality. Perhaps to counteract any bias against the film as lightweight and superficial, the *Heaven Can Wait* (1978) image of Warren Beatty as angel was later buttressed with critical raves to suggest a film of a higher quality than others in the market; *Grease* depends almost entirely on the images of John Travolta and Olivia Newton-John, suggesting primarily that these stars will differentiate the movie from other teen movies and secondarily that the stars will make the film of a higher quality than other films; *Days of Heaven* (1978) also operates primarily on a variation in product variety through suggesting that the sensual experience of the film will be quite different than the viewer's experience of any other film.

With the addition of the concept of product differentiation, the marketplace can be conceived as split into many different, smaller markets, each catering to specific audience segments with distinct demand functions. The marketplace is split, as is the "good" of film itself; film can be conceptualized more fruitfully as a product with a large number of attributes which can be varied to meet the needs of specific audiences. This atomized model of the film marketplace obviously has some problems in practice (e.g., "cross-over" films, such as *Rambo: First Blood Part II* and *Flashdance*, which transcend a single defined market segment, would complicate the model considerably), yet it also offers some specific routes to explain the status of the current film marketplace. In

Product Differentiation: Paramount Pictures, 1978 (a) Heaven Can Wait: *Warren Beatty as angel, later matched by critical raves.*

(b) Grease: *stars as differentiating factor.*

Your eyes...
Your ears...
Your senses...
will be overwhelmed
in 70mm and Dolby®stereo*

(c) Days of Heaven: *a distinctive sensual experience.*

addition, the model of market segmentation and product differentiation can be utilized to examine studio products and strategies in the marketplace. In particular, high concept can be conceptualized as a specific form of differentiated product targeted at a defined audience segment. The large-scale high concept hits, such as *Batman, Lethal Weapon* (1987), and *Home Alone* (1990), become so potent through transcending this one audience segment and expanding into the broad population of moviegoers.

High Concept as Product Differentiation

In his analysis of the relationship between film content and economic determinants, Joseph R. Dominick comments that "the tighter the oligopoly and the risk, the more similar will be the 'look' of films produced by each studio."[125] Dominick argues that the new technologies have not increased the variety of films produced; Hollywood is only producing more of the same. While the genres of film may be the same, I disagree with Dominick's contention regarding the aesthetics of these films.[126] The most successful studios are those which can identify and exploit a particular market segment in their films. In particular, Paramount realizes this strategy through a significant percentage of its release schedule. For example, in targeting the teen audience, Paramount released *Explorers* (1985), *Pretty in Pink, Summer School* (1987), and *Ferris Bueller's Day Off;* while in targeting the older male audience segment, Paramount concentrated on action films such as *The Untouchables* (1987), *The Presidio* (1988), *Black Rain* (1989), and *The Hunt for Red October* (1990). While Paramount is most clearly aligned with the high concept film, Touchstone/Disney also presents a distinctive type of project. Accordingly, in the past several years, studio films *have* become differentiated through their look and style. For example, one can talk about the "personality" of a Paramount film: the visual style, genre (Paramount tends to concentrate more on the teen comedy or the "fish out of water" comedy than on drama), and marketing approach. While I would not want to claim that a studio's production schedule is uniform, there does appear to be continuity between some elements of certain studios' output.

The continuity suggests that a form of product differentiation is being undertaken by the majors. The advantages of this strategy are many. As Edward Chamberlain summarizes, "Where the possibility of differentiation exists, sales depend on the skill with which the good is distinguished from others and made to appeal to a specific group of buyers."[127] Studio manipulation of product characteristics intersects with the category of high concept: the most financially successful studios in the late '80s (Paramount and Disney) have been the studios most associated with the term high concept. High concept seems to be a more exact category of differentiation because, in several respects, there are decisive breaks from the usual narrational and compositional structure of the Hollywood film. In this section, I will highlight the breaks which offer a differentiated product.

As a form of product differentiation, high concept operates through two channels: through an emphasis on style, and through an integration with marketing and merchandising. Kenneth Clarkson and Roger LeRoy Miller discuss style changes as a type of product differentiation unrelated to quality or durability.[128] Innovations in style result in the obsolescence of the already existing products, with the most dramatic examples coming from the auto and fashion industries. This strategy—shifts in style to garner larger market shares—thereby aids the elimination of competing products. Style in the high concept films embodies many facets: style in the production, narrative, and use of genre. The most obvious of these traits is the high-tech look of the production. Relying on a tradition which architectural historian Reyner Banham referred to as "the Second Industrial Revolution" for its emphasis upon electronic devices and controlled environments, these films offer a distinctive look.[129] Former Disney Production Vice-President Peter McAlevey refers to the style as "a high tech gloss." This explanation seems useful, as it refers to the superficial rendering of high technology which controls the films.[130] The style of these films represents one configuration of attributes (production, narrative, design) which serves effectively to differentiate the high concept films.

The other major differentiating factor of high concept involves packaging, rather than product design. High concept films have a greater focus upon their marketing and merchandising than other mainstream Hollywood films. In part, this emphasis is due to these films being marketed and merchandised to a particular audience segment. The majority of the films are targeted to a certain audience in conception, thereby making their media campaigns much more specific and directed. In general, the films are skewed to a younger group, although the large-scale, high concept hits do cross over into other audience segments during their run.[131] The difference between the promotion of the high concept films and other mainstream Hollywood films seems to be a reliance on the image and the replication of this image through different media. By image, I am referring to both the figures from the print campaign ads and the "persona" of the entire film (i.e., the connotations which the entire campaign, including publicity and promotion, creates for the film). The viewer's impression of the film is strengthened by the repetition of the image from the ad campaign, media buys, and, most importantly, the licensing of the film through different products. While all films are supported by ad campaigns, only a minority are based on a concept which lends itself to this cross-fertilization of promotion. For example, *Top Gun*'s concept depends on strong visuals (e.g., jets cutting across the sky, aerial combat, muscular young pilot falling in love with beautiful blonde instructor) and a generically based story (the World War II–era combat films) which lead easily to the film's presentation in the media. Other Paramount films (perhaps *Heartburn* or *Children of a Lesser God*) contain concepts which cannot be contained succinctly through promotion, and which therefore do not operate via the same form of product differentiation. The image-based media campaigns represent segment-based product differentiation. Through its advertising, the company is able to appeal to particular market segments, thereby differentiating its product from the rest of the films in the market. Frequently this strategy augments the differentiation in terms of style, which also marks the high concept film.

Of the majors, Paramount and Disney have been most successful in practicing these forms of product differentiation. The fact that these companies have both the most distinctive products and highest revenues (1986–1989 market shares of 18.0 percent for Paramount and 14.5 percent for Disney) is by no means coincidental. Many of Paramount's films play into utopian fantasies; as Tony Schwartz suggests, "A remarkable number of Paramount's movies mine the mainstream fantasy of struggling against odds to realize a dream."[132] Just as important is Paramount's adherence to established genre patterns. While other studios offer films which defy genre description, Paramount works within genre: from the musical (*Footloose, Staying Alive, Flashdance*), the adventure/action film (*Raiders of the Lost Ark, 48 HRS.* [1982], *Indiana Jones and the Temple of Doom* [1984], *The Untouchables*), the "fish out of water" comedy (*Trading Places* [1983], *Beverly Hills Cop, "Crocodile" Dundee* [1986], *Planes, Trains and Automobiles, Crazy People* [1990]), to the teenage comedy (*Pretty in Pink, Some Kind of Wonderful*). Paramount does undertake cross-generic products, however. Consider the *film noir* comedy *The Blue Iguana* (1988), the comedy-drama *Shirley Valentine*, and most impressive, from a boxoffice standpoint, the comedy-romance-thriller *Ghost* (1990). Typically, though, these films are not integral to the company's release schedule, or, to use Paramount's terminology, these films are not the "tent poles" of the schedule.[133]

Nevertheless, Paramount's genre films are certainly not classical genre examples either. More than other studios, Paramount utilizes the viewer's knowledge and understanding of mass/popular culture. The audience's recognition of, for example, musical conventions (in the case of *Staying Alive* or *Flashdance*), action/adventure serials (the *Indiana Jones* series), television series (*Star Trek, The Untouchables*), and even board games (*Clue* [1985]) gives the studio license to "update" the films through the visual style and production design of the films. The studio's style has been described as "urban, hipper, gutsier," and this evaluation certainly grows from the surface appearance of the Paramount films.[134] The fusion of this stylishness with the saturated genre narratives offers the method that Paramount has utilized to differentiate its product. Producer Don Simpson's assessment of *Flashdance*'s success could well describe Paramount's modus operandi: "I thought there was a chance for popular art, not high art, in the concept. *Flashdance* had a quality known as top spin, in which the casting, the concept and the look and sound of the movie all come together."[135]

The product from Disney follows some of the same guidelines as the Paramount films. The connection is not coincidental: Disney's creative team of Michael Eisner, Jeffrey Katzenberg, and Richard Frank all worked at Paramount in the early 1980s under the tutelage of Barry Diller. The connection between the two studios begins with the close control which both have over the projects and, in particular, over the films' budgets.[136] With Touchstone, Disney solved its own diversification problem by creating an adult-oriented film arm. Significantly, Disney did not dilute the tradition of the Disney name and its connection with family entertainment. In a statement which indicates the importance of product differentiation for the company, Richard Berger, president of Disney Pictures, explains the reason for the two divisions: "People don't know who [which studio] made *Star Wars* or *Raiders*, but they can tell you who made *Tron*."[137]

While maintaining Disney product, the company also produced consistent Touchstone product. With *Down and Out in Beverly Hills* in 1986, Touchstone began to produce films which contained many similarities, while still remaining individual projects. The company has profited from a series of comedies featuring established actors, directors, and tight comic timing.[138] The comedies have mainly been light-hearted social commentaries containing larger-than-life personalities, such as Bette Midler, Jim Belushi, or Robin Williams. The difference between these stars' other films and their Disney films underlines Disney's method: the films are able to contain the stars' personae, rather than being overwhelmed by them. The comedies (such as *Ruthless People, Outrageous Fortune* [1987], *Three Men and a Baby, Good Morning, Vietnam* [1987], *Turner and Hooch* [1989], *Three Fugitives* [1989], and *Sister Act*

[1992]) have also been balanced by more personal projects, such as the anthology film by Woody Allen, Francis Coppola, and Martin Scorsese, *New York Stories* (1989), and John Boorman's *Where the Heart Is* (1990). In this way, Disney has been able to develop continuing working relationships with more famous "auteur" directors, while still having the financial security of its comedies.

Among the other majors, it's more difficult to discern distinctive studio styles. David Puttnam's Columbia promised to offer an alternative to mainstream Hollywood product. Working from a personal desire to make socially relevant films, Puttnam's release slate during his brief tenure included *Housekeeping* (1987), *Hope and Glory* (1987), *The Last Emperor* (1987), *A Time of Destiny* (1988), and *The Old Gringo* (1989). The rationale behind these decisions seems to be a need to make high-quality films, leaving the marketplace to its designs. Interestingly, there was economic reasoning to Puttnam's mandate; the Puttnam slate seemed designed as a shift in the *quality* (rather than variety) of film to gain a larger market share. Still, at this time, only Paramount and Disney have successfully practiced in-house product differentiation (via their high concept projects) on a sustained basis.

With the blockbuster as its point of departure, the high concept film has been shaped by the development of the new delivery systems and the increased concentration and conglomeration of the film industry. High concept, differentiated through its style and integration with marketing/merchandising, speaks to the structural changes in the industry. These films, centered on bold, marketable images, are designed to target a specific audience and to convey a strong image carrying the film through all the release windows. High concept can be described most productively, therefore, as one strain of contemporary American cinema whose style has a direct economic motive. This economic strategy depends on conceiving the market for film as splintered through product differentiation and market segmentation. Through well-defined market segmentation and the aesthetic difference of these films, some of the major studios, particularly Paramount, have created a space for high concept within film history.

4 Marketing the Image: High Concept and the Development of Marketing

The ties between high concept and marketing are both numerous and strong. On the most fundamental level, the style of the high concept films depends on slick, arresting images which, at times, distance the viewer from the narrative. These images in turn drive the marketing of the high concept films through being replicated across a variety of media (e.g., print ads, one-sheets, television commercials, trailers) and merchandised product (e.g., book tie-ins, soundtracks). The viewer's awareness of the film generally begins and is sustained through these primary marketing images.

The high concept/marketing connection develops from several interlocking historical and institutional shifts in the market for film. Indeed, as suggested previously, the "first wave" of conglomeration in the film industry led to a contraction of the economic risk involved in mainstream studio filmmaking, evident through the lower number of releases and the development of the roadshow, the youth film, and the blockbuster. This tightening of the industry is also illustrated through a shift in film distribution strategy. The move to saturation releases rather than limited or platform releases for major studio films in the mid-1970s onward marks a significant break in the established studio distribution pattern. This shift also fostered changes in film marketing methods, redesigning the pattern of film marketing to support saturation releases. Not coincidentally, both alterations in distribution and marketing function most effectively with high concept films, which foreground style and marketing hooks. Thus one can draw significant

Billy Jack: *four-wall phenomenon (1971).*
Copyright © by Warner Bros. Inc.

parallels between the development of several film marketing innovations in the 1970s and the development of high concept. Working from this perspective, I will chart these innovations and describe their utilization with the high concept films, with particular emphasis on the methods through which these marketing forms privilege (or seem designed to privilege) high concept.

Changing Distribution Patterns

Interestingly, the first major marketing revision was introduced by an independent producer, Tom Laughlin, whose low-budget film *Billy Jack* (1971) pioneered a form of distribution referred to as "four-walling." The film received poor box-office revenue during its initial run, yet Laughlin believed that the audiences would indeed respond to the pacifist–martial arts film.[1] With the help of marketer Max Youngstein, *Billy Jack* was reopened in May 1973 extremely widely in the Southern California area with an unheard of one-week ad expenditure of $250,000. The producer also leased the theaters outright throughout the entire broadcast area reached by the television spots.[2] Laughlin differentiated each television spot to appeal to a specific audience segment: "Believing that *Billy Jack* is a picture that is all things to all men, Taylor-Laughlin's spots covered all possible angles. The spots sold love angles, milked the counter-culture, appealed to action fans, karate cultists, youth, the middle-aged, and the non-filmgoer."[3] The response was phenomenal: the first week's gross of $1,029,000 represented the largest boxoffice take in Southern California film history.[4] This method of distribution was repeated on a market-by-market basis throughout the country with similar results.

The majors were attracted not only by the success of Laughlin's film, but also by the follow-up successes of two four-walled wildlife pictures, *Vanishing Wilderness* (1973) and *Cry of the Wild* (1974).[5] Soon majors such as Warner Bros. and Fox, and independent Avco-Embassy, were planning to four-wall films.[6] The marketing methods utilized for *Billy Jack* quickly were appropriated by the majors: the reallocation of media spending away from print and heavily toward television; customizing the advertising campaign to appeal to the particular demographics of a region; saturation release throughout a well-defined region; and the leasing of theaters within the television signal region. With the exception of the leasing of theaters, the majors responded positively to these methods. The traditional release schedule for a film had been a print-intensive campaign and an exclusive first run in a small number of theaters, finally opening up to a wider release in the suburban and sub-run theaters. Eventually this distribution pattern, and the accompanying marketing efforts, were revised. For those films which could generate a high level of anticipation on the part of the public, saturation releases with advertising campaigns centered on television became a preferred strategy.

After *Billy Jack, Magnum Force* (1973; the sequel to *Dirty Harry*), Charles Bronson's *Breakout* (1975), and, most prominently, *Jaws* all opened in saturation patterns.[7] While the Bronson and Eastwood films had obvious marketing hooks, *Jaws*'s opening was viewed as more bold; opening in a fairly wide (at the time) 409 theaters, the film received a saturation television advertising campaign.[8] Whereas in the past, this type of opening had been reserved for films which the studios judged to have little playability, the opening of *Jaws* signified the adoption of this release and marketing pattern for high-quality studio pictures. The strategy worked extremely well for *Jaws*, which grossed $7.061 million in its opening weekend.[9]

Following *Jaws*, high quality studio films developed even broader saturation releases; in 1976, *King Kong* (with a 961 theater opening); in

1977, *The Heretic: Exorcist II* (703 theaters), *The Deep* (800 theaters), *Saturday Night Fever* (726 theaters); in 1978, *Grease* (902 theaters) and *Star Trek—the Motion Picture* (856 theaters) continued to expand the pattern of saturation release and intense television advertising. The broader release pattern was solidified by the phenomenal opening grosses of those films which had pre-sold elements. For instance, *The Deep*, based on Peter Benchley's bestseller and starring Nick Nolte, Robert Shaw, and Jacqueline Bisset, set a domestic boxoffice record for Columbia, grossing $8.124 million in 800 playdates, while *Grease*, starring John Travolta (following *Saturday Night Fever*) and pop singer Olivia Newton-John, grossed $9.310 million in 902 theaters the following year.[10] Justifying the broader release strategy for *The Heretic: Exorcist II*, Terry Semel, at the time executive vice-president in charge of domestic distribution, cited research which indicated the film had the greatest want-to-see of any Warner Bros. film released in the time period and that, "Exhibitors have demonstrated the same interest. Therefore, we have booked the film more widely than any other, enabling audiences from coast-to-coast to see it on the same day."[11]

These films can be seen as the forerunners of the more mature examples of high concept, which integrate marketing and style into a cohesive unit. Generally, the development of this marketing and distribution strategy characterizes the high concept film: the strong images and the pre-sold elements within both the film and the marketing campaigns are able to translate to the medium of television, thereby creating viewer awareness and interest. Consequently, high concept films are likely to benefit from the saturation approach, whereas films dependent on audience word-of-mouth require the more traditional, tiered release and marketing approach. Writing in 1976, Stuart Byron offered this cautionary note on Hollywood's move to saturation openings: "Certainly, wide openings are not suited to all pictures; a pattern which maximizes profits on *Jaws* would probably have minimized them for *Shampoo*."[12] While valid, Byron's statement does not anticipate the ways in which Hollywood would shift toward making more films such as *Jaws* with pre-sold properties, merchandising and marketing hooks, and striking visuals—i.e., high concept movies.

Awareness Marketing: High Concept in Print

High concept films work well in a saturation release because their marketing fulfills the requirements demanded by this release pattern. To be more specific, a saturation pattern requires, first and foremost, wide public awareness and interest in the film by its opening weekend. Even if the film suffers from poor word-of-mouth, high awareness and want-to-see interest translate into a healthy opening weekend boxoffice. Due to their inherent marketing hooks, high concept films usually are able to build this awareness and want-to-see interest. For a film to be a hit, though, this strong level of awareness and interest must be accompanied by both solid word-of-mouth and the continued appearance of the film in the marketplace through marketing. High concept films can garner high awareness and then *maintain* this awareness through a comprehensive marketing approach including print, trailers, television commercials, and, to a greater extent than for low concept films, merchandising and music tie-ins. Of course, word-of-mouth also factors into the boxoffice success or failure of a high concept film, but the marketing channels working for the high concept movies offer a substantial "head start" in the marketplace. An examination of the principles and development behind the "awareness" marketing (e.g., print, trailers, and television commercials) and "maintenance" marketing (e.g., merchandising and music) will illuminate how the diverse marketing routes work together to build the "head start" for the high concept film.

Starting with the arena of print advertising, a useful contrast between high and low concept print advertising can be drawn from Steven Spielberg's *Jaws* and Robert Altman's *Nashville*. In an examination of American film in the period of 1975 to 1985, critic J. Hoberman begins by contrasting these two seminal films from 1975.[13] The contrast is made initially in terms of genre: "If *Nashville* could be said to have deconstructed the disaster film, Steven Spielberg's *Jaws* gave the cycle a second lease on life."[14] The contrast between these two films exists not only on the level of genre, however. Indeed, the films' marketing campaigns reveal many of the key principles behind the print campaigns for the high concept films. Consider the *Jaws* print ad: the artwork shows a naked woman swimming, with a huge open-mouthed shark looming beneath the surface of the ocean. The shark seems almost ready to prey upon the unsuspecting swimmer. This image is accompanied by copy, which varied across the campaign: "The terrifying motion picture from the terrifying No. 1 best seller" to "She was the first. . . ." The marketers were attempting to encapsulate the film through a single image in the print campaign. Appropriately, the image conveys the enormous threat of the shark through several different means: by the relative size of the shark within the image, by the sinister set of teeth in the shark's mouth, by the unsuspecting nature of the swimmer, and by the swimmer's nakedness, which connotes a certain vulnerability. The image became prominently featured through several different media: principally with

The Jaws *advertising image: a singular image and marketing approach (Jaws, Universal, 1975).*

a "tie-in" edition of Peter Benchley's best-selling novel and in the massive television advertising campaign. This replication eventually made the image instantly recognizable and identifiable. Most significantly, however, *Jaws* was capable of being reduced successfully to a single image, since the film embodied many high concept traits: a generically based story and characters, strong contrast between good and evil, and arresting imagery. These components fostered the singular image and marketing approach.

Conversely, Robert Altman's *Nashville*, also released in the summer of 1975, developed a much more intricate print campaign. Former Paramount marketing vice-president Charles O. Glenn described the campaign: "The new general market-minded ad for the film [which at the time of the article was playing only in 249 theaters] shows *Nashville's* cast of 24 characters emblazoned — patchwork style — on the back of a denim jacket, with the film's title enclosed in a car's license plate." [15] Two different copies were utilized: the first positioned the film as "a story of lovers and laughers and losers and winners," the second carried a series of adjectives ("Wild. Wonderful. Sinful. Laughing. Explosive."). The two lines were alternated, both accompanying the patchwork design.

While the film received extremely positive reviews, *Nashville* grossed less than $9 million in its initial release. [16] The film's comparative failure at the boxoffice seems due, at least in part, to the low marketing potential of the project which was all too evident in the ambiguous, and therefore problematic, ad campaign. The shot of the twenty-four actors on the denim jacket fails as an approach to market the film for two reasons: the actors were largely unknown, with the possible exception of Lily Tomlin and Henry Gibson (both from *Rowan and Martin's Laugh-In*), and the collection of small head shots failed to reduce adequately in newspaper and print ads. The medium of newsprint also has limitations in terms of the clarity of illustration and diagram reproduction; this factor reinforces the need for a clean, bold image, such as the *Jaws* shark, which can withstand these limitations.

Additionally, with the *Nashville* ad, the copy attempted to convey a wide spectrum of emotions in a small space. The film could be seen as a comedy ("laughers"), drama ("winners and losers"), romance ("lovers"), or any combination of these genres. The connection of the copy to the ad is also ambiguous: how does this mix of genres relate to the denim jacket (for instance, is the jacket worn by the film's protagonist?) and the title (i.e., does the city Nashville suggest such contradictory themes?). The net effect of the artwork and copy was a campaign which tried to be too diverse in its appeal. This problem is replicated in the

Nashville: *not easily reduced to a single marketing image* (Nashville, Paramount, 1975).

title of the film—a documentary about the city? an exposé of country music? —which lacks the visual, distinctive quality of a title like *Jaws*. Ultimately, though, the problems with the *Nashville* campaign illustrate a basic problem in terms of marketing for those projects which do not fall within the realm of high concept. Certainly, given its expansive narrative and complex social themes, *Nashville* could not be easily reduced to a single marketing image without severe distortion, or oversimplification, of the film's content.[17]

The marketing campaign of *Jaws* indicates the direction which film marketing would follow during the next decade. The reliance on strong, reproducible images, the saturation campaign, and widespread product tie-ins steadily became standard marketing practices after the success of films such as *Jaws*. In addition, the difference between the *Jaws* and *Nashville* campaigns illustrates some of the key principles upon which the marketing of high concept films (represented in an early form by *Jaws*) are based. Focusing on the once primary film marketing medium of print, these differences in film marketing represented by these principles can be located.

The first print marketing trait of a high concept film is a very close match between the film's marketing campaign and the actual content of the film. While this principle holds in general for all film marketing, with the high concept film's perfect reducibility in terms of narrative and image, the approximation can be made with much more accuracy. An image is chosen which will remain true to the spirit of the film, while simultaneously accentuating the film's marketing assets. Former Polygram marketing executive Nancy Goliger describes this process, using the example of *Midnight Express* (1978). Goliger states that, "on the one hand, you have a film about a kid who has dealt in drugs, and the nightmare which he goes through. On the other hand, you have a courageous, heroic story about a young man who is incarcerated because of a moment of weakness. Both statements are true."[18] The campaign for the film offered artwork showing Billy Hayes surrendering to the Turkish police, set against a large passport stamped "CANCELLED." The copy accompanying the image stated that this was a true story, and viewers were advised to bring all the courage that they could to the film. The complete print ad positions the film as an inspiring story of individual heroism and courage; without mentioning the hero's drug smuggling, the ad suggests a young man, detained for some unknown (possibly false) reason, who must escape from a foreign country. Certainly the image elides Hayes's guilt through presenting him as amenable (surrendering to the foreign authorities) and through asking the viewer to empathize with Hayes by bringing courage to a viewing of this

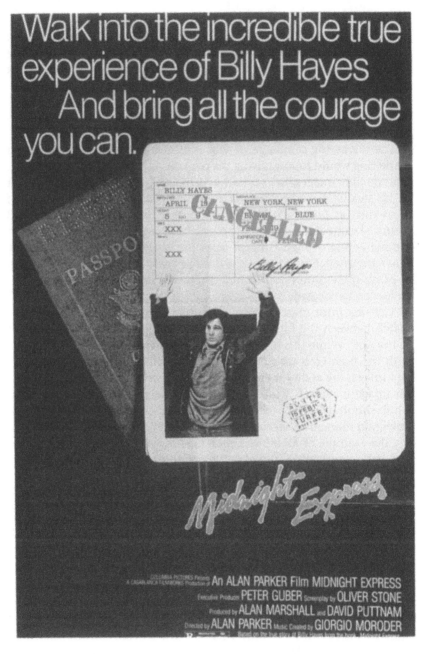

Midnight Express: *accentuating the marketing assets of a project (*Midnight Express, Columbia, 1978*).*

"incredible, true" situation. Of course, the dramatic emphasis of the film follows just the same trajectory as the ad, stressing the inequities of the Turkish law and the "courageous" effort of a young American lost within this system. The ad image can pinpoint this dramatization of a "black-and-white" situation.

As high concept films are designed to appeal to a specific audience segment, the print ad reflects this attempt to reach a target audience. Consider the print campaign for a high concept film such as *Endless Love* (1981): a close shot of Brooke Shields and Martin Hewitt in the moment before kissing, set against the copy "she is 15, he is 17. the love every parent fears." The ad foregrounds the erotic connection between two young people, an obsession which clearly frightens their parents. This reading mirrors all the relevant narrative developments of the film: the sensuality of the young love affair, the obsession (indicated by the kiss matched to the title "Endless Love"), and the objection of the parents. While the simplicity of the narrative permits its reduction to a single advertising image, it is important to note that the ad is targeted specifically at a teen audience, particularly to teenage girls. The ages in the copy, the young stars, and the promise of a romance designed to infuriate parents combine to attract a young demographic through the advertising.

With the high concept films' emphasis on style in the production and the narrative, some of the marketing campaigns reiterate style as a prominent feature. Paul Jasmine's tinted photograph of Richard Gere, featured in the *American Gigolo* print ad, offers a striking example of this usage. The shot shows an Armani-suited Gere gazing sensuously across an elegantly furnished room, with shadows from venetian blinds falling across his body.[19] While the image conveys little of the film's thriller plot, it does convey the extremely stylish nature of Gere's world and a general "noir" feeling suggested by the venetian blinds and shadows. Since Schrader's film is mainly concerned with issues of style, the marketing image, therefore, *does* also accurately represent the film. A large part of the film's commercial success has been attributed to the enticing marketing campaign; as one rival distributor commented at the time, "It [the film] was zip commercially, but they squeezed more dollars out of it than I would have thought possible. They positioned the picture so people believed that it delivered—many of them even after they saw it."[20] Because of the match between the image and the film's emphasis on style, the audience's expectations were fulfilled. Indeed, an alternative advertising campaign which was proposed for the film would have been much less appropriate. The original image showed Gere with a dead body sprawled at his feet—an approach emphasizing the thriller aspect, which the film actually downplays in its development.[21]

The simplicity of the narrative permits its reduction to a single image (Endless Love, Universal, 1981).

He's the
highest paid
lover in
Beverly Hills.

He leaves
women feeling
more alive
than they've
ever felt
before.

Except one.

Style in production, narrative, and marketing (American Gigolo, Paramount, 1980). Copyright © MCMLXXX by Paramount Pictures Corporation.

The marketing of high concept films is structured also by the choice of an image which is reducible, concise, and transferable into other media. These campaigns emphasize strong, singular images which make an immediate impression on the potential viewer. The high concept films usually are accompanied by campaigns featuring just such potent images. For example, Frank Mancuso, former chairman of Paramount, characterizes the campaign for *Escape from Alcatraz* (1979) as successful partly due to strong graphics and reducibility: "We developed a strong piece of art . . . there was one ad for the whole country—Clint with determination and will, breaking with his fist through a piece of granite—it captured the essence of the story and it reduced very well." [22]

Such a simple, powerful marketing image can be traced to the campaigns of Saul Bass, who is most often associated with the films of Otto Preminger and Alfred Hitchcock. Bass's distinctive style is frequently linked to the opening credits of certain films, which he also designed. His most memorable images include the limp black arm for *The Man with the Golden Arm* (1955), the severed body for *Anatomy of a Murder* (1959), the arms raised in revolt for *Exodus* (1960), and the spiral containing two falling figures for Alfred Hitchcock's *Vertigo* (1958).[23] In most cases, Bass extracts from the title credits a basic symbol which is simple in graphic design. The genius of his work, and the inspiration for the high concept campaigns, is derived from his ability to select simple images which both define the film's theme and make the posters instantly recognizable and striking. In this manner, Bass's work anticipates the replication of key images through marketing and mass merchandising so characteristic of high concept. Indeed, film marketing had not "matured" enough to fully capitalize on Bass's work.

The type of image popularized by Bass lends itself to the alterations in size necessary for print, and, more importantly, to the creation of an identity for the film.[24] Consider the simplicity of the two images used to market *E.T. the Extra-Terrestrial*. The first image offers a tight close-up of E.T.'s finger reaching out to touch the young hero Elliot's finger; in the second, a child, in extreme long shot, rides a bicycle across the moon, while E.T. is huddled safely in the bicycle's basket. The former offers a very simple graphic image which nonetheless establishes the film as the emotional story of connection between E.T. and a young child. Most significantly, the image's simplicity creates an identity for the film, since the graphic can be marketed through the different media and, especially in the case of *E.T.*, can also be merchandised. The film's second campaign offers an image which is not as immediately identifiable, although, in conjunction with the first campaign, the bicycle becomes more effective, since the film's fantastical elements (e.g., the

E.T. *Image: Fingers Touch* (E.T. the Extra-
Terrestrial, *Universal, 1982)*.

E.T. *Image: Flying across the Moon (*E.T. the
Extra-Terrestrial, *Universal, 1982).*

child's ability to fly) are highlighted.[25] The fantasy connoted by the second image complements the premise presented in the first campaign. Additionally, the bicycle image benefits from its replication of one of the film's key scenes, in which Elliot escapes with E.T. by cycling into the air. While the second image was not as widely dispersed as the first, its modesty and power no doubt helped Steven Spielberg choose the image as the logo for his Amblin Entertainment production company. The logo instantly recalls *E.T.* (and its incredible grosses), through recalling one of the film's most spectacular scenes, every time that a film is produced under the Amblin banner.

In several notable campaigns for high concept films, the marketing image has been augmented by slight variations within the ad image across the film's run. In this way, the reader's attention is focused on the image for two reasons: first, due to the initial graphic design; second, by the minute differences in design week-to-week. Often these differences are motivated by seasonal factors. As an example, consider the initial marketing campaign for *Three Men and a Baby*: the shot features

the three bachelors (Tom Selleck, Steve Guttenberg, Ted Danson) looking quizzical while Tom Selleck holds a urinating infant. The Annie
Leibovitz shot firmly established the film's identity and theme. To
maintain interest, though, the image was manipulated several times;
for example, at New Year's, the four characters were wearing party hats,
and later as the Super Bowl approached, they donned football helmets.
While the initial image remained basically the same, these small ad-
ditions served to revitalize the image and the public's interest in the
film. Similar strategies were also utilized in the campaigns for *Airplane!*
(1980), *The Goonies* (1985), *"Crocodile" Dundee* (1986), and *The Naked
Gun* (1988).

Akin to the self-consciousness of this strategy are campaigns which
recall or spoof earlier films' marketing campaigns. Several comedies
have utilized this strategy to capitalize on an already strong, recognizable marketing image. *Revenge of the Pink Panther* (1978) initially used
the tag line "Just when you thought it was safe to go back to the movies" (reference: *Jaws*), and a panther posed like Warren Beatty in the
Heaven Can Wait ad.[26] The campaign for *Rabbit Test* (1978) presented
variations of the print ads for *Jaws, King Kong, A Star Is Born,* and *Star
Wars,* with rabbits replacing the usual advertising figures. *Short Circuit*
adjusted its advertising campaign to feature an interview with the
movie's robot hero, No. 5, who comments, "All the ads said 'No. 5 is
alive.' It was humiliating. Did the *Cobra* ads say 'Sylvester Stallone is
alive?' "[27] Additionally, in international markets, the comedy *Top Secret!* (1984) featured a poster with the line "The Hero is a Berk," with
star Val Kilmer wielding a whip—an allusion to the copy and image
from *Indiana Jones and the Temple of Doom* ("The Hero is Back").[28]

The connection between high concept and strong marketing images
may not *always* be present. A film can be high concept in its design,
yet without the appropriately striking marketing campaign. *Innerspace*
(1987) failed to have both an appropriate title and an effective marketing campaign. Although the film does embody many of the qualities of
high concept (e.g., an exploitable premise, strong visuals, stars), the
campaign neglected to use bold graphics. Instead, the main artwork featured a huge hand with an extended thumb on which one could barely
discern a tiny space ship and astronaut. The image lacked the strong,
bold composition most often found in the high concept campaigns.
Consequently, the image also did not reduce adequately, further limiting its chances of crossing into different media.[29]

Along similar lines, the campaigns for the high concept films *The
Hunger* and *Heartbreak Hotel* (1988) failed to match the films' stylish
look and easily digestible narratives. *The Hunger,* offering bisexual

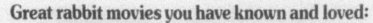

*Evoking marketing images from high concept films as a selling strategy (*Rabbit Test*, Avco Embassy, 1978).*

AN ADVENTURE OF
INCREDIBLE
PROPORTIONS

Steven Spielberg presents

Innerspace

A Joe Dante Film

This summer take a trip you'll never forget.

Innerspace A Guber-Peters Production
Starring Dennis Quaid Martin Short Meg Ryan Kevin McCarthy
Director of Photography Andrew Laszlo, A.S.C. Production Designer James H. Spencer
Music by Jerry Goldsmith Co-Produced by Chip Proser
Co-Executive Producers Frank Marshall and Kathleen Kennedy
Executive Producers Steven Spielberg, Peter Guber and Jon Peters
Story by Chip Proser Screenplay by Jeffrey Boam and Chip Proser

High concept film without the matching advertising image (Innerspace, *Warner Bros.*, 1987).

The Hunger: *problematic ad* (The Hunger,
MGM/UA, 1983).

vampires in a high-tech, new wave New York, opted for a print ad which is confusing and ambiguous. The illustration shows David Bowie and Susan Sarandon looking down at Catherine Deneuve, whose head is thrown back, allowing her blond hair to flow across the ad. Placed against her hair is a pendant which the vampires use to kill their victims. This ad is problematic for several reasons: the choice of the illustration, rather than a photograph, seems strange, since the images of the three stars in the drawing can barely be discerned; the pendant fails to reproduce adequately, so that it could perhaps be interpreted instead as a crucifix or even an earring, either of which furthers the confusion; the tag line "nothing human loves forever" is open enough to suggest a film about polygamy, sexual experimentation, or infidelity to a greater extent than a film about vampirism. With *The Hunger*, therefore, the design and construction of the film follows the high concept "specifications" for style, yet the marketing campaign neglects these qualities.

The narrative of *Heartbreak Hotel* falls clearly within the region of high concept, with the "hook" being the kidnapping of Elvis Presley by a young boy to rejuvenate his Midwest small town and family. With the built-in marketing hook of Elvis Presley and his music, the marketing campaign could capitalize on Presley, with perhaps the nostalgia and the "fish out of water" aspect of the story as secondary marketing emphases. The film's print ad demonstrates that an effective high concept campaign relies on an image, which can be replicated, rather than on words to convey meaning. For high concept, copy in the ads should be kept to an absolute minimum to ensure full identification with the image in the ad. The print ad for *Heartbreak Hotel* — a Cadillac, with four people in the front seat, and the Elvis figure lying in the back — however, relies on many copy lines to explain the story, which, when combined with the image of the car, makes the film look like a "road" movie. The simplicity of the concept and its commercial attractions are lost in the dark, ill-defined image and the lengthy plot description in the ad. The vast majority of campaigns for the high concept films operate in the opposite direction: finding an image which matches the film's content, while remaining basically simple in its composition.

Many of the high concept films emphasize pre-sold elements within the film to increase the audience's identification with the material: stars, familiar stories or situations, remakes, sequels, and series films are prominent pre-sold elements within the film. Stars are particularly important, from an economic standpoint, as a pre-sold element. As veteran advertising designer Tony Seiniger comments, "The hardest kind of film to sell is a film that has no marketable cast. . . . If it's not what everybody in production likes to call a 'high-concept' picture, the

*The simplicity of the concept lost in the advertising image (*Heartbreak Hotel, *Touchstone, 1988).*

campaign becomes very difficult."[30] While many examples of this tactic are obvious, perhaps the combination of approaches will explain their power in practice. Consider the campaign for the Barbra Streisand–Ryan O'Neal film, *The Main Event* (1979). The primary image was a shot by fashion photographer Francesco Scavullo of Streisand and O'Neal in a sparring pose: Streisand wearing shorts and T-shirt, O'Neal dressed as a boxer. The copy read "A Glove Story." The campaign works on several levels, many of which are based upon a presumed audience familiarity. Firstly, the shot is graphically bold: the outlines of the two bodies are clear, as well as the difference between male and female. The sharp contrast between the two, and the starkness of the figures, combine to form an easily identifiable marketing image. Perhaps the primary connotation of the image is that the film concerns a "battle of the sexes." The difference between the two figures and the boxing pose indicate that this will be a story of a warring man and woman. Simultaneously, though, this very difference, the mock serious fighting expressions, and our familiarity with the stars indicate that the tale will be told as a romantic comedy. This indication is also augmented by the copy ("A Glove Story"), a "play on words" which promises romance, fighting, and comedy.

Perhaps the most important signifiers, though, are the pre-sold elements of the image: Barbra Streisand, Ryan O'Neal, and their previous films. Streisand represents the quintessential driven and independent woman, while O'Neal is known for his light comedy. These personae influence the reading of the image, clarifying the combat theme and, with the strong Streisand against the romantic O'Neal, the match seems just about even. Additionally, the stars had previously teamed in the successful screwball comedy *What's Up Doc?* (1972), so the combination was already familiar to audiences. Of course, this previous film also colors the reader's expectations of the new film. Finally, the copy "A Glove Story" operates, at least partially, as a reference to Ryan O'Neal's greatest boxoffice success, *Love Story*. The coy twist on the title indicates that some amusing reworking of romantic conventions is in store, while reminding the reader of O'Neal's status as a romantic figure. The "presold" elements (primarily the personae of O'Neal and Streisand, and their previous films) greatly influence the viewer's appreciation and understanding of the ad's other elements.

The principles behind the high concept print campaigns — the close match between content and marketing, the emphasis on style, the reducibility to a single image — are repeated in the visual marketing forms: trailers and television commercials. Given the time limitations of a trailer and even moreso a television commercial, the requirement of

The Main Event: *pre-sold elements as marketing focus* (The Main Event, *Warner Bros., 1979*).

both forms is to create an image of the movie, including the genre, premise, and stars. This image may be varied subtly from trailer to trailer and commercial to commercial depending on the audience segment which the studio is trying to reach. Television, particularly with the development of cable, has become increasingly significant in targeting these different audience segments. The ability to "narrowcast," that is, to specifically target a well-defined audience segment, has developed with the increase in cable channels. As *Variety*'s Richard Gold commented on the phenomenon in 1989: "The blossoming of cable TV is enabling studio marketeers to target a fragmented audience with WIRV-like multiplicity. The high-octane action pic that might appeal to the ESPN viewer and the high-toned period piece that could find favor with the Arts & Entertainment devotee can now be pitched accordingly."[31] In this manner, television commercials can be utilized to shoot at additional audience segments in addition to the basic target audience.

Maintenance Marketing: Selling through Music and Product

Print ads, trailers, and television commercials are crucial to building awareness for the high concept film. While all three marketing forms also maintain an image of the film in the marketplace after the premiere, high concept films are sustained in the market through music and merchandising tie-ins. Both became increasingly significant in the marketing equation at the same time as high concept developed as a focus for the industry. In fact, these marketing forms themselves matured due to their success with the high concept movies. Economically, merchandising, in music and other forms, is tied also to the conglomeration of the industry; many of the conglomerates involved with film industry distribution own companies which can produce merchandised product centered on their films. For instance, Gulf & Western controls both Paramount, distributor of *Star Trek II: The Wrath of Khan*, and Pocket Books, publisher of the film's novelization.[32] So merchandising not only maintains an image of the film in the market, but also appeals to the conglomerates' desire for synergy between their different companies and products. The adjustments in film marketing caused by the move to saturation releases are continued through the encroachment of music and product merchandising as a film marketing force through the '70s and '80s.

Although film companies have always been linked with the music industry for promotional tie-ins, the ability to pre-market a film using music and the cross-overs between music, film, and other media is a relatively contemporary phenomenon. As Joel Sill, vice-president of music at Warner Bros., comments on this change: "The song score has become a marketing tool. A record not only synergizes within the film, but reaches out to the core youth market that the film wants to attract."[33] Despite the success of the early rock musicals (e.g., the Elvis Presley films and *A Hard Day's Night* [1964]), music received very limited use as a marketing tool until the mid-1970s. For the most part, through the end of the 1960s, music tie-ins were connected to the large-scale, opulent musicals, such as *West Side Story* (1961), *Mary Poppins* (1964), *The Sound of Music* (1965), and *Funny Girl* (1968). Alexander Doty credits the unexpectedly high sales of youth-oriented soundtracks (e.g., *Easy Rider* [1969], *Butch Cassidy and the Sundance Kid* [1969], *Midnight Cowboy* [1969], *Love Story*) as one significant advance for the influence of music in marketing.[34] Nevertheless, these films failed to capitalize on the music in their films as an approach to market the film before its opening.

The connection between films and music marketing actually must be attributed, at least partially, to three individuals who realized the potential of the music-film mix: Jon Peters, Robert Stigwood, and Peter Guber. Guber describes the developing form of music marketing as "unique visual marketing" in which pre-selling the film with music was attempted "when studios understood that films were heard, seen, and thought about in a unique way by the youth audience."[35] Guber's statement does encapsulate this major marketing change, although the music has been used as a target for many demographic categories beyond the youth market. The development of this phenomenon and its relation to high concept can be characterized most fruitfully through an examination of these three producers and their marketing strategies during the '70s and '80s.

While viewed initially with amusement given his background in hairstyling and his entry into the film business through girlfriend Barbra Streisand, Jon Peters had established himself as one of the leading producers in the industry by the early '80s. Peters's influence as a producer seems initially located in his shrewd ability to pre-market a film using music and striking images. Peters's first film as producer offers many insights regarding his method. The project was conceived as a single-phrase line between John Gregory Dunne and wife Joan Didion: "James Taylor and Carly Simon in a rock-and-roll version of *A Star Is Born*."[36] This concept immediately places the film into the realm of high concept: a recognizable storyline made vital through placement into the current era and through the potential exploitation of music. From this concept, the film developed, and eventually Peters and Barbra Streisand became attached to the project as producer and star,

*Jon Peters: marketing through music and a striking image (*A Star Is Born, Warner Bros., 1976).

respectively. The completed film does follow the widely known outline of the earlier films. Apart from this tie, both Streisand and co-star Kris Kristofferson were placed in roles which perfectly matched their earlier on- and off-screen personae: Streisand as a talented, energetic, and aggressive pop singer on the rise; Kristofferson as a hard drinking, cynical rock star whose career is on the wane.

Even more significantly, Peters realized the potential in the soundtrack. Instead of a simultaneous release of film and soundtrack, Peters released the soundtrack and first single ("Evergreen") two weeks prior to the film's December 1976 opening.[37] This strategy, bolstered by Streisand's musical popularity, helped to ensure that the film's single was frequently played by the time of the actual opening, raising the level of awareness for the film at the most crucial time.[38] In addition, Peters chose to market the film through all media with the same provocative image: a Francesco Scavullo photograph of a naked Streisand and Kristofferson in a passionate clinch. This image marketed the film through print, television, soundtrack, novelization, and many other forms. The combination of the music as a marketing force, the replicated artwork in the media, and the familiarity of the project's basis and stars all evidenced *A Star Is Born*'s high concept strategy.

Peters followed this project with the thriller *Eyes of Laura Mars*, set in the world of fashion photography. The film solidified many of the earlier marketing methods. Although the project did not possess the presold elements of *A Star Is Born*, Peters developed a remarkable marketing campaign centered on another Scavullo photograph: an ominous shot of white eyes staring from star Faye Dunaway's darkened face. The image managed to connote the fashion and advertising visuals central to the film and its sense of chic horror. As an image, the piercing eyes quickly transferred into other media: through the soundtrack album cover, novelization, fashion, and photography magazines. The ad, designed by Tony Seiniger, even received the top prize at the eighth Key Art Awards, an annual industry-sponsored contest judging effective advertising campaigns.[39] Following the success of *A Star Is Born*, Peters released the soundtrack for *Eyes of Laura Mars* before the film's opening. The soundtrack capitalized on the burgeoning disco trend, as Peters included songs such as "Native New Yorker" (by Odyssey), "Boogie Nights" (by Heatwave), and "Shake Your Booty" (by K. C. and the Sunshine Band).[40] Peters also diversified his risk on the soundtrack by including "Prisoner (Love Theme from *Eyes of Laura Mars*)" — a more subdued, haunting song performed by Barbra Streisand.

By the release of *Eyes of Laura Mars*, the marketing approach adopted by Peters was even identified within the industry by trade paper *Variety*:

Francesco Scavullo's image for Eyes of Laura Mars *(Eyes of Laura Mars,* Columbia, *1978).*

*The chic world of high fashion photography
in a high concept film (Eyes of Laura
Mars, Columbia, 1978). Copyright ©
MCMLXXVIII, Columbia Pictures Industries,
Inc.*

"Peters says he'll run advertising on all his pictures much like the campaign for *A Star Is Born*. With his current film that means billboards of
the pic's logo, a graphic design for Faye Dunaway's face, already posted
for several weeks to 'make people aware it's coming,' early release of
Streisand's tune on the airwaves and a media blitz in newspapers, television, radio and magazines.''[41] While *A Star Is Born* developed Peters's
music marketing approach, *Eyes of Laura Mars* is probably more significant as the film which helped emphasize the distinctive style of the high
concept film, since the film's chic world of high fashion photography
helped set the emphasis on style in the high concept narratives.[42]

Before joining with Peter Guber to form the Guber-Peters Company,
Jon Peters focused almost entirely on projects which utilized music as a
primary marketing force.[43] In a move which indicates that Peters comprehended the importance of market segmentation, Peters carefully devised an unusual music and marketing campaign for *The Main Event*.
While the soundtrack contained only one Streisand song (the disco
theme) in two versions, Peters realized a method to maximize the
soundtrack's presence in the marketplace. Two singles of the song "The

Main Event" were released prior to the film's opening: one seven-inch version for radio airplay, and a twelve-inch remix version for discos. The longer version became very popular, in part, because the film was released in 1979 at the height of the disco boom. Still, only the seven-inch version was available on single. If listeners wanted to own the longer version, they were forced to purchase the entire soundtrack, which contained both versions. As Peters predicted, "They'll eat up the longer version, but they won't be able to get it [separately] in stores."[44] Through this tactic, Peters was able to attract younger disco listeners to a full-length soundtrack album — which, of course, featured the recognizable Scavullo photograph used to market the film.

Through these three films, Peters helped to construct this new form of marketing. The cross-fertilization between music, product, and film made possible through this method has become a hallmark of high concept. With the additional tie-ins related to the music marketing, the film's "image," in all respects, became more apparent in the marketplace. Perhaps the attempt to foreground the conjunction of style and marketing, through the films and the music tie-ins, had inspiration from Peters's prior career, which also stresses the importance of selling a style and a new look. Regardless, the implications of his marketing approach for high concept are numerous. High concept films, based on a simplicity and abstraction of images, provided the ideal vehicle through which to market films through music. The music complemented the image without overwhelming the familiar, generically based narrative. In turn, the music further increased the modularity of the films, segmenting the film into narrative "units" set to the songs. Both of these traits would be deepened and extended in later high concept films.

In some respects, the method of marketing films through music is based on integrating one medium (music) with another medium (film), while exploiting the market opportunities made possible through this intersection. Entrepreneur Robert Stigwood deserves much of the credit for developing these opportunities. As Stigwood commented in 1978, at the height of his filmmaking career, "For a long time I looked at those long lines of people at rock concerts and wondered why you couldn't have the same kind of crowd for a movie. That kind of *excitement*. An audience that's really turned on by music but loves movies too."[45] Stigwood was able to harness this "excitement" initially through productions based on bold, hyperbolic visuals matched with a rock soundtrack: *Jesus Christ Superstar* (1973), *Tommy* (1975), *Saturday Night Fever*, and *Grease*. These films also follow upon the marketing principles evident in the Peters films by pre-selling through the music and an immediate visual icon extracted from the film.

Stigwood's history illustrates his developing awareness of both these marketing principles and the style of the high concept film. He began in the business as a music and theatrical manager. Stigwood's first lesson in the possibility of cross-over occurred early in his career. In trying to sell singer John Leyton, Stigwood was unable to find a niche until he cast Leyton as a pop star on a British television series, *Harpers West One*.[46] By persuading the producer of the series to allow Leyton to sing "Johnny Remember Me" on the television show, Stigwood set Leyton with his first hit single.[47] Significantly, Stigwood succeeded only through Leyton's exposure on a medium other than the radio, and through exploiting the opportunities from translating an artist across media.

While still representing performing artists, Stigwood continued his experiments in transferring properties. In television, Stigwood sold the rights to two British series which he controlled, and helped to pioneer the hit American series *All in the Family* and *Sanford and Son*. In theater, Stigwood realized the potential of *Hair* and transported the show to Britain.[48] These cross-over efforts paled in comparison to Stigwood's marketing efforts with *Jesus Christ Superstar*. Tim Rice and Andrew Lloyd Webber composed a full-scale rock opera based on the last seven days in the life of Jesus Christ. The authors first released the single "Jesus Christ Superstar" and continued to work on the full album. Realizing the potential inherent in the property, Stigwood decided to produce a stage version of the album. As RSO (Robert Stigwood Organization) executive Beryl Vertue comments, "All we knew was that he had seen this record selling, and he had this vision about turning the record into theater."[49] Stigwood's extravagant staging produced a huge success in London, while the Broadway version, costing $700,000 to stage, was considerably less profitable.[50] Following the movement of the property from one medium to the next, Stigwood produced the Universal film version. The film, directed by Norman Jewison, curiously joined the realism of the locations with extreme stylization. The results were decidedly mixed, with critical opinion lukewarm at best. Nevertheless, the project of *Jesus Christ Superstar* as a whole allowed Stigwood to extend many of his earlier marketing techniques. By producing a film transplanted from another medium, Stigwood was able to capitalize upon the pre-sold support of the initial projects. Since the cross-overs were occurring with music projects, the effect was mutually reinforcing; the film sold records connected both to the film and the stage show, while the records bolstered interest in the film and stage shows. This process became identified, within the film industry, as "synergy" between music and film.[51]

This process continued with Stigwood's film of *Tommy*, a rock opera

Roger Daltrey as Tommy: *a Robert Stigwood cross-media project (*Tommy, *Columbia, 1975). Copyright © 1975 Columbia Pictures Industries, Inc.*

album by the Who. With *Tommy,* Stigwood assembled all the elements of the project before seeking a distributor, seeking to remain in complete control of the project from its conception. Stigwood envisioned casting the film with recognizable stars from the rock world: Elton John, Roger Daltrey, Pete Townsend, Eric Clapton, and Tina Turner. Secondly, Stigwood hired Ken Russell to direct the film. While the film of *Jesus Christ Superstar* shows little emphasis on directorial style, Russell's work had been distinguished by outrageous visual imagery in films such as *The Devils* (1970), *Women in Love* (1970), and *The Music Lovers* (1971). After raising the money for the film independently, Stigwood struck a distribution deal with Columbia Pictures through the support of Columbia executive Peter Guber. With the new input from the "guest star" artists, and buoyed by the Elton John single "Pinball Wizard," the film's soundtrack easily became a success; released in conjunction with the film's March 1975 release, the album was certified platinum by November 1975.[52] Perhaps more so than in previous Stigwood efforts, the film developed the emphasis on style so evident in the high concept films.

With the many guest appearances and the different styles of performance, *Tommy* naturally developed in a modular fashion. Russell appeared to be pioneering what would later be called "music video."
Critic Charles Michener's review of the film describes its similarity to
the music video: "To a prerecorded sound track utterly without spoken
dialogue and consisting entirely of the 'opera's' rock songs and sound
effects, Russell has fused a kaleidoscope of images that pulsate with the
incredible precision of a rock drumbeat in a visual counterpoint to the
music."[53] *Tommy* reinforced the pattern of marketing through music by
expanding the collection of artists/singers (from AOR ["album-oriented
rock"] artists the Who and Eric Clapton, to soul star Tina Turner to pop
star Elton John) in the film, by developing the modular music video set
pieces which could be used for exploitation, and by strengthening the
connection between music and strong visuals, which could easily be
abstracted in the film's marketing.[54]

All the early marketing experiments culminated with Stigwood's production of *Saturday Night Fever*, released by Paramount Pictures nearly
three years after *Tommy*. First, Stigwood altered the timing of music
released in conjunction with the film. Stigwood released the soundtrack
about six weeks prior to the film's opening to allow more lead time for
the first single ("How Deep Is Your Love?").[55] This strategy bolstered the
single's rise to the top of the charts just as the film opened. After the
initial single, several other songs were promoted as singles: "Stayin'
Alive," "Night Fever," "If I Can't Have You." Stigwood and RSO president Al Coury staggered these singles so that the film was represented
at the top of the pop charts for the next several months. The phenomenal success of this strategy helped fuel the strong repeat business for the
film and sales of the soundtrack album (25 million units—the second
biggest LP of all time).[56]

The film represented another successful cross-over for Stigwood,
since it was based on a *New York* magazine article, "The Tribal Rites of
the New Saturday Night," by Nik Cohn. More significantly, Stigwood,
realizing the potential of the actor from television's *Welcome Back Kot-
ter*, cast John Travolta in a role which had very strong ties to his already
established television identity and his burgeoning musical career.[57] The
film's key advertising artwork also established an identity for the film
through a very striking and apt image: Travolta and Karen Lynn Gorney
on the disco dance floor, with Travolta in the foreground striking a
pose pointing his right arm high in the air. This image was replicated
through all the marketing media; like the *A Star Is Born* image, the
Travolta image became the source for immediate visual recognition of
the film, and even a focus of parody.[58] Finally, *Saturday Night Fever* also

CATCH THE FEVER

IF YOU'RE NOT SURE YOU HAVE THE FEVER NOW, AFTER TODAY, YOU'LL SAY YOU ALWAYS DID.

...Catch it

PARAMOUNT PICTURES PRESENTS JOHN TRAVOLTA KAREN LYNN GORNEY
"SATURDAY NIGHT FEVER" A ROBERT STIGWOOD PRODUCTION
Screenplay by NORMAN WEXLER Directed by JOHN BADHAM
Executive Producer KEVIN McCORMICK Produced by ROBERT STIGWOOD
Original music written and performed by the BEE GEES
Soundtrack album available on RSO Records

John Travolta in Saturday Night Fever: *the image became part of American popular culture, even parodied in films such as* Airplane! *(1980) (*Saturday Night Fever, *Paramount, 1977).*

The music and marketing potential of the Beatles, Peter Frampton, and the Bee Gees dissipated in Sgt. Pepper's Lonely Hearts Club Band *(Sgt. Pepper's Lonely Hearts Club Band,* Universal, *1978). © 1978 Stigwood Group, Ltd.*

extended the emphasis on style evident in the earlier Stigwood films, from the visual style in the film's dance scenes to the privileging of style within dance, dress, and demeanor.

The film represented the most commercially successful attempt, at that time, to integrate the marketing of a film with its content and style. The blend of marketing and film was achieved due to *Saturday Night Fever's* allegiance to traits of high concept. The movement toward the emptied characters and plotline, modular structure, and emphasis on style within the narrative combined to create a film favoring, even encouraging, the integration of marketing, merchandising, and content. This formula was replicated with Stigwood's next two films, both released in 1978: *Grease* (based on the Broadway musical) and *Sgt. Pepper's*

Lonely Hearts Club Band (based on the Beatles album). While *Grease* successfully consolidated Broadway tunes with '70's pop (Bee Gees, Olivia Newton-John), *Sgt. Pepper* failed to attract audiences despite utilization of the same marketing and merchandising routes.[59] Part of the problem with *Sgt. Pepper* seems to be the lack of a generically based storyline on which to base the film. Although research proved that the film had an unusually high level of pre-awareness, word-of-mouth was uniformly negative. Stigwood's film possessed excellent marketability, but very poor playability.

The Stigwood oeuvre also illustrates another change related to the reception of the high concept films. The strong connections between high concept, marketing, and music—the cross-fertilization of marketing efforts and their inseparability from the film—encourage an endless consumption of the high concept films. Through the films and their media representation, viewers repeatedly attend the same film. David Ansen characterizes this trait in the following manner: "[Stigwood's] movies have the same easily digested, stand-up-and-boogie style: they seemed designed, like records, to be played again and again."[60] Especially with these musically based high concept films, the marketing through music seems designed to encourage this repeat viewing phenomenon. Indeed, the incredible success of films such as *Grease* and *Star Wars* is not based upon their broad appeal to all age/sex categories, but rather their success at achieving repeat viewings. Olen J. Earnest studied this pattern with *Star Wars*, and noted the following: "Thus, at the end of the traditional summer moviegoing season, not only had *Star Wars* [which opened in May] started tapping the difficult to reach infrequent moviegoer, but the film was generating exceptional levels of repeat viewing . . . through the end of August, four out of every ten moviegoers showing up at the boxoffice had already seen *Star Wars* one or more times."[61] Therefore, the marketing of the film through music, in a case such as *Grease*, might be seen as one factor building this repeat phenomenon, which has been so vital to the success of many high concept films.

The influence of Peter Guber as a marketing force seems based primarily upon the efforts he has made to institutionalize the connection between music and the movies during his initial tenure at Columbia Pictures (beginning in 1968) and through his own productions. While at Columbia, Guber championed *Tommy* as a project, despite the opposition of the other studio executives. Nevertheless, Guber's chief contributions occurred with his move into independent production in 1975. "Peter Guber's' Filmworks" grew out of Guber's association with Columbia; the mandate was to develop and produce films which would be released through Columbia. Guber's first film, *The Deep* (1977), ex-emplifies many of the techniques which have been instrumental to his success.[62] As author Michael Pye states about Guber's involvement with *The Deep*: "Guber turned most of the apparent disadvantages into publicity."[63] On the one hand, Guber relentlessly produced publicity during the making and launching of the film, focusing on Nick Nolte's first film (after his television success with *Rich Man, Poor Man*), Peter Benchley's connection to *Jaws*, the perilous conditions making the film largely underwater, and, of course, Jacqueline Bisset's wet T-shirt. Si-multaneously, Guber fostered the development of the music and mer-chandising marketing routes.

During the filming, Guber merged his film company with Neil Bo-gart's record company, which featured Kiss and Donna Summer. The result—Casablanca Records and FilmWorks—was an organization de-signed to exploit the synergy between records and films. In many re-spects this move marked the logical consequence of the marketing ex-periments from producers such as Jon Peters. An in-house recording arm could only serve to strengthen the ties between the company's film and appropriate musical accompaniment. With *The Deep*, Guber used Donna Summer to record the theme song, "Down Deep Inside," which was released on the Casablanca label. The company's next project, *Thank God It's Friday* (1978), represents a more extensive commitment to the music/marketing connection. The film is centered around a single evening at a Los Angeles disco, and features guest appearances by Donna Summer and the Commodores. Casablanca partnered with Mo-town Records for the film to expand the range of artists on the sound-track. *Thank God It's Friday* is set to the soundtrack music at virtually all times, creating what Guber refers to as "a kind of visual album."[64]

Guber followed these successes with *Midnight Express*, then merged with Jon Peters in 1981 to form Guber-Peters Entertainment. The com-pany united two of the individuals who best realized the potential of marketing contemporary music in film. While their individual works pioneered the high concept film through the integration of music, mar-keting, and film, the collaborative films seem to strike a balance be-tween high concept projects and more low concept films. Many of their films do follow the music marketing route, though: consider *Endless Love*, a film which was propelled by the Diana Ross–Lionel Richie single during its initial run. Other music-based projects include *VisionQuest* (1985), *Who's That Girl* (1987), and *Flashdance*.

One of the most interesting marketing experiments from the com-pany has been the film *Clue* (1985), perhaps the only film to be based upon a board game (until *Super Mario Bros.* [1993], which reconsiders

Peter Guber combines the music and market-
ing hooks of Donna Summer and the Com-
*modores (*Thank God It's Friday, Columbia,
1978). Copyright © MCMLXXVIII, Colum-
bia Pictures Industries, Inc.

the strategy through new technologies, adapting a video game into a dramatic film). *Clue* offers a project completely driven by a marketing and merchandising scheme, and opening weekend audiences probably were attracted to the film primarily by their familiarity with the game. More importantly, though, *Clue* suggested that Guber-Peters were continuing to develop more significant marketing experiments based upon recognizable "cross-over" material in other media.

Considering the increasing awareness of contemporary music as a marketing tool, music video logically extends this form of marketing. In particular, music videos have been tied closely to the film through the use of film excerpts, strengthening the other parts of the music-marketing route. Guber-Peters's *Flashdance* illustrates the possibilities of this approach. The film's marketing campaign was based on the provocative and graphically simple shot of Jennifer Beals in her torn sweat-shirt. The print campaign helped to establish the image for the film, but simultaneously, the film's music provided the focus for a campaign of mutually reinforcing components. Since the music tie-ins were already present within the film, *Flashdance* offered a unique opportunity to experiment with music *and* music video as marketing hooks. Paramount's Frank Mancuso described the possibilities in the following terms: "We started zeroing in on the visual elements of the film and the music. *Flashdance* seemed quite exceptional in both these areas. We went after it quite heavily, figuring it was a different kind of movie — so much was told visually and through the soundtrack that these became our primary marketing elements."[65] The film was initially marketed through advance buys on MTV, and through music video from the modular set pieces within the film.[66] These music videos might be montages of different scenes from the film (e.g., Irene Cara's 'Flashdance') or might be a modular sequence (e.g., the workout scene set to Michael Sembello's "Maniac") which lends itself to direct extraction from the film. Of course, the music videos energize both awareness and interest in the song, soundtrack, and film. Increasingly, music videos for a single song occur in more than one version, with each presenting an "interpretation" of the song via different scenes from the film. The effect of this replication is an even greater saturation of the music marketing apparatus; as Jon Lewis comments on the *Purple Rain* music videos: "MTV has aired both versions of 'When the Doves Cry' — enabling the VJ's to play it more than almost any other song."[67] Like the music soundtrack and the product merchandise, music video extracted from film represents another form of extended marketing: a method of maintaining audience awareness for a film long after it has entered the marketplace.

Merchandising and Ancillary Tie-ins

Accompanying these changes in marketing were significant advances in film merchandising. As with the marketing developments, the merchandising of film also favors those films which can be easily reduced to a single image. This reducibility lends itself to the tactile representation of film, that is, the licensed products constructed around the film and its characters. Similarly, merchandising serves the same economic function as marketing through music and strong images: the licensed products extend the "shelf life" of the film by replicating the film's characters, action, or setting through the products. As Brad Globe, head of licensing and merchandising for Amblin Entertainment, comments on this phenomenon: "Licensing is not just about generating revenues. We're really very concerned that the licensing program have a positive impact on the movie and create some consumer awareness for the film."[68] Although films have been merchandised since *Snow White and the Seven Dwarfs* in 1937, merchandising has become increasingly influential within the past two decades as a form of marketing.[69] Indeed, only within the last decade have studios initiated in-house merchandising units within their marketing departments. This period of merchandising growth represents another significant method through which the high concept image may be presented to the public.

Historically, several films from the early 1970s advanced the influence of merchandising as a marketing force. While the majority of merchandising before this point had been almost exclusively for the children's market, the studios began to aim their licensed promotions beyond this small, yet lucrative, set.[70] *Love Story* producer Robert Evans was partly responsible for one of these merchandising booms. At Evans's suggestion, Erich Segal wrote a book, based on his screenplay, which was released by Harper & Row for Valentine's Day of 1970. The book turned into a phenomenal success, spending over nine months on the *New York Times* bestseller list, and created a high level of anticipation for the film, which was released the following Christmas.[71] The horror film *The Omen* (1976) further demonstrated the power of novelizations, with sales of over 3 million paperback copies during the release of the film.[72] Book tie-ins have become the norm in the industry, so that today the majority of major studio releases are supported by a novelization.

On a much larger scale, Paramount's *The Great Gatsby* (1974) engineered a revolutionary merchandising campaign; producer Robert Evans and former Paramount promotion director Charles O. Glenn assembled a product tie-in scheme valued at $6 million to create "a third level of awareness" for the film.[73] In keeping with the emphasis upon style and romance, four brands were selected to represent the film: Ballantine's Scotch, Glemby hairstyling studios, Robert Bruce's men's sportswear, and du Pont's "classic white" line of cookware.[74] Consider the Ballantine's ad, for example, which privileges style above all other qualities, claiming in a description of the Jazz Age that "Ballantine's was there. Like the era, the scotch with style." While F. Scott Fitzgerald's daughter, Scottie Lanahan Smith, complained that "you have turned *The Great Gatsby* into pots and pans," Paramount was able to establish firmly the nostalgic, romantic image for the film, as evidenced by the strong exhibitor advances, through these extensive promotions.[75]

Two years later, Paramount's *King Kong* mounted an even more involved merchandising campaign. In many ways, the remake *King Kong* offers an unusual number of high concept traits which integrated the film with its promotion: primarily, a pre-sold classic story, the visual presence of Kong as a character, and the simplicity (on a narrative and visual level) of a beauty and the beast story. Producer Dino De Laurentiis orchestrated several merchandising opportunities designed to

*Merchandising F. Scott Fitzgerald's American classic (*The Great Gatsby, Paramount, *1974).*

broaden the base of the story. Adults were to be attracted to the Jim Beam *King Kong* Cocktail and the Jim Beam *King Kong* Commemorative bottles; the youth market was targeted with *King Kong* sportswear; the children by 7-Eleven *King Kong* cups, *King Kong* peanut butter cups, and *King Kong* GAF Viewmaster slides.[76]

A similar situation occurred with Warner Bros.' *Superman* in 1978. With the property so familiar through comic books, cartoons, and television, *Superman* mobilized all of Warner Communications with its merchandising plan, which included eight tie-in *Superman* books, the John Williams soundtrack, T-shirts, and almost one hundred licenses to toy manufacturers.[77] This film's merchandising efforts suggest that the extremes of high concept are integrated completely with merchandising: a film which can be completely reduced to a single pre-sold image inevitably becomes a merchandised product. The reading of the film is mediated by the viewer's knowledge of the merchandised products which so accurately represent the film's content.

In terms of economic importance, merchandising boomed in 1977

King Kong Promotional Tie-Ins

JAMES M. BEAM DISTILLING CO.

"KING KONG is the largest monster ever made for a movie" is the theme of Jim Beam's advertising, which will run through March 1977, in 8 national magazines as well as in over 1,800 newspapers.

The second thrust will include the introduction of the KING KONG cocktail in all of their January through March magazine and newspaper advertising. All display and point-of-purchase material featuring the cocktail plus the recipe will be distributed nationally to their retail trade, cocktail lounges, taverns and restaurants.

So you can have a headstart in making the cocktail, here is the recipe:

1 oz. Jim Beam over ice—¾ oz. grenadine— fill with orange juice—add a wedge of lime.

And, as part of their famous series, they have created a KING KONG Commemorative Bottle—the first time they have ever produced a bottle to salute a motion picture.

SEDGEFIELD SPORTSWEAR COMPANY

For the teen and college-age market, Sedgefield, one of the largest manufacturers of jeans, jackets and sportswear, has created a real collector's item — a plastic keychain that has within it a tiny reproduction of the full-color KING KONG poster and a few strands of the actual hair from KONG himself. Special display cards and posters will be used to herald the offering in their 5,000 retail outlets.

Full-page four-color ads will appear in approximately 15 publications such as "Rolling Stone," "Playboy," "Esquire," and "Sports Illustrated."

Further, Sedgefield has launched major campaigns with leading department stores in the top 75 markets. These promotions will produce two full-pages of newspaper ads, half of each ad devoted to the film and half to the jeans. Everything from footprints, to photos, to a 10-foot mockup of KONG will be featured inside the stores.

"FAMILY CIRCLE"

KING KONG is on the cover of the January issue of "Family Circle," the largest women's magazine in the world with approximately 10,000,000 circulation. They have created an Iron-On Transfer, bound inside the issue, with instructions for its application.

SCHRAFFT CANDY COMPANY

A KING KONG milk chocolate and peanut butter candy bar has been created by Schrafft's. KING KONG's head is emblazoned on the orange wrapper as well as the words "inspired by the new motion picture KING KONG."

Television advertising will appear on a number of network game shows including "The Price is Right," "The Gong Show," "$20,000 Pyramid," and "The Don Ho Show."

Point-of-purchase materials will promote the candy and the film in supermarkets and candy stores everywhere.

GAF CORPORATION

Tieing in with the children's audience, GAF will have an extensive advertising and promotional campaign for their Viewmaster unit consisting of twenty-one 3D pictures made right on the KING KONG set. GAF will ship the reels and giant KING KONG display units to approximately 20,000 retail outlets and supermarkets.

In addition, they are making a premium offer of 2 KING KONG posters which will be heavily promoted with inserts in their film-processing envelopes.

Television advertising to reach the young audience during December, January and February will run on Saturday and Sunday morning kid-strips and on such afternoon favorites as the Mickey Mouse Club.

7-ELEVEN STORES

On January 1st, six million special KING KONG 16 oz. hi-impact styrene cups will go into use in 7-Eleven stores across the country to promote the chain's special Slurpee drink. The cups feature 6 drawings of the mighty KONG in different heroic moments of his odyssey. 7-Eleven which anticipates the promotion will be carried by approximately 5,000 stores, is looking to the cups to help build a winter-time audience for the Slurpee drink. They plan major market television buys and locally will use posters and banners across the front of their stores. For young collectors they believe the different cups will stimulate multiple sales of Slurpee. Additionally, a special cup featuring KING KONG astride the World Trade Center Twin Towers is being offered to theatres along with special point-of-purchase material for theatre lobbies.

King Kong: *merchandising possibilities at time of release* (King Kong, Paramount, 1976).

Character-based merchandising (Star Wars, Twentieth Century–Fox, 1977).

with George Lucas's *Star Wars*. The film certainly did not have the pre-sold ability of, for example, *King Kong*. Twentieth Century–Fox's John Friedkin declared at the time of release: "The film [*Star Wars*] opened May 25, and on May 24 you couldn't give it away."[78] Another Fox executive, Mark Pepvers, has commented that, "George Lucas created *Star Wars* with the toy byproducts in mind. He was making much more than a movie."[79] In fact, Lucas sought to control all merchandising rights for the film, with the final contracts specifying an even revenue split between Fox and Lucas after Fox's administrative costs were covered.[80] Since the film has been licensed to over fifty companies, with Kenner Toys producing seventy *Star Wars* products alone, sales figures are not readily available, although within the first year, merchandising had accounted for at least $300 million for *Star Wars*.[81] Part of the film's phenomenal success as a licensing property has been its diverse set of characters. The film's entourage has been parlayed into numerous products, further enhancing the world created by Lucas. The film's completely novel environment and characters have been so striking that Kenner

Toys has been able to go beyond the figures in the film by adding new characters to its *Star Wars* line in keeping with the film's mythological world.[82]

The mature period of merchandising can be located as starting with the successful and innovative programs of *The Great Gatsby, King Kong, Superman*, and especially *Star Wars*. Simultaneously music soundtracks, which represent another merchandised item, also flourished with the rise in music as a marketing tool. Currently, all studios have merchandising divisions, and licensing as a marketing practice has grown into a $56 billion industry.[83] Of this figure, the largest forms of merchandised products include toys/games, gifts/novelties, publishing, sporting goods, apparel, and housewares.[84] The integration of merchandising with film (and in particular, high concept film) has become so complete that projects are being conceived with the merchandising hooks as a primary marketing focus. Apart from George Lucas, Steven Spielberg's *E.T.* has received much attention due to Spielberg's remarks that he had carefully deliberated the marketing and merchandising possibilities of E.T. before filming had begun.[85]

While all projects aspire to a phenomenal merchandising enterprise such as *Star Wars*, commercially successful films do not necessarily translate to strong merchandising. For instance, *Gremlins* (1984), *Who Framed Roger Rabbit?* (1988), and *Willow* (1988), all hits, proved major disappointments in terms of merchandising.[86] An additional level of media association, such as a television series, can bolster the fate of merchandised product derived from films. For example, the merchandising scheme for *Batman*, in 1989, benefited from the comic books and old television series, both of which greatly strengthened the potential of merchandised product from the new film. A year later, *Teenage Mutant Ninja Turtles* was offered incredible pre-sold recognition for its tie-ins through the Ninja Turtles comic book, television cartoon series, and preexisting Turtles products.[87] This secondary level of association can even occur after the film's release. Consider that television cartoon series were developed around both *Ghostbusters* (1984) and *Beetlejuice* (1988) to maintain interest in the merchandised product from the original films.[88]

Moving beyond the younger markets, merchandising has developed even in R-rated projects such as *Rambo: First Blood Part II* and *RoboCop*. The more adult projects tend to transfer much more into ancillary tie-ins, rather than merchandised toys or products. Styling trends have been created by films such as *Flashdance* (the off-the-shoulder sweatshirt), *Top Gun* (bomber flight jackets), *Saturday Night Fever* (three-piece white suits), and *Baby Boom* (soft-edged business suits).[89] Although the effect may be fairly immediate, the impact is usually a greater awareness for the film rather than a direct financial profit for the studios from merchandise.[90] The synergy between fashion trends and film has been matched by several promising new merchandising venues such as direct mail, studio catalogs, and in-theater sales.[91] *Top Gun* and *Flashdance* producers Don Simpson and Jerry Bruckheimer have begun to realize the marketing possibilities of these more nebulous tie-ins. As Ronald Grover comments on these producers, "The duo were eager to cash in on such film inspired fads. And they were upset over Paramount's failure to move quickly enough to beat others who capitalized on *Flashdance* clothes or flyer style jackets after *Top Gun*. Simpson and Bruckheimer recently forced the studio to create a new merchandising unit."[92]

Merchandising, like marketing through strong print images, music, and across media, is a key variable of the high concept equation. These marketing forces developed at the same time as Hollywood began to investigate marketing-driven projects. The interest in this kind of project could be traced back to the conglomeration of the industry, which sought a more financially conservative, less risky approach to filmmaking. With saturation releases creating a need for high awareness, the marketing forms — through commercials, music, and merchandising — developed to service this requirement. In turn, high concept, as a kind of filmmaking, worked with these new marketing forms most successfully. The result of this marketing mechanism was an industry in which high concept became an increasingly significant focus for the major studio.

The roots of this system can be located through a series of ads in *Variety* from 1974. These ads illustrate the growing importance of marketing in the industry and the direction through which the marketing-oriented high concept films would develop. In the ads, readers were asked to "Watch 20th Century–Fox, Warner Bros. and Irwin Allen build the blockbuster of the century . . . "[93] The remainder of the ad was composed of *The Towering Inferno* logo accompanied by a series of empty boxes showing the names of the film's characters. In the ensuing weeks, the boxes were filled in with superstars (Paul Newman, Steve McQueen, et al.) and stars (Robert Wagner, O. J. Simpson, et al.). Significantly, the ad illustrates many of the key marketing components behind high concept: an identifiable logo, pre-sold elements (e.g., stars and a best-selling book), a marketable concept, a merchandising tie-in (e.g., a book reissue), and a modular approach to filmmaking (i.e., "build" the film from matching different marketable parts). The interdependence of high concept with these marketing apparati offers films whose "narration" is as much a function of their innovative marketing campaigns as their storylines.

5 High Concept and Market Research: Movie Making by the Numbers

Although market research in the film industry can be traced back to forecasts of market demand for movies in 1915, market research did not become an integral part of the film industry until the late 1970s.[1] The development of more nuanced methods of audience analysis, along with key changes in the institutional framework of the industry, aided the entrenchment of market research within the studios at that time. By the early 1980s, market research had become so integral to mainstream Hollywood filmmaking that every major studio devoted a significant portion of its marketing budget to market research.[2] At the current time, the market research managers and vice-presidents within the studios in turn coordinate their efforts with independent market research suppliers specializing in field work, tabulation, and coding. Together these forces have created a significant position for market research in the pre- and post-production life of a film. This position, however, is based upon a methodology which privileges high concept as a style of mainstream filmmaking within Hollywood and which cannot adequately account for many other forms of production. In this chapter, I will situate the relationship between market research and high concept in contemporary Hollywood, with an eye toward explaining factors which have contributed to the development of market research within the industry.

The Growth of Market Research

Organized audience research has existed within Hollywood for several decades. Apart from studio sneak previews, independent companies, such as George Gallup's Audience Research Inc., Sindlinger & Company, and Leo Handel's Motion Picture Research Bureau, conducted studies for a number of studios from the late 1930s onward.[3] Bruce Austin attributes the development of these independent movie market research suppliers to two primary postwar factors: the introduction of television, which diminished the film audience, leaving the studios seeking methods to retain their audience, and the desire to appear economically responsible to Wall Street and the banking industry.[4] Market research during this period included audience response to sneak previews of films and more broad-based research detailing audience awareness of and interest in films, attendance patterns, and recall of film advertising.[5]

Market research began to gain a great deal more prominence, however, in the 1970s. This new stature followed from the earlier attempts to make the film industry appear to be a logical, economic business. As the founding studio moguls died or retired, the studios were acquired by conglomerates: MCA acquired Universal in 1962, Gulf & Western, Paramount in 1966, Transamerica, United Artists in 1967, and Kinney National, Warner Bros. in 1969.[6] With the number of film releases falling and costs rising, the conglomerates required more accountability on the part of their motion picture divisions; as Julie Salamon describes, "They [the studios] needed to put together a seasonal string of 'product' in an orderly way, and the corporate parents wanted to know that something besides somebody's seat-of-the-pants judgment was involved in the process. Research provided comfort to executives working in an industry where the average tenure in a high-ranking job was a couple of years."[7] Consequently, the conglomerates were more receptive to market research techniques, with many executives familiar with the processes from packaged-goods marketing and merchandising.

The conglomerates further fostered ties between consumer advertising and film marketing through acquiring executives from the consumer research arena: for example, Jonas Rosenfeld, former Vice-President of Advertising, Promotion and Research at Twentieth Century–Fox, was lured from the corporate division of Bristol-Meyers, while marketing vice-presidents Dana Lombardo at Disney and Richard Del Belso at Warner Bros. both had extensive experience in research at advertising agencies.[8] The conglomerates' application of the market research methods traditionally used in consumer research was greeted by the creative community with skepticism, at best, and hostility, at worst. Producer Keith Barish's response is representative of this hostility: "As the larger and larger companies take over studios, they start treating film as a product no different than soda pop or potato chips. Same cost controls, same reporting structure, same market testing."[9]

More significantly, a shift in the distribution pattern of film in the 1970s also aided the institutionalization of market research. As has already been established, with the success of "four-wall" films, the major studios began to open films in saturation, as opposed to platform, releases centered on television advertising.[10] Universal's opening of *Jaws* in June 1975 was the starting point of this distribution trend, which soon increased so that an eagerly anticipated film in recent times, such as *Batman Returns* (1992), could open in 2,644 theaters at one time.[11] This distribution strategy depends upon a high level of awareness of the film by the time of opening; if the film cannot open well in its first weekend, its chances for long-term success are extremely limited, since theaters will drop the film and the advertising support will be cut.[12] To build awareness and therefore the chances for a good opening, advertising through television, as opposed to print, became the norm. The increased cost of network and local TV buys over print advertising, along with the necessity to open a film immediately to a strong first weekend, sparked the interest of the studios in evaluating the efficacy of their advertising material.[13]

At the same time, market research as a field began to move beyond demographic profiles in predicting consumer behavior. In the 1960s, a school of research developed which sought to define consumers along psychological dimensions through discerning their needs, values, attitudes, and interests.[14] Referred to variously as psychographic or "value and lifestyle" research, this method allowed audiences to be divided beyond sex, age, and education. With the additional information, consumers could be segmented into dimensions which cluster similar attributes or individuals, thereby allowing companies to market their products more specifically. Therefore, the studios were able to target specific groups through testing their television commercials and then arranging their media buys with television shows that would attract the desired audience. These two forces—the movement toward saturation campaigns based upon television advertising and the greater segmentation of the market through psychographic research—fostered the widespread adoption of market research within the film industry. Consequently, market research has made a significant dent in the film industry, to a point where entertainment analyst Jeff Logsdon has recently estimated that at least 75 percent of the top two hundred films yearly are market researched in some form.[15]

The Model of Market Research within the Film Industry

By the 1980s, a fairly uniform set of market research surveys had become common practice within the film industry. Of course, different studios chose to emphasize different market research functions, although in the press, most studio marketing executives stressed that market research played a minor role in the success of their films. The set of market research surveys which became instituted can be divided into those studies conducted pre-production and studies conducted post-production. As Thomas Simonet notes, pre-production studies are composed primarily of concept testing, casting tests, and title tests.[16] Concept testing involves breaking down a script into a short concept, which is then read to respondents so that the attractive (read "marketable") elements might be identified. Similarly, casting tests are designed to identify marketable stars and the match between a star and a particular concept, while title tests gauge the connotations suggested by a particular title.

The majority of market research within the industry, however, occurs after the production has been completed. Recruited audience screenings are attended by those who have been selected to meet certain sex, age, and lifestyle quotas. After the screening, audience members complete surveys describing their overall evaluation of the film, how strongly they would recommend the film to a friend, their description of the film, their media usage habits, and demographic (sex/age) characteristics. A subset of the audience may be retained for a focus group in which a moderator probes the survey questions in greater depth. In addition to recruited audience screenings, post-production market research also includes testing advertising material, such as print ads, trailers, and television commercials. These tests are designed to evaluate the interest and image created for the film by the advertising material.[17]

This model of market research is somewhat problematic from both a methodological and an analytical perspective. In particular, the pre-production market research has received criticism for being prescriptive: for dictating creative decisions based upon a quantitative score or set of scores. The post-production market research has been judged less harshly, since this research is more evaluative of a finished product for marketing purposes, rather than prescriptive for an evolving product.

Considering the pre-production research, perhaps the most significant methodological problem is the inability to account for innovative film concepts, or as a veteran marketing consultant comments, "Anything that is innovative is hard for market research to clue in on."[18] Consequently movies which adhere strictly to genre tend to be more attractive in concept form than films which might be described as cross-genre or outside genre. Therefore, a romantic comedy, such as *Pretty Woman*, would be easier to concept test than the comedy/family drama *Avalon*, whose cross-genre storyline would be almost impossible to reduce to a concept. The implications of this factor for high concept are clear: high concept, adhering closely to genre and previous successes, offers an immediate reference point for the respondent. Therefore, high concept films would probably test higher in concept form than low concept films, other factors held constant.

In addition, another limitation in the pre-production research involves the difficulty of expressing the visual or aural nature of the medium. Films which are heavily dependent upon striking visuals, such as *Blade Runner, The Hunger,* and *One from the Heart,* or upon their soundtracks, such as *Purple Rain, Flashdance,* and *Something Wild* (1986), cannot be conveyed accurately through a marketing concept. Consider, for instance, a possible concept for *Purple Rain*: "*Purple Rain* is a dramatic musical, starring Prince, featuring eight new Prince songs shot in music-video style." While all these claims are true, the concept, through its form, fails to convey the music and visual style of the film. A respondent listening to the concept would indicate interest based primarily on the appeal of Prince, rather than on the film. Similarly, casting tests tend to privilege stars within their familiar genre. Concept testing responds mainly to star-driven projects, and high concept, which often relies on stars as a form of insurance, fits neatly with this paradigm.

Partly to compensate for these limitations, market researchers often resort to a rhetoric which poses another set of problems. The rhetoric of market research is centered to a certain extent around hyperbole. These concepts might link the film to be tested to past successes of the same genre. For example, the firefighter film *Backdraft* (1991) could be positioned in a concept as "an incredibly exciting, death-defying drama in the tradition of *The Towering Inferno*." An interest level on the film based on this concept would be biased, since the respondent would be making the equation between *Backdraft* and *The Towering Inferno;* interest in the new film would be based largely upon assuming that the two films are equivalent, which, of course, may be an incorrect assumption.

The choice of adjectives in a concept description also can affect the interest level: for example, in positioning the film as an adventure,

Backdraft could be presented as "suspenseful," "intense," or "the most thrilling adventure of your lifetime." The market researchers cannot discern the extent to which interest is due to the basic storyline and, more significantly, the extent to which the wording of the concept has altered basic interest. This error in measurement has been noted by the studios: as reported in an article about leading film and television market researcher Joseph Farrell, " 'Joe was off in forecasting *The Rocketeer* [1991], because, when presented to the public, it was compared to *Raiders of the Lost Ark*,' recalls one marketing executive. 'This summer's [1992] *Cool World* was described as continuing where *"Roger Rabbit* takes off.*"* That's "advertising," not "concept." ' " [19]

Although post-production research involving recruited audience screenings is more widely accepted within the industry, these surveys also remain problematic in terms of method. One of the main difficulties with audience screenings as a method to extrapolate future success involves sampling: following the basic tenet of statistical analysis, the market researchers select a sample of moviegoers to represent the general population of moviegoers. [20] One major difficulty with this process is deciding on the characteristics of the general population of moviegoers: in particular, whether this general population is, in fact, an abstract target audience which the filmmakers have designed the film for, or is more representative of the spectrum of moviegoers. [21] The issue of sampling becomes even thornier considering that audience members at the screening are not just differentiated by sex and age, which target audiences are often defined by, but also by geographical location, income level, and educational background. [22] Extrapolation of the recruited audience research results beyond the limited audience sample at the screening becomes a precarious endeavor due to these inherent sampling problems.

These limitations in method historically have worked in conjunction with the increasing conglomeration of the film industry to privilege the high concept film whose economic risk is minimized through emphasizing the familiar over the original. [23] The economic appeal of the high concept film is based upon the immediate point of reference for the audience; as Tom Pollock, chairman of the MCA motion picture group, states, "The reason studios make them [blockbusters] is because of marketing. They have instant identity." [24] This instant identity strongly facilitates market research which, as a method, inherently favors those films which the respondent can compare to previous familiar films. Therefore, the movement toward the "packaging" of films within the past two decades correlates with the encroachment of market research;

the strong argument would be that market research has, in some sense, shaped and certainly has furthered high concept filmmaking.

Case Study:
Determining Boxoffice Revenue

The sampling and design problems in these short-run projects are replicated in more long-run projects implemented in market research. While the short-run projects are constructed around specific films and their marketing strategies, the long-run projects commissioned by the major studios attempt to gauge attitude and taste changes across time. The methodological limitations of market research and the tendency toward production of high concept films can be comprehended through the close analysis of a long-run market research project.

In many respects, high concept should be the most amenable of any filmmaking to market research. The connection between market research and high concept derives from the commercial emphasis of these films: these "formula" films are designed to be "appreciated" as much as possible by the target audience, and, it is hoped, by other audience segments as well. Certainly, the industry usage suggests that the high concept film "ensures" financial success due to the presence of several elements, including storyline, genre, stars, and bankable directors. If these high concept films can be broken down into their constitutive elements, then these films would fit more readily than other types into a model describing the components of a single film. Consequently, long-run market research surveys tracking the popularity of different film types should be more accurate in accounting for the packaged, formulaic high concept films than for the more low concept projects, which defy simple categorization by genre, stars, marketing hooks, etc. Market research, therefore, in both short- and long-run projects, favors and furthers the high concept film.

One way to investigate the connection between market research and high concept is to develop a statistical model explaining the determinants of "popular" film. Using films released in the heyday of high concept (1983–1986), I will build a model which accounts for the final boxoffice gross of each film.[25] The goal of the model will be to determine whether high concept films, and their commercial success, can be accounted for more accurately than other films by this method of analysis. The model will be specified so that the boxoffice gross is explained by those factors having a probable positive impact on the gross of the film. Through such a model, the relative impact of the different variables accounting for boxoffice gross can be determined. The model, therefore, can be used to predict future boxoffice gross if the values of the explanatory variables are known beforehand. Such an attempt at forecasting would be a possible long-term market research project in the film industry.

The overall sample of films from 1983 to 1986 also will include a subset of high concept films. Three separate facets define the films as high concept for this particular project: the style of the films, their links to merchandising and licensing, and the "repetition" through either remakes, sequels, or series. Regarding the latter aspect, high concept can be seen as a type of "economy" on the part of producers: the repetition of bankable material to guarantee audience interest. The most obvious forms of this repetition are remakes, sequels, or series films, which together represent one "formula" for commercial success. A comparison between the overall sample and the high concept films will illuminate any differences in the high concept films' relation to popularity.

Theorizing the Positive Influences on Boxoffice Gross

Quantitative audience research has a substantial history in mass communications, with the material more specifically in film audience studies summarized in Bruce Austin's *The Film Audience: An International Bibliography of Research*.[26] Barry Litman's "Predicting Success of Theatrical Movies: New Empirical Evidence" offers a useful point of departure for this study, both in terms of the variables considered and the results derived.[27] Litman's goal is also the determination of success for theatrical features; his choice of variables — the factors which explain theatrical success — basically grows from the three areas that he feels are important to success: "the creative sphere, the scheduling and release pattern, and the marketing effort."[28] Litman specifies the following variables as having an impact on theatrical rentals: the adjusted negative cost, the distributor, the award nominees and winners, the Motion Picture Association of America (MPAA) rating, the critics' star rating, the superstars in the cast, the genre, the number of first-run theaters, the newspaper advertising intensity, and the release date.[29] Litman offers many useful "proxies" for variables which would seem to be inherently unquantifiable. In other words, he presents alternative variables for factors which are difficult or impossible to include in a statistical model. For example, Litman judges that a director's reputation would have an effect on revenues "if a director was nominated for an Academy Award during the four years prior to his film in the sample or won an award during the previous seven years."[30]

Some aspects of Litman's model have been developed further in other studies. For instance, Bruce Austin has considered the effect of critical reception on boxoffice gross.[31] Through questionnaires and interviews as the basis for his research, Austin argues for the importance of criticism and movie reviews as a guide for attendance. Generally, though, reviews are more significant for the frequent, rather than occasional, patron.[32] Austin's other major finding in this area supports the "elitist" trait of major critics: an evaluation of 788 films by consumers and critics suggests that "consumers evaluated the movies significantly more positively than the critics."[33] These conclusions suggest that some form of critical rating—either by the critics or the public—would be worthwhile to include in the model.

Thomas Simonet and Kenneth Harwood weigh the relationship between the film director and boxoffice revenue.[34] They find that critically favored directors are not necessarily the same as financially successful directors, and that audiences do not respond to directors as "auteurs." Looking at the issue from a different angle, though, Simonet, in a solo study, does show a strong positive relation between the prior boxoffice success of directors and the boxoffice success of their subsequent films.[35]

Much more academic and industrial interest has focused on the contribution of boxoffice stars to gross. Starting with the industry-funded Gallup research ("Continuing Audit of Marquee Values"), Hollywood has continually tried to discover the "market value" of a performer. As researcher David Ogilvy stated, "I calculated how much each star contributed to the receipts of a picture and told our clients how much he should be paid."[36] Gorham Kindem's "Hollywood's Movie Star System: A Historical Overview" offers a synthesis of several past analyses which have sought to link stars with revenue. While much attention has been paid to the period of the studio system and the economic significance of boxoffice stars to the mode of production, Kindem makes an interesting contribution to these arguments.[37] Moving into the past two decades, Kindem argues for the increasing interdependence between media stars and content: "Performers like Sally Field, John Travolta, Goldie Hawn, Olivia Newton-John, Henry Winkler, Barbra Streisand, and Kris Kristofferson became stars on television or in the recording industry before their star status was fully exploited by the film industry."[38] Therefore, the bankability of these (different) media stars acts as an insurance marker for filmmakers.

Another factor which might be considered regarding bankable performers is the correspondence of performer with genre. As director John Badham states, "There's an audience that will show up to see *Rocky IV* even if it's 105 minutes of black leader. On the other hand, *Over the Top* is a picture that's in terrible trouble: There Stallone is stepping out of his genre, like Eastwood in *Bronco Billy*."[39] Even within my sample of films, Badham's comment rings true: Bill Murray is bankable in a comedy like *Ghostbusters*, but not in the somber drama *The Razor's Edge* (1984); John Travolta attracts customers in the musical sequel *Staying Alive*, but not in the drama/exposé *Perfect*; Steve Martin is winning to audiences in comedic roles, such as those in *Father of the Bride* (1991) and *Housesitter* (1992), but not so in dramatic fare, such as *Pennies from Heaven* (1981) and *Grand Canyon* (1991). One possible adjustment to the Litman model would be to limit the boxoffice stars to certain genres if the identification between star and genre seems especially strong.

Finally, Austin also has isolated the influence of the MPAA ratings on audiences in his study "Do Movie Ratings Affect a Film's Performance at the Ticket Window?"[40] Utilizing a questionnaire which described possible film scenarios and their MPAA ratings, subjects were asked to rank their preference for several film projects. Austin discovered that the likelihood of attendance at both PG- and R-rated movies was significantly greater than for both G- and X-rated films, and that there was no significant difference between PG- and R-rated films in terms of likelihood of attendance.[41] Austin's studies, in conjunction with the other research projects on factors influencing attendance, offer some important variables to be included in the model explaining boxoffice revenue.

Specification of the Model

The variable to be explained in the model—i.e., the element that will be accounted for in terms of all possible influences—is theatrical gross accruing to the distributor per film. A. D. Murphy's *Boxoffice Register* offers both weekly and cumulative yearly figures for boxoffice gross. I am considering all those films between 1983 and 1986 (inclusive) which have grossed more than $1 million at the boxoffice, in order to create as large a sample as possible. The vast majority of releases are included within this group since, if a film is given a wide release, a total revenue of at least $1 million is extremely probable. The years 1983 through 1986 represent the mature period of high concept, in which the major studios had fully adjusted their production schedules toward this form of production.[42]

The set of explanatory variables derives from all those factors which could have a positive influence on boxoffice gross. The first explanatory variables involve the distributor for each film.[43] The six major distributors are Paramount, Twentieth Century–Fox, Universal, Columbia, Warner Bros., and MGM/UA. During the period of the sample, MGM/UA was split into two individual companies (MGM and UA) which utilized the same distribution arm in conjunction. For this analysis, I am considering the output of both companies as part of only MGM/UA. The mini-majors are Orion, Tri-Star, and Disney/Touchstone. These companies typically did not have as large a release slate as the majors, and they lacked the advantages of economies of scale offered through extensive production and integration of the different windows of release. Companies such as De Laurentiis Entertainment Group, Cannon, New World, New Line, and Embassy are considered as independents. The expectation is that the majors will have a greater positive impact on boxoffice gross compared to the independents, who cannot match the distribution and marketing expertise of the majors.

Ratings can potentially influence the size of the boxoffice revenue through limiting admittance to R-rated features or through acting as a positive or negative guide to a film's adult content. To account for this factor, the second set of variables, from the MPAA rating system, accounts for the categories G-PG-PG13-R. The X rating was excluded, since no films in the sample had been assigned this rating.

The third explanatory variable concerns release date. Since the phenomenally successful release of *Jaws* in 1975, summer has been increasingly seen as the most favorable period for release. Indeed, currently 40 percent of boxoffice revenues are derived from the summer period.[44] This pattern has developed in conjunction with the targeting of a youth audience for pictures. Alternately, the Christmas vacation period has remained very important as a release season. Traditionally this period includes prestige, Oscar-hopeful movies, yet several blockbusters have started their runs during the Christmas season. Both periods have been expanding so that, for the film industry, summer now begins before Memorial Day in May, and Christmas slightly before the Thanksgiving Day holiday in November.[45] To discover if, in fact, these periods do have a positive effect on boxoffice revenue, I introduced variables for the two periods. I would expect that both variables would have a positive effect on theatrical gross, signifying that a Christmas or summer release adds to the revenue of a film compared to other release periods. Release dates are from the first wide-release week for the film listed in the *Boxoffice Register*.

Market researchers often base initial audience "want-to-see" interest in a project on the title and stars of the film. Foregrounding the stars in this fashion indicates the significance which the film industry accords stars, treating the star as the most significant form of human capital ("talent") in a film project. To evaluate this factor as a positive influence on boxoffice, the presence of bankable stars in a film constitutes the fourth explanatory variable in the model. Utilizing a method from Litman's study, I am considering the top ten boxoffice stars from the Quigley Publications' "Annual Poll of Circuit and Independent Exhibitors in the United States." For the current year, a film has a bankable star if it features any actor or actress from the three prior top-ten lists.[46] Therefore, a film released in 1986 contains a bankable star if it contains any person from the top ten for 1983–1985. The complete list of the stars for each year is presented in Table 3. (Tables 3–9 appear at the end of this chapter.)

Similarly, the variable accounting for the bankable directors is also constructed based on track record. The directors of the top twenty films in each of the past three years were compiled: if any of these directors made a film in the current year, the model would include a variable specifying a "marketable director" for that film.[47] Since a director may have helmed more than one top film in the past three years, the list of marketable directors for each year is less than sixty. A listing of the marketable directors for 1983–1986 is given in Table 4. The data for the top twenty films was derived from the *Boxoffice Register* and *Variety*'s chart of "The Big Rental Films" for each year. The expected effect of the bankable director on boxoffice gross would be positive, since a director with a previous top twenty film would be expected to produce another bankable film.

The advertising of most films includes, at some point, critical blurbs in the copy. Ranging from the relatively highbrow (Janet Maslin, say, or Vincent Canby) to the unabashedly populist and reductive ("Two Thumbs Up" Siskel and Ebert), critical opinion acts as a signal of film quality for potential ticket-buyers. In the model, therefore, I included an index of critical reception, based on an average of overall reviews from national critics, as an explanatory variable. *Boxoffice* magazine, an industry trade paper targeted primarily at exhibitors, publishes its "Review Digest." Each film in the digest is assigned a rating from 1 (very poor) to 5 (excellent). This cumulative rating is based upon an average of the individual ratings from *Boxoffice*, *Variety*, the *Los Angeles Times*, the *New York Times*, and *USA Today*. The sample of films is remarkably comprehensive: the Digest only omitted 54 (out of 512) films from my larger sample of all releases. For the missing critical ratings, I utilized a conversion of critic Leonard Maltin's ratings.[48]

A series of seven variables account for the genre of each film. The possible genres are drama, comedy, action/adventure, horror/mystery/suspense, family, musical, and science fiction. Each film was placed within a single genre. Cost figures are also utilized as explanatory variables. While Litman constrained his study to include only those films on which he could find cost data, I propose instead to specify a variable for high-cost films: to be designated if a film has a negative cost of over $15 million, and omitted otherwise.[49] Data on these high-cost films is available in *Variety's* annual "Big Buck Scorecard." For those high-cost films, another variable listing the actual cost (as a number over $15 million) was entered. One would expect that somehow the enhanced production values in the high-cost films should correlate with larger box-office grosses.

The final explanatory variables involve the Academy Awards. Two numerical variables list the number of nominations and the number of awards won for each film. The expectation is that these awards would add to the boxoffice gross of the winning films. Therefore, the actual full model, accounting for all the positive influences on gross, is composed as follows: boxoffice revenue is explained by distribution company, MPAA rating, release pattern, bankable stars, bankable director, critical reception, genre, cost, and awards.

A statistical technique, multiple regression analysis, will be used to assess the relationship between boxoffice revenue for the films from 1983 to 1986 and the entire set of factors which are specified as having an influence on boxoffice revenue. This technique mathematically estimates the *relative* effect of each of these factors on boxoffice revenue. In addition, multiple regression analysis can be used to attempt prediction of future boxoffice revenue.[50]

Estimation of the Model and Results

The model considers virtually all the major releases from 1983 to 1986, comprising a sample of 512 films. Table 5 presents summary statistics for the data set. The vast majority of the films (81 percent) were released by majors; a "Restricted" rating (48 percent of the sample) proved to be the most frequent rating by the MPAA; and few films contained boxoffice stars (only 11 percent of the sample) or were made by bankable directors (which comprised 16 percent of the sample). About half of all films (54 percent) were merchandised in one form or another, although few possessed the high concept style (15 percent) or were a sequel or part of a series (17 percent). Among genres, comedy (30 percent), drama (23 percent), and action (21 percent) occurred most frequently.

Correlation analysis indicates how closely two variables move together.[51] In other words, this statistical procedure illustrates whether one variable increases or decreases in value as another variable increases or decreases in value. Variables that move together in the same direction are positively correlated, while variables that move in opposite directions are negatively correlated. In addition, regardless of how the two variables move together, there may be a strong, weak, or no correlation, or relationship, between the two variables. Table 6 shows the simple correlations between boxoffice gross and each explanatory variable. As expected, since the variables were chosen for having a positive influence on boxoffice, almost all of the specified variables correlate positively with boxoffice gross: as each of the positive factors influencing gross increases, so does boxoffice gross. Among the genres, there is little correlation between any one genre and boxoffice gross. The major discrepancy between Litman's findings and my own occurs with the science fiction genre: Litman found a stronger correlation between gross and sci-fi. This finding could be due to the earlier revival of science fiction films during the period (late 1970s) of Litman's study. Among studios, Paramount shows the highest correlation with gross, implying that, compared to other studios, Paramount is most strongly related with boxoffice gross. This finding is especially interesting given the large number of high concept films with which Paramount has been associated.

All the variables related to criticism and evaluation show a positive correlation with gross; Academy Award nominations are more highly correlated with gross than either Academy Awards or critical rating. Summer correlates positively with gross, which breaks from Litman's model, in which summer release correlated slightly negatively with gross. Litman's sample also exhibited a strong correlation between Christmas release and gross, whereas Christmas release and gross showed a slight positive correlation in my model. Finally, all three high concept variables correlate positively, with the strongest correlation being between gross and the high concept style. This finding indicates that the high concept variables are related to boxoffice gross.

Between the explanatory variables, several interesting correlations can be made relating to the different studios. These findings illustrate the relationship between the studio and each of the factors influencing boxoffice gross. The results appear in Table 7. First, although Paramount is most correlated with revenue, the studio ranks low (eighth out of ten) in its correlation with the cost variable. This would seem to indicate that Paramount is among the most cost-efficient of the studios, especially since there is also a strong correlation between Paramount and boxoffice stars. Warner Bros. shows strong correlation with cost, boxoffice stars, and bankable directors. Among the mini-majors, Disney's early promise is definitely evident: Disney exhibits the strongest correlation with critical response and merchandising, while showing little correlation with boxoffice stars or high cost. Paramount also shows the strongest correlation with the high concept variables, followed by Disney. Among genres, Universal shows the highest correlation with comedy, independents with the horror and action genres (the most popular of the exploitation genres), and Disney with the family pictures.

Every variable, except Academy Awards, adds significantly to the explanatory power of the model, meaning that statistically each variable deserves inclusion in the model.[52] The most refined statistical model can be found in Table 8. This model accounts for or explains 45 percent of boxoffice revenue through the explanatory variables specified in the model.[53] The relative effects of some variables on boxoffice gross warrant mention.[54] The high-cost variable has a large and negative effect, which is especially interesting, indicating that an excessive budget film will decrease the overall gross of a film by $18.6 million! This surprising statistic indicates that high-budget films actually lower the prospects for revenue. Films in the sample such as *Something Wicked This Way Comes, The King of Comedy* (1983), *The Cotton Club* (1984), *The Bounty* (1984), *Once Upon a Time in America* (1984), *King David* (1985), and *Enemy Mine* (1985) each cost more than $20 million, while grossing substantially less than 50 percent of its budget. These big-budget disasters greatly outweigh proportionately high-budget hits such as *Return of the Jedi, Rambo: First Blood Part II*, and *A View to a Kill* (1985). All the majors, except Universal, have a positive effect on gross. The model indicates that, compared to the other studios, Universal actually has a negative effect on boxoffice revenue. In other words, the impact of Universal as an element in a potential film "package" is negative: the distributor actually detracts from the potential gross. As expected, both Paramount and Warner Bros. carry the largest positive impact on gross, thereby attesting to their superior distribution and marketing practices.

The estimated statistical model offers a predicted value for the boxoffice for each of the films, meaning that the model specifies predicted boxoffice revenue for each film based on the values for all the factors (e.g., release date, studio, cost, etc.) influencing gross. This predicted value should be close to the actual or observed boxoffice gross which the film accrued. An analysis of the plotted "observed" (real-world) versus "predicted" grosses from this regression uncovers some trends among the types of films which may be projected through this form of statistical analysis. The largest errors in prediction occur among the positive outliers, those films which have phenomenally large grosses.[55] For example, *Back to the Future* grossed $188.77 million in adjusted 1983 dollars; the regression specified a figure of $63.01 million, which is amongst the largest predicted in the model, yet obviously quite far away from the actual gross. *Top Gun* is another outlier problem: an actual gross of $154.6 million, with a predicted gross of $87.8 million. Again, a very high figure for the model, but not very close to the actual gross.

Other large errors are associated with large-budget "surprises": films which were highly touted, yet failed to live up to their expectations. *The Right Stuff* (1983), *Brainstorm* (1983), and *Brazil* (1985) fit into this category. In many ways, these films were expected to perform much more strongly, and their eventual failure remains a mystery. The most striking case would be *The Right Stuff*, which was well received by the critics, garnered many Academy Award nominations, and was considered a fascinating and very American subject. The film grossed only $21.5 million: well below the expected revenue, and far below the predicted value of $78.3 million. This discrepancy indicates one of the potential difficulties in predicting boxoffice gross: there are many cases of a film such as *The Right Stuff*, with all the "commercial" elements in place, which failed to attract audience interest regardless.

Given the emphasis of the high concept projects on simple and definable storylines, it is interesting that the model's large errors also occur with films which have been widely criticized for their confusing narratives. Consider the narratives of, for example, *The Hunger*, *The Keep* (1983), *Against All Odds* (1984), *The Cotton Club*, and *Swing Shift* (1984).[56] All of the narratives of these films are torn in several different directions, confounding the viewer's expectations and the limitations of their genres. These films cannot be conceptually reduced in the same manner as *Flashdance* or *Top Gun*. For example, what is the concept behind Francis Coppola's sprawling gangster-musical *The Cotton Club*? These "complicated" film narratives produced boxoffice revenues far below their predicted values in the regression model. In part, an argument could be made for their failure in terms of high concept: the lack of a clear concept behind these films hampered their performance at the boxoffice.

Alternately, the model works best predicting action and horror films. Action films which fit the model well include *Ten to Midnight* (1983; observed $7.1m, predicted $7.53m), *Conan the Destroyer* (1984; observed $24.8m, predicted $24.3m), *The Terminator* (1984; observed $34.7m, predicted $38.7m), *Delta Force* (1986; observed $15.1m, predicted $17.5m); horror films include *Firestarter* (1984; observed $14.2, predicted $13.8m), *Impulse* (1984; observed $2.5m, predicted $2.7m), and *Cat's Eye* (1985; observed $8.0m, predicted $8.1m). These predicted values encompass a wide range, indicating that the model is able to predict low- and high-grossing horror and action films. The model also operates most successfully in the prediction of strict genre films (such as the action and horror picture); cross-genre films seem more difficult

The problem of predicting cross-genre films
(The Cotton Club, Orion, 1984). Photo by
Adyer W. Cowans, © 1984 Orion Pictures
Corporation.

to predict accurately. Another strength of the model is in the prediction of sequel or series films such as *Staying Alive, Superman III* (1983), *Porky's II: The Next Day* (1983), *Oh God, You Devil* (1984), *Exterminator II* (1984). Finally, the model also works best with films from the major studios, which can assure a film of widespread distribution and adequate marketing.

To identify the differences in the high concept films compared to the rest of the films released, I isolated a subset of only high concept films. High concept films are defined in the model for this subset as those films which carry the high concept style and are also merchandised. A group of 67 films (from 512) were classified as high concept (see Table 9). The most striking contrast between the high concept sample and the larger sample is the mean for boxoffice revenue: $47.8 million for the high concept films, $14.5 million for the rest of the sample. The increased revenue is also matched by a greater percentage of high-cost films (37.3 percent vs. 18.8 percent) and distribution by majors (97 percent vs. 78 percent). The high concept films also tend to include more action and musical films, and are twice as likely to feature a boxoffice star. In terms of release date, high concept films are more likely to be released in the summer compared to other films. As expected, Paramount's share of the high concept films (16.4 percent) is greater than any other studio's, and the independent distributors' share of the high concept films is substantially smaller than their share of all films. This factor is probably due to the higher production cost of the high concept films more readily being supported by major studios than by independents.

In conclusion, this type of statistical modeling, indicative of one kind of market research project within the industry, relies on dividing a film into elements. The film becomes the sum of its parts, such as the stars, bankable director, merchandising tie-ins, and genre. The modular, packaged high concept films, with marketing hooks inherent in the projects, lend themselves to this kind of analytical breakdown. Consequently, it is not surprising perhaps that the statistical model illustrates that high concept is actually more predictable than other forms of production. The model works most successfully with genre-bound, linear narrative and pre-packaged films—all categories which overlap with high concept.

If high concept films are more predictable through market research in terms of gross, then high concept lowers the risk and uncertainty within the movie marketplace. The attractions of this are obvious. While this factor is attractive to the industry, methodologically the link between high concept and market research is flawed. The short-run biases in market research, such as the allegiance to genre and past media references which favor high concept, are replicated in the longer run projects, as exemplified by my model. Regardless, this type of long-run market research project also presents more substantive methodological problems which should also be taken into account when evaluating the results. These additional concerns illustrate the difficulty in relying on quantitative data when deciding on film productions.[57]

Manipulation, Control, and High Concept

If market research is designed to target, present, and highlight the most marketable elements of the film, then high concept is the most accessible type of film for this process due to its inherent construction as a strictly commercial venture. The development of high concept within the industry parallels the encroachment of market research at the same time. Clearly cause-and-effect is difficult to argue in terms of market research and high concept, but market research certainly does serve high concept films to a greater extent than, for example, the non-star, cross-genre films, as is evidenced by the boxoffice gross model.

Ideologically, market research recalls the prophecies of media influence from the Frankfurt School. Indeed, Herbert Marcuse could have been directly addressing market research in the film industry through posing the question, "Can one really distinguish between the mass media as instruments of information and entertainment, and as agents of manipulation and indoctrination?"[58] This statement embodies the paradox of market research. On the one hand, market research does act as a straitjacket in the film industry, limiting content and material which is objectionable to test audiences and respondents. This straitjacket, in many ways, could be interpreted in ideological terms as a dictatorship created by market research. On the other hand, market research merely shapes motion picture "products" in response to the tastes and feelings of the greatest number of people. In this way, populism rules in the world of market research.

If all mainstream films are the meeting of commerce and art, market research tips the scales much further toward commerce. It is hardly surprising that market research concept testing placed *Wind, Stay Tuned,* and *Honeymoon in Vegas* at the bottom of all Summer 1992 films in terms of audience "want-to-see" interest.[59] Regardless of the films' quality, the lack of clear genre allegiance and stars, as well as the unusual/offbeat quality of each film, signified their lack of appeal for market research. Of course, each of these films also lacks discernable high concept qualities. Greeted by the dismal initial interest scores, the studio marketing department understandably shifts effort to those films which show more promise. Consequently, those films which should receive *greater* marketing help — in creating a coherent image of the film for the public — are pushed aside by the majors. This cycle is replicated by films which test poorly in preview screenings. For instance, Robert Altman's against-the-grain teen comedy *O.C. & Stiggs* was "dumped" by MGM after dismal research screenings in 1984, as was the 1991 baseball drama *Talent for the Game,* which Paramount relegated to straight-to-video after research testing.[60]

The institutional control exacted by market research extends to the fine-tuning of the mainstream Hollywood films. Ruled by a methodology which seeks to maximize the satisfaction or utility of the greatest number of potential moviegoers, market research also inevitably embodies the value system belonging to this majority.[61] Indeed, the control of market research is a control of the norms, both aesthetic and social. Thus, any denunciation of the mainstream film industry in terms of moral turpitude — such as Michael Medved's diatribe *Hollywood vs. America: Popular Culture and the War on Traditional Values* — is completely untenable. Medved claims that Hollywood films promote attitudes *against* the values of a majority of Americans: for instance,

Mannequin: *designed for maximum appeal to a young, female demographic (*Manne-quin, *Twentieth Century–Fox, 1987). Photo by Gale Adler, copyright © 1987 Gladden Entertainment Corp.*

Medved has been quoted as stating, "The point is that Hollywood pro-motes an attitude that the majority of Americans don't share — that the family is in meltdown, that the family is dead as an institution."[62] Mar-ket research, though, virtually ensures that Hollywood films carry the prevailing values, attitudes, and tastes of the American public. There-fore, Medved's attack is misguided: he should really be attacking the public as a whole for endorsing these popular movies, rather than sug-gesting that Hollywood, instead of merely reflecting dominant beliefs, is shaping beliefs and actively lowering moral standards.

High concept could be interpreted as the product of an industry driven by market research. To claim that high concept films are com-pletely dictated by quantitative scores would be a strong misrepresen-tation; even within high concept, there is latitude for creative decisions which do not lend themselves to a questionnaire. Taken to the extreme, the end result of market research would not be the light romantic comedy *Mannequin* (1987), as some critics have suggested.[63] Executive-produced by market researcher Joseph Farrell, the successful *Manne-quin* — telling of a beautiful mannequin coming to life for a romance with a store clerk — was designed from its inception for maximum ap-

peal to a young, female demographic, with casting, advertising, and release date all centering on this goal.[64] Rather, the extreme is represented
by the operation called "Future Films": a mysterious production company whose entry into Hollywood was heralded by an advertising
campaign in the industry trade papers: "PUBLIC NOTICE: Six years of
confidential research. Thousands of interviews and tests done. Is the
discovery about PEOPLE or TECHNOLOGY?" Beneath this copy are two
drawings: a smiling researcher, pen and clipboard in hand, talks with a
mother and daughter, and a panel of monitors illustrates impressive
bar and flow charts against such titles as "Comedy," "Western," "Romance," and "Actress Age."

This campaign was followed by the announcement of Future Films:
a production company wholly devoted to market research in the choice
of screenplay, story elements, and even running time. As Robert Cefail,
Future Films' chief executive officer, describes, after exhaustive public
research across the nation, "In late 1986 I tabulated the No. 1 type of
film that people wanted to see and tested it against the films in development. The No. 1 film people wanted at that time was a romantic
comedy set in the present during springtime. The place would be a big
city and the lead actors would be 28 to 32 years old. . . . The comedy
that was most needed at that time was witty and intelligent humor and
they didn't want any mixture of it with stupid slapstick. The time length
of the movie should be 1 hour and 52 minutes."[65] Planning to make
"McMovies," Cefail organized a national survey of public taste in which
respondents would call a 900 number (at the minimum cost of $2) and
then answer questions about potential plots, subjects, stars, and storyline traits.[66]

The underlying agenda of Future Films can be discovered through
part of its press release: "See why our American public feels completely
neglected regarding their tastes in movies: *Dying Young*—91% want up-
beat endings & *Casual Sex*—89% prefer stories with 'good old-fashioned
romance' over casual relationships and unusual practices."[67] This "iron-
ing" of potentially disruptive subject matter again makes Marcuse seem
unusually prescient in stating, "Many of the most seriously trouble-
some concepts are 'eliminated' by showing that no adequate account of
them in terms of operation or behavior can be given."[68] Indeed, the
agenda of Future Films is really not profit, but ideological control. Un-
masked by the *Los Angeles Times* and a witty *Village Voice* article by Russ
Baker titled "Putting the Cult Back in Culture," Future Films was tied
closely to Scientology; as Baker comments, "Future Films may be the
latest, thinly disguised attempt by Scientology to gain widespread acceptance and suck thousands into the movement."[69] Given its regime

of market research, the group sought to control masses through presenting media produced according to carefully framed market surveys. The illusion of control by the public is, in fact, control by those designing and framing the questions.

Certainly the majors operate in a much less extreme fashion than the Orwellian scenario above, but the "lesson" offered by Future Films could be applied to high concept: simply stated, that market research represents an ideology of the masses which serves to shape the form and content of films produced within this institutional structure. Innovation—aesthetic or social—is not a facet of the structure, and occurs either as an aberration or outside the system altogether. Despite this rather stern pronouncement, there are factors within the system which have been shifting the relationship between market research, the film industry, and, by extension, high concept.

Factors Influencing the Decline of Market Research

The alignment between market research and the film industry which has developed over the past two decades may be faltering, however. The adjustment in this relationship seems due to two principal factors: the movement away from the high concept syndrome and the development of the baby boom generation as an audience force. The lessening of Hollywood's emphasis on the high concept film derives in part from increasing cost in producing and marketing these films. According to the MPAA, the average film budget rose to $26.8 million in 1990, up from $18 million in 1988.[70] This increase has been driven by the escalating cost of the high concept films reliant on big stars, large-scale productions, and pre-sold properties. Consider that in 1990 alone, *Total Recall* cost $60 million, with an additional $35 million in advertising costs, *Die Hard 2* also cost approximately $60 million, with $30 million in ad costs, and *Days of Thunder* was only slightly less expensive at $50 million, with $27 million in ad costs.[71] As the costs increase, these films are also rushed into distribution to save on interest payments. For example, in order to recoup its cost as soon as possible, *Days of Thunder* was released only five months after the beginning of principal photography.[72]

Just as significantly, production cost increases for the high concept films have been met with dramatic increases in advertising and marketing costs. With studios spending $50–60 million on a large-scale film, insurance for a substantial recoupment is available in advertising which establishes and reinforces the image of the film. In the past decade, television advertising has accounted for 60–70 percent of total advertising expenditures, with key buys being commercials during primetime on the midweek evenings prior to a weekend opening.[73] Television networks have been sharply escalating rates to the studios, or as Fox marketing and distribution chairman Tom Sherak comments, "Thursday night is a big night to spend money, if your picture comes out the next day, and the TV companies make us pay for that."[74] Indeed, in 1990, the average movie marketing budget increased 26 percent to $11.6 million, while the marketing cost of major studio releases jumped 20 percent over 1989, to an average of $26 million per film.[75]

The phenomenal increase in production and marketing costs for these commercial films has created a climate in which films such as *Dick Tracy*, grossing $104 million, and *Batman*, grossing $253 million, have failed to break even in domestic theatrical release.[76] The apparent decline of high concept became particularly evident to the studios in 1990 with the simultaneous failure of several big-budget, action-oriented sequels (*RoboCop II, Rocky V, Another 48 HRS.*) and star-power films (*Days of Thunder, Havana, Air America*). At least in the press, the studio executives have been distancing themselves from the high concept films as the staple of their production schedule. Typical of the response is Disney chairman Jeffrey Katzenberg's widely circulated memo titled "The World Is Changing: Some Thoughts on Our Business," in which he describes the industry as facing a period of great danger and uncertainty.[77] Responding to the increasing unprofitability of the big-budget blockbusters and, in particular, to *Dick Tracy* as an example of this phenomenon, Katzenberg concludes, "We should now take a long and hard look at the blockbuster business . . . and get out of it."[78]

As an alternative to the high concept films, Katzenberg and other executives frequently cite a need for original, inventive stories as a focus rather than large productions, stars, and pre-sold properties; as Katzenberg comments, "We must not be distracted from one fundamental concept: the idea is king."[79] The role of market research in this process is more problematic, however. While market research can gauge the audience interest in the high concept films composed of identifiable stars, properties, and genre allegiance, this method cannot adequately account for film narratives which lie outside existing boundaries. Therefore, in shifting the focus to "original" stories, the industry is simultaneously decreasing the role which market research might play in the filmmaking process. Indeed, even in the memo, Katzenberg emphasizes that market research, which carries the aura of "science," should not dictate creative decisions since "there is nothing scientific about the movie business."[80]

To exacerbate this shift away from market research, the composition of the filmgoing audience targeted by market research has also been changing. The evolving age distribution of the population, given the growth of the baby boomers, has produced a society with increasing consumer affluence: for example, the household incomes of baby boomers will grow 56 percent by the year 2000, compared to only 5 percent for those under thirty-five years of age.[81] In addition, as the baby boomers and their families mature, leisure time will grow, especially as their children age and begin to leave home.[82] The effects of these demographic changes have been experienced already within the film industry. Whereas during the past two decades Hollywood focused primarily on the youth market, the filmgoing audience had been maturing during this period. Consider, from 1984 to 1989, that filmgoers aged twelve to twenty-four dropped from 54 percent to 44 percent as a proportion of total theatrical admissions, while filmgoers aged twenty-five to forty-nine increased from 39 percent to 46 percent. More significantly, in 1990, the over-forty audience jumped 24 percent, while the under-twenty-one audience dropped 4 percent from the previous year.[83]

This shift in audience demography has created some unexpected trends in popular films. First, as the baby boomers with children become increasingly critical to industry success, films which appeal to *both* adults and their children have become more popular: for instance, the Spielberg/Lucas adventures, *Three Men and a Baby*, *Look Who's Talking*, the new Disney cartoons (*The Little Mermaid* [1989], *Beauty and the Beast* [1991], *Aladdin* [1992]), and most strikingly *Home Alone*.[84] In addition, this adjustment in demographics has been met with a number of boxoffice successes whose appeal has been decidedly adult: *Dangerous Liaisons* (1988), *The War of the Roses* (1989), *Parenthood* (1989), *Driving Miss Daisy* (1989), and *Thelma & Louise* (1991). These successes largely fall outside the domain of market research, however. The lack of adherence to genre, pre-sold properties, and star power creates films which cannot be encapsulized in market research concepts.

Consequently, executives have been forced to reevaluate their traditional market research approaches; as Arthur Cohen, President of Worldwide Marketing at Paramount Pictures, describes, "Contemporary moviegoers are now a very educated populace. They're more sophisticated, so marketing becomes a more intricate task."[85] Implicit in Cohen's statement is an understanding that the older baby boom generation filmgoers are more resistant to persuasion and therefore more resistant to film marketing as an enterprise.[86] The younger moviegoers can also be targeted with more precision. Indeed, a study by Dennis Tootelian and Ralph Gaedeke of teens across the western United States demonstrated that television was by far the most important source of information for movie and entertainment choices.[87] As movie marketing consultant Ira Deutchman summarizes, "[The adult audience] is not as easy to target as a youth audience."[88] The more mature audience segment is also less predictable in terms of film preference compared to the youth market, choosing to attend films on a situational rather than regular basis. All these qualities of the baby boom audience members — the greater sophistication in filmgoing, the higher resistance to marketing, and the unpredictability of attendance — serve to undermine further the usefulness of market research as a tool for the film industry.

The marriage between market research and the film industry may be in decline, therefore, given the shift away from the market research–ready high concept productions and the movement toward adult-oriented films which cannot be reduced effectively to the rhetoric of market research. While market research will continue to serve a certain style of mainstream Hollywood filmmaking, the limitations of the methods, which privilege the familiar over the original, may prove to be increasingly unsatisfactory to Hollywood. If Hollywood continues to focus attention on the adult-oriented films, for which audience demographics make a strong case, more and more studio executives may react to market research as has former Twentieth Century–Fox chairman Joe Roth. In an impassioned speech, Roth vowed that his studio will completely break with a heavy reliance on research or, as he kindly referred to the market researchers, "the voodoo makers" of the film industry.[89]

Table 3. Listing of Bankable Boxoffice Stars for the Regression Model

For 1983:

Burt Reynolds	Richard Gere	Dustin Hoffman
Paul Newman	Clint Eastwood	John Travolta
Harrison Ford	Sylvester Stallone	Sally Field
Alan Alda	Dudley Moore	Sissy Spacek
Bo Derek	Richard Pryor	Barbra Streisand
Goldie Hawn	Dolly Parton	Steve Martin
Bill Murray	Jane Fonda	

For 1984:

Clint Eastwood	Richard Gere	Jane Fonda
Eddie Murphy	Chevy Chase	Paul Newman
Sylvester Stallone	Tom Cruise	Alan Alda
Burt Reynolds	Dudley Moore	Bo Derek
John Travolta	Richard Pryor	Goldie Hawn
Dustin Hoffman	Dolly Parton	Bill Murray
Harrison Ford		

For 1985:

Clint Eastwood	Prince	Dustin Hoffman
Eddie Murphy	Dan Aykroyd	Richard Gere
Sally Field	Meryl Streep	Chevy Chase
Burt Reynolds	Sylvester Stallone	Tom Cruise
Robert Redford	John Travolta	

For 1986:

Sylvester Stallone	Harrison Ford	Prince
Eddie Murphy	Michael Douglas	Dan Aykroyd
Clint Eastwood	Meryl Streep	John Travolta
Michael J. Fox	Sally Field	Dustin Hoffman
Chevy Chase	Burt Reynolds	Richard Gere
Robert Redford	Tom Cruise	Chuck Norris
Arnold Schwarzenegger		

Source: Adapted from *The International Motion Picture Almanac.*

Table 4. Listing of Marketable Directors for the Regression Model

For 1983:

I. Kershner	J. Bridges	J. Glen	T. Hackford
R. Benton	T. Chong	J. Sandrich	C. Higgins
C. Reiner	B. Fosse	A. Stevens	N. Meyer
J. Abrahams	H. Ramis	J. Boorman	T. Hooper
H. Needham	S. Rosenberg	M. Hodges	J. Huston
M. Apted	R. Maxwell	T. Gilliam	H. Hudson
H. Zeiff	S. Cunningham	J. Henson	C. Eastwood
J. Landis	R. Lester	J. Derek	T. Kotcheff
S. Pollack	S. Poitier	O. Scott	J. Milius
S. Kubrick	I. Reitman	D. Davis	H. Becker
R. Kleiser	B. Van Horn	S. Stallone	B. Reynolds
G. Nelson	S. Gordon	M. Rydell	J. Layton
S. Spielberg	A. Alda	B. Clark	J. Avildsen

For 1984:

S. Spielberg	J. Boorman	J. Huston	J. Badham
R. Lester	M. Hodges	C. Eastwood	A. Lyne
S. Poitier	T. Gilliam	T. Kotcheff	S. Dragoti
C. Higgins	J. Henson	J. Milius	W. Hill
I. Reitman	J. Derek	H. Becker	H. Ramis
B. Van Horn	O. Davis	S. Pollack	P. Brickman
S. Gordon	O. Scott	B. Reynolds	S. Lumet
H. Needham	S. Stallone	J. Layton	J. Alves
A. Alda	M. Rydell	T. Gilliam	I. Kershner
J. Glen	B. Clark	J. Avildsen	J. Brooks
J. Sandrich	T. Hackford	R. Marquand	R. Donner
A. Stevens	N. Meyer	J. Landis	T. Hooper
T. Chong	R. Attenborough		

For 1985:

S. Spielberg	H. Becker	W. Hill	L. Nimoy
S. Stallone	S. Pollack	H. Ramis	H. Wilson
M. Rydell	B. Reynolds	P. Brickman	R. Zemeckis
B. Clark	J. Layton	S. Lumet	H. Ross
T. Hackford	T. Gilliam	J. Alves	R. Howard
C. Higgins	J. Avildsen	I. Kershner	A. Magnoli
N. Meyer	R. Marquand	J. Brooks	B. Levinson
T. Hooper	J. Landis	R. Donner	B. De Palma
J. Huston	J. Badham	R. Attenborough	R. Tuggle
H. Hudson	R. Lester	J. Henson	P. Hyams
C. Eastwood	A. Lyne	I. Reitman	B. Streisand
T. Kotcheff	J. Glen	J. Dante	J. Kanew
J. Milius	S. Dragoti	M. Brest	

Table 4. (*continued*)

For 1986:

R. Marquand	S. Lumet	L. Nimoy	J. Kanew
S. Pollack	J. Alves	H. Wilson	G. Cosamatos
J. Landis	I. Kershner	R. Zemeckis	P. Weir
J. Badham	J. Brooks	H. Ross	J. Paris
R. Lester	R. Attenborough	R. Howard	A. Heckerling
A. Lyne	J. Henson	A. Magnoli	M. Ritchie
S. Stallone	C. Eastwood	B. Levinson	L. Teague
J. Glen	I. Reitman	B. De Palma	P. Bogdanovich
S. Dragoti	S. Spielberg	H. Hudson	T. Burton
W. Hill	J. Dante	R. Tuggle	G. Miller
H. Ramis	M. Brest	P. Hyams	J. Hughes
P. Brickman	J. Avildsen	B. Streisand	

Table 5. Distribution of the Entire Sample

	Entire Set
Sample Size	512
Boxoffice revenue: mean	$18.86m
standard deviation	$28.19m
Films released by majors	80.6%
Films released by independents	19.4%
Films released during Christmas season	10.9%
Films released during the summer season	33.0%
Films released apart from Christmas or summer	56.1%
Films containing a boxoffice star	10.7%
Films containing a bankable director	16.4%
High-cost films	21.2%
Films with G or PG rating	37.4%
Films with PG13 rating	14.6%
Films with R rating	48.0%
Genre breakdown	
Comedy	30.2%
Drama	23.0%
Action	21.1%
Horror	9.4%
Science fiction	5.8%
Family	5.1%
Musical	5.1%
Studio breakdown	
Warner Bros.	12.7%
Universal	11.3%
20th C–F	10.7%
Columbia	9.8%
MGM/UA	9.8%
Paramount	9.2%
Orion	7.4%
Tri-Star	6.4%
Disney	3.5%
Independent	18.9%

Table 6. Simple Pairwise Correlations between the Dependent Variable (Boxoffice Gross) and Several Independent Variables

Cost	0.255	(0.395)	Action	0.081	(−0.164)
Major Distributor	0.204	(0.321)	Horror	−0.062	(0.067)
PG13 rating	−0.007	*	Family	−0.045	(−0.051)
R rating	−0.108	*	Musical	0.023	(0.067)
Xmas release	0.128	(0.469)	Science fiction	0.037	(0.216)
Summer release	0.224	(−0.029)	Paramount	0.164	(0.097)
Critical rating	0.265	(0.395)	20th Century–Fox	0.030	(0.030)
Academy Nominations	0.337	(0.233)	Universal	−0.010	(0.031)
Academy Awards	0.212	(0.295)	MGM/UA	−0.038	(0.027)
Bankable Director	0.227	*	Columbia	0.053	(0.104)
Bankable Star	0.276	(0.276)	Warner Brothers	0.098	(0.185)
Merchandising	0.272	*	Orion	−0.039	*
High Concept Style	0.371	*	Tri-Star	−0.006	*
Remakes/Sequels/Series	0.182	*	Disney	0.005	*
Drama	−0.118	(−0.002)	Independent Distrib.	−0.200	*
Comedy	0.068	(0.071)			

The figures in parentheses are the simple correlations found in Litman's 1980 study.
* Variable missing from Litman's study.

Table 7. Simple Pairwise Correlations between Explanatory Variables

Between cost and . . .		Between critical rating and . . .	
Warner	0.102	Disney	0.129
Universal	0.085	Orion	0.101
20th C–F	0.081	Warner	0.086
Disney	0.056	20th C–F	0.046
Tri-Star	0.038	Columbia	0.023
MGM/UA	0.005	Universal	0.005
Columbia	−0.010	Paramount	−0.007
Paramount	−0.016	Tri-Star	−0.045
Orion	−0.074	MGM/UA	−0.048
Indeps	−0.202	Indeps	−0.184

Between boxoffice star and . . .		Between bankable director and . . .	
Warner	0.114	Warner	0.179
Paramount	0.086	Columbia	0.067
Columbia	0.055	Universal	0.057
20th C–F	0.001	Paramount	0.041
Universal	−0.004	MGM/UA	0.014
Tri-Star	−0.013	Tri-Star	−0.008
Orion	−0.026	20th C–F	−0.051
MGM/UA	−0.029	Disney	−0.055
Disney	−0.066	Orion	−0.085
Indeps	−0.119	Indeps	−0.160

Between high concept style and . . .		Between merchandising and . . .	
Paramount	0.091	Disney	0.113
Universal	0.054	Tri-Star	0.100
20th C–F	0.028	Universal	0.059
MGM/UA	0.025	Warner	0.048
Columbia	0.025	Columbia	0.041
Warner	0.017	Orion	0.038
Disney	0.007	Paramount	−0.003
Orion	−0.016	20th C–F	−0.006
Tri-Star	−0.022	MGM/UA	−0.011
Indeps	−0.163	Indeps	−0.240

Table 8. Regression on Boxoffice Revenue—Best Linear Model

Dependent Variable: Boxoffice revenue for theatrical movies, 1983–1986 ($ million)

Independent Variables	Estimated Coefficient	Standard Error	t-Ratio
Summer release	8.615*	2.112	4.079
Critical rating	4.781*	1.152	4.151
Cost	−59.220*	18.885	−3.136
Size of cost	4.179*	1.442	2.879
(Size of cost) squared	−0.058*	0.025	−2.313
Academy nominations	4.911*	0.653	7.522
Boxoffice stars	14.126*	3.308	4.271
Bankable director	3.414	2.788	1.224
Merchandising	6.003*	2.145	2.798
High concept style	19.330*	2.821	6.852
Tie-ins	7.581*	2.683	2.826
Paramount	13.408*	3.593	3.732
20th Century–Fox	4.482	3.381	1.326
Universal	−1.274	3.316	−0.384
MGM/UA	0.049	3.443	0.014
Columbia	2.388	3.494	0.684
Warner Bros.	5.352**	3.223	1.661
Comedy	11.942*	2.840	4.814
Action	14.694*	2.769	5.305
Horror	8.042*	3.679	2.176
Science fiction	7.667**	4.440	1.723
Constant	−22.018*	4.298	5.123

R-squared: 0.452.   R-squared adjusted: 0.429.
Sample size: 512.
*Significant at 5% level.
**Significant at 10% level.

Table 9. Distribution of the High Concept Sample

	High Concept	Rest of Full Sample
Sample size	67	445
Boxoffice revenue: mean	$47.86m	$14.50m
standard deviation	$56.12m	$17.34m
Films released by majors	97%	78%
Films released by independents	3%	22%
Films released during Christmas season	14.9%	10.3%
Films released during the summer season	43.2%	31.5%
Films released apart from Christmas or summer	41.9%	58.2%
Films containing a boxoffice star	23.3%	8.9%
Films containing a bankable director	23.8%	15.3%
High-cost films	37.3%	18.8%
Films with G or PG rating	34.4%	37.7%
Films with PG13 rating	17.9%	14.2%
Films with R rating	47.7%	48.1%
Genre breakdown		
Comedy	22.4%	31.4%
Drama	20.9%	23.3%
Action	26.8%	20.2%
Horror	4.5%	10.1%
Science fiction	12.0%	4.9%
Family	0%	5.8%
Musical	13.4%	3.8%
Studio breakdown		
Warner Bros.	13.4%	12.6%
Universal	15.0%	9.6%
20th C–F	12.0%	10.6%
Columbia	13.4%	9.2%
MGM/UA	10.4%	9.7%
Paramount	16.4%	8.1%
Orion	5.9%	7.6%
Tri-Star	5.9%	6.5%
Disney	4.4%	3.4%
Independent	3.0%	21.3%

6 Conclusion: High Concept and the Course of American Film History

From the landscape of postwar American film, high concept films have developed as a potent commercial and aesthetic force in contemporary Hollywood. The most overt qualities of high concept—the style and look of the films—function with the marketing and merchandising opportunities structured into the projects. The result is a form of differentiated product adhering to the rules of "the look, the hook, and the book," as I described the traits of high concept in the introductory chapter. The high concept style, the integration with marketing, and the narrative which can support both of the preceding are the cornerstones of high concept filmmaking.

The differentiated product of high concept has been fostered by shifts in the economics, technology, and institutional structure of the motion picture industry. These shifts were precipitated by several major technological advances—primarily the rise of television, cable, and home video—and the concurrent rise in conglomeration of the film industry. The effects of these changes were identifiable: the differentiation of film from other media, the necessity of film "playing" across a wide range of media, and the move toward more commercially "safe" product, with inherent marketing hooks which would ensure a return on investment. Throughout the mid- to late-'70s, the larger structural changes were reinforced by the development of more "micro" adjustments in the film marketing and distribution: saturation releases, music and merchandising as marketing tools, and market research in both short- and long-range projects. Films such as *Jaws*, *Star Wars*, and *Grease* embody many of the traits which would become characteristic of high concept in the years following their release in the mid- to late-'70s. The structural and marketing/distribution changes bonded together to privilege high concept as a focus for mainstream Hollywood filmmaking.

High concept is powerful in its command of the contemporary film industry partly because the system behind these films is self-replicating. High concept breeds more high concept. Consider the routes traveled by a high concept and low concept film through the film industry and into the marketplace. High concept project X—with a marketable, presold property, stars, and a bold look—tests well in the market research process, since respondents recognize the "reference points" in the project. Testing well in market research gives the distributor added confidence in the movie, and a large advertising budget is specified. The advertising plan, which includes detailed merchandising, creates strong awareness of the movie. This awareness translates into a good opening weekend boxoffice. The studio bosses are pleased, making a note to produce more movies just like project X. The strong theatrical boxoffice ensures adequate support for marketing the film in cable and home video.

Project Y, on the other hand, made to appease an action star who has just appeared in the studio's big summer picture, is an adaptation of Henrik Ibsen's classic drama *An Enemy of the People*.[1] Market research respondents show little interest in the big action star as a tormented Norwegian doctor in a period film—the concept and advertising materials test poorly. The studio starts to get cold feet, deciding to cut its advertising support. Of course, the movie also has limited merchandising potential. The studio becomes increasingly nervous over alienating fans of the action star. The consequence is that the marketing campaign is underfunded and is developed primarily around the prestige quality of the film. Prestige counts for little in terms of movie awareness, though. The film has low awareness, and opens poorly in a saturation pattern. The low gross at the theatrical window creates little support for the film at all subsequent windows. The "lesson" from projects X and Y for the studios could be seen in a potential monologue taking place the Monday after project Y's opening, "We tried to make a high-toned film, but no one cared. There just isn't the audience to support those movies on a large-scale level. All the numbers indicate that it is most prudent to proceed with movies like project X. Let's green light 'Project X: Part Two.' " Another point is notched for high concept.

The shift in demographics and rising costs may be signaling a yellow light for high concept, yet it is important to realize that high concept has been continuing, and no doubt will continue, to some extent, into the future. As I have suggested, high concept has been molded by strong institutional and industrial forces during the post–World War II era. These foundations of high concept remain in contemporary Hollywood. Consequently, while factors may be scaling down the larger high concept projects, it is inevitable that Hollywood will always be seeking a pre-sold, moderately priced high concept product, such as a cinematic adaptation of the television series *The Addams Family* (1991), *Wayne's World* (1992), or *The Beverly Hillbillies* (1993). As such, high concept cannot be adequately periodized, given the lack of a clear break from this form of production.

The power of high concept within the industry of the past two decades is substantial, however. Consider, for instance, the general development of American film history. How will the era of the 1970s and '80s be characterized in film history classes of the next century? I would argue that a consideration of the traits of high concept would be central to any characterization of the period.

The Transformation of the Auteur

To gauge the importance of high concept, consider how a film historian might chart the death of the rich period of experimentation in American film of the late '60s and early '70s. As indicated in the chapter on industrial and aesthetic history, this period is frequently described in auteurist terms. An examination of the fate of these auteurs illuminates just how powerful high concept became within the industry and how high concept, in many ways, irrevocably altered the career paths of these auteurs. In 1981, Gerald Mast, in his concluding chapter to *A Short History of the Movies*, commented, "Like the film industries of Europe and Japan, the American cinema has become a directors' cinema. . . . The American director has become one of the film's stars, and it is significant that many directors of the last decade can make films without any major star at all (*The Last Picture Show, Thieves Like Us, Star Wars, Days of Heaven*), an unheard of practice for major films until 1968."[2] Mast proceeds to identify Woody Allen, Robert Altman, Francis Coppola, Martin Scorsese, Paul Mazursky, and Peter Bogdanovich, among others, as exemplary auteurs.

If you extend the "short history" by ten years, the careers of these auteurs illustrate the progression of American film. As already recounted, Robert Altman falls into the category of auteurs who failed to adapt to high concept, and consequently he was forced to work outside the mainstream film industry. Indeed, Altman's *The Player*, released in 1992, can be interpreted as a thinly veiled satire of the mechanism which ousted him from the film industry—a world in which films are pitched as "*The Gods Must Be Crazy*, but with a television actress instead of a coke bottle" or "*The Graduate Part 2*, except Mrs. Robinson has suffered a stroke." Altman describes his own exile from Hollywood in terms of a shift toward commercially risk-free products. Telling of his inability to secure funding for his films from the mainstream industry, Altman comments, "What comes back is something based on computer data: 'We don't find a place for what you tell us this picture is going to be. We don't find an example of where that will succeed.' People don't work on feelings or hunches. They work on what they think is intellect. And you cannot intellectualize art."[3]

Directors such as the late Hal Ashby, Bob Rafelson, William Friedkin, and Peter Bogdanovich, all acclaimed for their work in the early '70s, follow a trajectory similar to Altman's.[4] From 1970 on, Ashby directed a series of diverse social comedies and dramas which commented articulately on the concerns of the times: *The Landlord* (1970), *Harold and Maude* (1971), *The Last Detail* (1973), *Shampoo* (1975), *Coming Home* (1978), and *Being There*. The latter film, released in 1979, represents Ashby's final work of artistic substance. After this time, his idiosyncratic projects were deemed virtually unreleasable (such as the comedies *Second Hand Hearts*, in 1980, and *Lookin' to Get Out* in 1982), and his career ended with the workmanlike *Eight Million Ways to Die* (1986) and, amazingly enough, a Neil Simon comedy, *The Slugger's Wife* (1985).

Unlike either Altman or Ashby, both Friedkin and Bogdanovich were more narrowly genre-oriented. Regardless, they also failed to adapt successfully to the changing marketplace of high concept. Friedkin's blockbusters of the early '70s — *The French Connection* (1971) and *The Exorcist* (1973) — actually do have some traits in common with high concept: the emphasis on style and the striking look of both films, the pre-sold property of *The Exorcist*. Yet Friedkin's career floundered after these successes, in part due to the narrative ambiguity of films such as *Cruising* (1980) and *To Live and Die in L.A.* (1985), both of which carry the high concept style without the linear, recuperable genre narratives.[5]

Bogdanovich's status as an auteur now seems based on his critically acclaimed work, *The Last Picture Show* (1971), and, to a much lesser extent on *Targets* (1968), *Paper Moon* (1973), and possibly *What's Up Doc?* (1972). With the exception of *Mask* (1985), his heavy-handed genre re-creations and broad farces — *Nickelodeon* (1976), *They All Laughed* (1982), *Illegally Yours* (1988), *Noises Off* (1992), *The Thing Called Love* (1993) — failed to connect with either audiences or critics after the mid-'70s. The lack of style and marketing hooks in his films augmented the precariousness of the Bogdanovich oeuvre.

In another arena altogether, Francis Coppola and Martin Scorsese represent those directors who have been able to adapt somewhat more successfully to the economic dictates of high concept. Coppola's career in the past two decades has been shaped by the 1982 failure of his $26 million Las Vegas romance/musical *One from the Heart*, and the ensuing disintegration of his Zoetrope Studios.[6] Reeling from the critical reviews and public indifference to this film, as well as the loss of his studio, Coppola chose to direct two films back-to-back. These films, both adaptations of S. E. Hinton youth novels, illuminate much about Coppola's attitude toward the economics of the industry in the '80s. *The Outsiders* (1983), featuring a cast of teen idols including Matt Dillon, Diane Lane, Rob Lowe, and Tom Cruise, is a straightforward teen melodrama, marked by only moments of excessive style. With the teen cast and pre-sold property, the film grossed a solid $25.7 million. Coppola's second 1983 S. E. Hinton adaptation — *Rumble Fish* — returned Coppola to the heavy stylization of *One from the Heart*, and is obviously a more personal interpretation than his previous film. With its black-and-white cinematography, unconventional camera work and cutting, and an expressionistic soundtrack of industrial noises by Stewart Copeland, the marketing assets were overwhelmed by the director's sense of style. As a result, despite the assets of a teen cast and a pre-sold property, *Rumble Fish* grossed one-tenth ($2.5 million) of *The Outsiders*. This movement between personal projects, often highly stylized, and projects which make strong concessions to the marketplace distinguishes Coppola's career in the aftermath of *One from the Heart*. For instance, the risk of *Tucker: The Man and His Dream* (1988) is offset by the commercial appeal and marketing hooks of *The Godfather, Part III* (1990) and *Bram Stoker's Dracula* (1992).

Scorsese has experienced his own catastrophes at the hands of the mainstream industry, from the large-scale flop of his big-budget *New York, New York* (1977) and *The King of Comedy* (1983) to the abrupt cancellation of *The Last Temptation of Christ* by Paramount in 1983.[7] As with Coppola, Scorsese has accommodated the industry through either pursuing projects with pre-sold elements (such as *The Color of Money* [1986] or *Cape Fear* [1991]) or operating on a low budget outside the mainstream industry via affiliation with smaller companies, such as Cineplex-Odeon (*Last Temptation*) or Geffen (*After Hours*). Currently Scorsese moves between these modes of production, although the respectable grosses of *Goodfellas* ($46.8 million) and *Cape Fear* ($78.1 million) may allow Scorsese more freedom in his choice of projects, such as his $30 million historical romance, *The Age of Innocence* (1993).

In addition to either ignoring or adjusting to the changing marketplace, a few directors have been able to negotiate a space within the

The commercial failure of One from the Heart *led Coppola to the more marketable, teen-oriented* The Outsiders *(One from the Heart,* Columbia, 1982; *The Outsiders,* Warner Bros., 1983).

mainstream industry in which they are granted almost complete autonomy over their films. Of the late '60s auteurs, only Woody Allen has
negotiated this route successfully, primarily due to strong critical support characterizing him as one of the only film "artists" working in
America. Despite a solid gross from only one film (*Hannah and Her Sis-
ters*; $39.4 million in 1986) since 1979, Allen has been able to sustain a
remarkably consistent output over a long time period, averaging about
one film per year. With the support of Orion and Tri-Star Pictures, Allen
continues to make films undaunted by the economic constraints experienced by others working within the system.[8] This enviable position is
shared by few other directors. Freedom is more often seized by commercially successful directors, such as Oliver Stone, who may be given
relatively free rein to pursue personal projects. Indeed, only a director
with the commercial (and critical) clout of Stone could make a large-
budget, major studio film like *JFK* (1991) so openly critical of American
institutions, society, and history.

In sum, most of the auteurs praised for their innovation and originality in American film have been forced to respond to the more commercially centered marketplace of high concept. As a result, the work
from this group, and, by extension, the general quality of mainstream
filmmaking, has been less memorable compared to the period of experimentation in the late '60s and early '70s. In this manner, the influence of high concept can be appreciated, with this type of filmmaking
acting to squeeze other less marketable and perhaps more aesthetically
challenging films from the landscape of American film.

Television and the
Ideological Agenda of High Concept

To extend the auteur argument
slightly further, it is interesting to contemplate the rise of the "Network
TV" generation of auteurs who have developed during the period of
high concept. Timothy Corrigan anticipates this tendency in the strong
connection which he posits between the two media: "'Shareability' is a
way of describing the ability of a high-concept film to recuperate large
budgets in advance by being marketable to the audiences of both television and theaters. This accounts, I would add, for the common, easy
mobility of actors and directors between television and film (usually
bringing television styles with them)."[9] This mobility extends to television actors turning to directing films; consider the success as auteurs
met by such '70s television personalities as *Laverne and Shirley*'s Penny
Marshall (*Big* [1988], *Awakenings* [1990], *A League of Their Own* [1992]),
All in the Family's Rob Reiner (*Stand by Me* [1986], *The Princess Bride*

[1987], *Misery* [1990]), *Happy Days'* Ron Howard (*Cocoon* [1985], *Parenthood* [1989], *Backdraft* [1991], *Far and Away* [1992]), and *Taxi's* Danny DeVito (*Throw Momma from the Train* [1987], *The War of the Roses* [1989]). The effective transition from television to film for these actors scarcely seems accidental. The movement toward high concept within the film industry favors the aesthetics of television: the reliance on character types, the strict genre parameters, and, of course, the modular structure. In addition, recall that high concept originally was conceived in relation to the ABC "TV Movie of the Week," which often focused on topical, or marketable, subject matters which could be sold in one line in *TV Guide*.[10] Both of these factors furthered the exchange among television, film, and high concept.

Perhaps the salient characteristic of television programming is its highly ritualized or formulaic quality — from the placement of programs within a fixed slot on the regular broadcast schedule to the fully recuperable plotline in the thirty-minute format. This quality also operates throughout high concept, and, at the risk of a generalization, this feature has been noted as one of the defining characteristics of American cinema in the past two decades. For example, Andrew Britton, in his exhaustive and compelling review of "Reaganite Entertainment," comments, "The structure, narrative movement, pattern of character relationships and ideological tendency of *Star Wars, Tron* and *Krull* are identical in every particular: the variations, if that is the word, are mechanical and external. . . . [The conventions of Reaganite entertainment] function, rather, to inhibit articulation, and the impediments to thematic development which they set up must be referred to this function."[11]

The ritualized quality of these contemporary American films embodies an ideological agenda which offers reassurance, according to Robin Wood. Building on Britton's initial thesis, Wood claims that the ideological function of popular American film, particularly the Lucas-Spielberg films, is to defuse the social threats, remaining from the late '60s, to patriarchal, bourgeois society.[12] Unquestionably the high concept films, geared so specifically to the marketplace, reflect the American zeitgeist, embracing the return to right-wing values and beliefs.[13]

The emphasis on consumerism and lifestyle as represented in the style of the high concept films clearly operates in a recuperative fashion. This tendency also is manifested within high concept, in part, through presenting the alternative to the bourgeois and patriarchal center — the other. For instance, in *Endless Love*, Jade's bohemian, ersatz-'60s family is offered only in terms of moral laxity: Jade's mother tries to seduce her daughter's boyfriend, the parents cannot control their children's be-

Moral "problems" created by '60s idealism
(Endless Love, Universal, 1981). Copyright
© 1981 Universal City Studios Inc.

havior, and the mother enjoys an extended voyeuristic interlude at the
expense of her underage daughter. The central "problem" of the film—
the obsessive love relationship between two young teens which destroys
both the bohemian family's house and family unit—could easily be interpreted as retribution for the "unstable" '60s-fixated family. Similarly,
in *American Gigolo*, while the chic, monied world of Beverly Hills ma-
trons is presented as desirable and an achievement, the "other" world
for gigolo Julian Kay is also clearly defined: the dark, secret milieu of
gay bars represented, not coincidentally, by the black pimp who frames
Julian. Director Paul Schrader makes the equation of homosexuality
and racial minorities; he offers a value judgment on this constructed
world with the valiant Julian refusing to work in this world until he
becomes a murder suspect.

The otherness of '60s idealism, ethnicity, and sexual difference is
augmented by a clear reinforcement of patriarchal capitalism. Under
the guise of the teen comedy genre, Paul Brickman's *Risky Business* offers a paradigm for this reinforcement. Teenager Joel (Tom Cruise), a
prospective business major graduating from high school, transforms
his parents' home into a brothel on the same night as his interview

with a representative from Princeton. Assuming that he has seriously jeopardized his chances for admission, Joel is surprised by his acceptance to the university, as well as the financial windfall reaped by becoming a pimp for a single night. The viewer learns the value of the entrepreneurial spirit, the link between capitalism and exploitation, and, most significant in the Reagan era, the methods through which the upper middle class reproduces itself. Indeed, Joel, the white-bread teenager living in a wealthy Chicago suburb, is supported financially and commended for his initiative in running a whorehouse, with his future secure given his (academically undeserved) entry into an Ivy League school. Of course, his partner in crime, the teen prostitute Lana (Rebecca DeMornay), forced to leave home by abuse at the hands of a stepfather, remains in her profession after Joel's success — despite her large role in initiating and implementing the scheme. The class divisions in the film are solidly reinforced. Opportunities for advancement are still available in the Reagan era, but these chances are limited to those who are already firmly ensconced in the affluent socioeconomic class. As with many high concept films, *Risky Business* follows the Robin

*Class divisions and the trajectory of "democratic capitalism" (*Risky Business, *Warner Bros., 1983). Copyright © 1983 Warner Bros. Inc.*

Wood trajectory of reinstating "racism, sexism, 'democratic capital-ism,' the capitalist myths of freedom of choice and equality of oppor-tunity, the individual hero whose achievements somehow 'make every-thing all right,' even for the millions who never make it to individual heroism."[14]

The Alternatives to High Concept

If the institutional structures are still operating to support the high concept films so steeped in a conser-vative ideology, what alternatives exist to transform the landscape of American film? One avenue for the aesthetic rejuvenation of American film is the exchange between the alternative and mainstream cinemas. David James proposes a definition of alternative film practice which foregrounds a social determinant: "All models of filmic distinctions, and especially all formalist models that propose distinctions between an alternative film style and the codes of the feature film industry, must then be doubled to include the social determinants of each; they must be returned to social practice. And any alternative practice, whether it be Black film, underground film, or women's film, may be understood as a response to the three other spheres of activity: the alternative social group, the dominant society, and the hegemonic cinema."[15] James stresses the link between minority interests and their representation through alternative filmmaking, and, of course, a long history of ex-perimental and avant-garde film has been associated with, for example, racial and sexual minorities. However, the significant equation that James makes is between the alternative and mainstream cinemas, illus-trating how the mainstream cinema assimilates traits of the avant-garde during the course of time.[16]

In the context of mainstream cinema, the adoption of avant-garde stylistics follows an economic motive — Hollywood will alter the domi-nant style of production given the potential for additional boxoffice revenue. This process has continued throughout the development of film history, even in the period of classical Hollywood cinema. Janet Staiger describes the contribution of "the innovative worker" whose aesthetic contribution to Hollywood cinema is encouraged given poten-tial economic benefits: "Instead of holding back the innovative worker, the Hollywood mode of production cultivated him or her as long as the results provided profits."[17] This argument holds just as readily in the contemporary industry, and high concept may be transformed by an aesthetic innovation shifting this style of filmmaking. Certainly this process cannot be charted in any linear, organized fashion. The model of the high concept style outlined in Chapter 2 is not static. Subtle aesthetic alterations in the high concept style are an ongoing phenomenon: each newly successful high concept film potentially offers an alteration to be assimilated by future high concept films.

The source of these alterations may be within the modes of production outside mainstream commercial cinema. The degree of assimilation of avant-garde artists within the mainstream industry obviously depends on the extent to which these artists are interested in engaging narrative in their creative projects. It seems extremely unlikely, for instance, that an experimental or structural filmmaker, such as Yvonne Rainer or Jonas Mekas, would ever interest Hollywood as a source of potential profits. The emphasis in their works on structure and process over narrative and linearity negates any concern from the mainstream. Of course, artists working in alternative cinema may well adopt styles of dominant filmmaking, in part, to offer a critique of these styles. Consider, for example, Tom Kalin's independent film *Swoon* (1992), which offers a contemporary perspective on the Leopold/Loeb murder case. The film is shot in a manner which evokes high concept: an emphasis on the fashion style of the characters, and shooting in grainy black-and-white through smoke and shadow. The effect is to suggest an identification with the style alone, and to offer a critique of this empty style, adopted from advertising, which obscures the moral degradation of the characters.

More feasible cases of assimilation from experimental work to the mainstream can be discovered in Tim Burton and David Lynch, both of whom exhibited strong ties to narrative before entering the mainstream industry. Burton gained attention from the mainstream industry due to a short film titled *Frankenweenie*, an off-center retelling of the Frankenstein legend involving a suburban family's dog. Burton's skewed outlook and very strong, surreal visual sense was then integrated into feature filmmaking with *Pee Wee's Big Adventure* (1985). Apart from immortalizing Paul Reubens's Groundlings character, the film was distinguished by a bold pop art design and a striking use of primary colors, both of which expressed the cartoonlike world of Pee Wee perfectly. Burton's subsequent assignment, *Beetlejuice*, similarly took advantage of his visual sense and his off-center point of view. Both of these features paved the way for Burton's enormously successful *Batman*, in which Burton brought his visual sense and skewed humor to the high concept project (due to its pre-sold nature and star casting). Arguably, *Batman*'s greatest achievement is its meticulous production design and cinematography, which offer a darkly revisionist version of the Batman familiar from comics and the '60s television series. While the film is clearly within the domain of high concept, which accounts partly for its commercial success, Burton was able to shift the parameters of high concept through his strong visual sense. Since the film grossed over $250 million, this form of differentiation will be acknowledged and encouraged by the mainstream film industry.

Lynch's entry into the mainstream is more tentative. With the support of the American Film Institute, Lynch's background is in experimental shorts such as *The Grandmother*, about a disturbed boy who plants a seed that grows into his grandmother.[18] Lynch's first feature was filmed over five years from 1971 through 1976. The result, *Eraserhead* (1977), became one of the foremost cult films of the '70s: an horrific, disturbing, and grotesque nightmare about a mutant baby. As with Burton, Lynch's gifts appear to be a visual sense and an appreciation for the bizarre within everyday life. Unlike Burton, Lynch's stylized world seems much more extreme and uncompromising: choker close-ups, unbalanced compositions, an attraction to darkness, and especially a Diane Arbus–like affiliation with the grotesque and abnormal. As a result, it is interesting to chart the extent to which Lynch has not been able to integrate into the mainstream industry. Indeed, perhaps the only mainstream film which fully integrated Lynch's vision with a cohesive narrative is his adaptation of *The Elephant Man* (1980); as critic Richard Woodward describes, "The mood of *The Elephant Man*, its palpable vision of blanketing darkness and pockets of light in industrial-age England, owes much to Lynch. And for the first time in his career, his gift for atmosphere was joined to a clear dramatic story: the relationship between the pathetically deformed John Merrick and his doctor."[19]

After the success of *The Elephant Man*, Lynch directed the $40 million science-fiction epic *Dune* (1984) for producer Dino De Laurentiis and Universal Pictures. In this case, Lynch's style overwhelmed the film, and the Lynchian characters could not fit neatly with the ostensible narrative. The result was an enormous critical and boxoffice failure, moreover a failure for Lynch's talents to mesh with a pre-sold project. As a consequence, unlike Tim Burton, Lynch failed to make a transition to major Hollywood filmmaking. His subsequent films have been released by independents, such as Goldwyn and the now defunct De Laurentiis Entertainment Group. His special talents have been mined by television (*Twin Peaks* [1990]), although the appeal proved to be limited. Lynch represents the case of an experimental film artist whose particular strengths cannot be assimilated by mainstream Hollywood and, as a result, whose strengths will not alter the dominant style of Hollywood filmmaking.

High concept may also be altered through the reconceptualization of the film marketplace. As marketing and market research have become

*David Lynch's dark vision combined with a linear narrative (*The Elephant Man, *Para-mount, 1980). Copyright © MCMLXXX by Brooksfilms Limited.*

more significant in delivering the film to the marketplace, there is an increasing tendency to "narrowcast": to target television buys to specific well-defined demographics.[20] The era of high concept also correlates with the targeting of a young demographic, but Hollywood is clearly interested in other breakdowns in demography beyond age. In particular, the majors wish to target ethnic groups, such as the African-American or Hispanic market. Hit films labeled as African-American oriented, such as *House Party, Boyz N the Hood* (1991), and *Do the Right Thing* (1989), certainly helped to give a director like Spike Lee the latitude to direct the $35 million *Malcolm X* (1992).[21] Through his track record at the boxoffice, Lee has been accorded a position like Woody Allen or Oliver Stone—i.e., one who can direct a film without strict pre-sold boxoffice appeal. If the studios are able to define submarkets according to ethnicity and successfully market films to this subdemographic, this niche marketing may signal a significant form of production beyond high concept. Of course, the argument revolves completely around the success with which such a market may be defined and located. For instance, simply targeting the African-American market is fairly meaningless, since the task of targeting the audience for *Mo' Money* (1992) is much different than targeting *To Sleep with Anger* (1990). Regardless of race, the former would be appealing to a much younger audience than the latter.

Apart from the influence of independent media artists, narrowcasting, and the general passing of the Reagan era, high concept will remain as a form of production within the industry. The style no doubt will be adjusted over time in response to the aesthetics of the most popular, commercially oriented films. To return to the question of periodization and the fate of films from the past two decades in American film history, I hope that this period would not be dismissed as unproductive or stale. Instead, the period offers a chance to examine a specific instance in which the balance between commerce and art in American film tilted strongly toward economics, influencing the construction of and market for film.

Notes

1. A Critical Redefinition:
The Concept of High Concept

1. David Ansen, "Rock Tycoon Robert Stigwood," *Newsweek*, July 31, 1978: 43.

2. "The Yellow Brick Road to Profit," *Time*, January 23, 1978: 46.

3. R. Serge Denisoff and William D. Romanowski, *Risky Business: Rock in Film* (New Brunswick, N.J.: Transactions Publishers, 1991) 235.

4. Ibid. 240.

5. Rentals include money returned to the distributor, not the amount actually taken in at the boxoffice, which is referred to as the boxoffice gross.

6. See Thomas Schatz's analysis of the generic transformation in the film in *Old Hollywood/New Hollywood: Ritual, Art, and Industry* (Ann Arbor, Mich.: UMI Research Press, 1983) 280–281.

7. Richard Dyer, *Only Entertainment* (New York: Routledge, 1992) 61.

8. Chris Chase, "Fosse's Ego Trip," *Life*, December 1979: 94.

9. Martin Gottfried, *All His Jazz: The Life and Death of Bob Fosse* (New York: Bantam, 1990) 393.

10. Kevin Boyd Grubb, *Razzle Dazzle: The Life and Work of Bob Fosse* (New York: St. Martin's Press, 1989) 228.

11. Diller began his professional career as assistant to the head of programming at the age of 23 in 1965. He continued to rise at ABC, eventually leaving in 1974 as the Vice-President of Prime Time Programming at ABC. See James P. Forkan, "Paramount Exec is Adman of Year," *Advertising Age*, January 8, 1979: S2, 1. Gary Edgerton recounts Diller's innovations in "High Concept, Small Screen," *Journal of Popular Film and Television*, Fall 1991: 114–127.

12. For an interesting historical account of the development of this program-

ming form, consult Richard Levinson and William Link, *Stay Tuned* (New York: St. Martin's Press, 1981) 1–5.

13. Reprinted in Claudia Eller, "Katzenberg Memo: Rivals' Reactions Range from Accord to Scorn," *Variety*, January 31, 1991: 1+.

14. Interview with Peter Guber, April 27, 1988.

15. High concept is used in both film and television as a means of defining a project. The term has similar connotations in the two media.

16. Peter Biskind, "Low Concept," *Premiere*, February 1988: 74.

17. Dawn Steel, *They Can Kill You . . . But They Can't Eat You* (New York: Pocket Books, 1993) 98.

18. Will Tusher, "Schwarzenegger as the Tooth Fairy?" *Daily Variety*, August 29, 1991: 3.

19. Stuart Byron and Anne Thompson, "Summer Rentals," *LA Weekly*, September 27–October 5, 1985: 13.

20. J. Hoberman, "1975–1985: Ten Years That Shook the World," *American Film*, June 1985: 36.

21. Richard Schickel, rev. of *Irreconcilable Differences*, *Time*, October 8, 1984: 82.

22. Patrick Goldstein, "Hollywood Squared," *Los Angeles Times*, July 26, 1987: Calendar section, 40.

23. Dale Pollock, "Flashfight," *Los Angeles Times*, July 10, 1983: Calendar section, 1+.

24. For a more positive evaluation of high concept in terms of an economic strategy, see David Ansen and Peter McAlevey, "The Producer Is King Again," *Newsweek*, May 20, 1985: 84–86.

25. Michael Wilmington, "Nice Girls Don't Explode Is a Dud," *Los Angeles Times*, May 29, 1987: Calendar section, 8.

26. Timothy Noah, "Valley of the Duds," *Washington Monthly*, October 1985: 18.

27. Owen Gleiberman, rev. of *King Ralph*, *Entertainment Weekly*, March 8, 1991: 42.

28. Jack Matthews, "He Wants to Add New Pages to UA's Illustrious History," *Los Angeles Times*, November 19, 1987: C1.

29. Personal interview with studio production executive, tape on file.

30. Robert C. Allen and Douglas Gomery, *Film History: Theory and Practice* (New York: Alfred A. Knopf, 1985) 86.

31. David Bordwell, Janet Staiger, and Kristin Thompson, *The Classical Hollywood Cinema: Film Style and Mode of Production to 1960* (New York: Columbia University Press, 1985).

32. For a model of the plot structure of the genre film in these terms, consult Thomas Schatz, *Hollywood Genres* (New York: Random House, 1981).

33. In particular, consult Barbara Klinger, "Digressions at the Cinema: Reception and Mass Culture," *Cinema Journal* 28, no. 4 (1989): 3–19.

34. Barry R. Litman, "Predicting Success of Theatrical Movies: New Empirical Evidence," National Convention for Education in Journalism, Boston, August 1980.

2. Construction of the Image
and the High Concept Style

1. See, for instance, J. A. Place and L. S. Peterson, "Some Visual Motifs of Film Noir," *Film Comment*, January/February 1974: 30–35; and Paul Kerr, "Out of What Past? Notes on the 'B' Film Noir," *Screen Education*, Autumn/Winter 1979/1980: 45–65.

2. Steven Heller and Seymour Chivast, *Graphic Style* (New York: Harry N. Abrams, 1988) 200.

3. Stuart Ewen, "Marketing Dreams: The Political Elements of Style," *Consumption, Identity & Style*, ed. Alan Tomlinson (London: Routledge, 1990) 42.

4. Janet Bergstrom, "Androids and Androgyny," *Camera Obscura* 15 (1986): 37–65.

5. See, for example, James M. Markham, "This Spring's Hot Movie Underlines the Uneasy Link between Art and Advertising," *New York Times*, April 3, 1988: H1.

6. Howard Kissel, rev. of *The Hunger*, *Women's Wear Daily*, April 28, 1983: 15.

7. "Sky Wars," *Cinefex* 29 (1986): 54.

8. Kristin Thompson, "The Concept of Cinematic Excess," *Narrative, Apparatus, Ideology*, ed. Philip Rosen (New York: Columbia University Press, 1986) 132.

9. Ibid. 134.

10. For a discussion of the impact of modern architecture in film, see Pilar Viladas, "Good Guys Don't Live in White Boxes," *Los Angeles Times Magazine*, November 1, 1987: 22–23.

11. Mike Bygrave and Joan Goodman, "Meet Me in Las Vegas," *American Film*, October 1981: 42.

12. Gregg Kilday, "Strip Show: The Comic-Book Look of Dick Tracy," *Entertainment Weekly*, June 15, 1990: 40.

13. Pauline Kael, *Taking It All In* (New York: Holt, Rinehart and Winston, 1984) 3.

14. The effect created by this referencing is very similar to the excess presented by Jack crying "Here's Johnny" as he axes the door to the bathroom in *The Shining*.

15. For a description of Altman's innovations in sound and the utilization of sound as a stylistic element in his films, see Charles Schreₓ. "Altman, Dolby, and the Second Sound Revolution," *Film Sound: Theory and Practice*, eds. Elizabeth Weis and John Belton (New York: Columbia University Press, 1985) 348–355.

16. Peter Lloyd, "The American Cinema: An Outlook," *Monogram*, April 1, 1971: 13.

17. Richard T. Jameson, "Style vs. 'Style,'" *Film Comment*, March/April 1980: 12.

18. Roland Barthes, "The Third Meaning," *Image Music Text* (New York: Hill and Wang, 1977) 52–68.

19. For an analysis of film stills from the classical era which seem "more real

than life itself" (as the jacket describes), consult Diane Keaton and Marvin Hei-
ferman, *Still Life* (New York: Fireside Books, 1985).

20. K. Thompson, "The Concept of Cinematic Excess" 139.

21. Alexander Doty, "Music Sells Movies: (Re) New (ed) Conservatism in
Film Marketing," *Wide Angle* 10, no. 2 (1988): 72.

22. In an interesting anecdote, composer Michael Sembello has stated that
his song "Maniac" was actually originally about a mass murderer. In the film,
dancer Alex works out to the song; one assumes that Alex is a "maniac" on the
dance floor.

23. Rick Altman, *The American Film Musical* (Bloomington: Indiana University Press, 1987) 345–346.

24. David Bordwell, *Narration in the Fiction Film* (London: Methuen,
1985): 66.

25. Beverle Houston, "Music Video and the Spectator: Television, Ideology
and Dream," *Film Quarterly* 38, no. 1 (1984): 4–5.

26. Klinger, "Digressions at the Cinema" 10.

27. Mimi White, "Crossing Wavelengths: The Diegetic and Referential Imaginary of American Commercial Television," *Cinema Journal* 25, no. 2 (1986): 51.

28. Roland Barthes, *S/Z* (New York: Hill and Wang, 1974) 16.

29. Diane Shoos and Diana George, "Top Gun and Postmodern Mass Culture
Aesthetics," *Post Script* 9, no. 3 (1990): 25.

30. Jon Lewis, "Purple Rain: Music Video Comes of Age," *Jump Cut* 30
(1985): 22.

31. R. Serge Denisoff and George Plaskettes, "Synergy in 1980s Film and Music: Formula for Success or Industry Mythology?" *Film History* 4 (1990): 273.

32. *Dick Tracy* was supported in the marketplace by three albums: the Madonna album, the (instrumental) soundtrack by Danny Elfman, and an album
of songs from the film that were not recorded by Madonna.

33. For a discussion of the development of sampling, consult William Maxwell, "Sampling Authenticity: Rap Music, Postmodernism and the Ideology of
Black Crime," *Studies in Popular Culture* 14, no. 1 (1991): 1–16.

34. Klinger, "Digressions at the Cinema" 14.

35. See, for instance, Tania Modleski, "The Rhythms of Reception: Daytime
Television and Women's Work" from E. Ann Kaplan, *Regarding Television—
Critical Approaches: An Anthology* (Los Angeles: AFI Monograph Series, 1983); and
John Fiske, *Television Culture* (New York: Routledge, 1987).

36. Nikki Finke, "Film Ads: Would They Lie to You?" *Los Angeles Times*, December 9, 1988: Calendar section, 1.

37. For an analysis of Hill's utilization of genre and the connection between
the film and MTV, see David Chute, "Dead End Streets," *Film Comment*, August
1984: 55–58.

38. Nick Roddick, rev. of *Staying Alive, Monthly Film Bulletin*, September 1983:
248.

39. See Lynn Langway and Julia Reed, "Flashdance, Flashfashions," *Newsweek*, July 4, 1983: 55.

40. Quoted in Pollock, "Flashfight" 1.

41. Consult, for instance, Jim Collins's discussion of the links between post-modernism, intertextuality, and media production in the '80s: "Postmodernism as Culmination: The Aesthetic Politics of Decentered Cultures," *Uncommon Cultures* (London: Routledge, 1989) 112–147.

42. For an interesting analysis of the average moviegoer's sophistication in recognizing references to other films, see Richard Crinkley, "The Art of the Cinemate," *Film Comment*, July/August 1985: 76.

43. In his model of narrative comprehension, the intertextual referencing, which I am claiming for the high concept film, is defined by David Bordwell as transtextual motivation, "The spectator may justify an expectation or inference on transtextual grounds. The clearest case is that of genre . . ." [*Narration in the Fiction Film* (Madison: University of Wisconsin Press, 1985) 36].

44. Markham, "This Spring's Hot Movie" H5.

45. David Bordwell and Janet Staiger, "Since 1960: The Persistence of a Mode of Film Practice," in Bordwell, Staiger, and Thompson, *The Classical Hollywood Cinema* 373.

46. Ibid. 373–374.

47. L. M. Kit Carson, "Breathless Diary," *Film Comment*, May/June 1983: 38.

48. Pamela Falkenberg, in considering the relationship of the two films, argues that the art cinema and Hollywood (not differentiating between historical periods in Hollywood) depend on each other for their definition: "Hollywood and the art cinema might be characterized as a bipolar modeling system in which each reproduces the other through difference—difference as the same difference." See "'Hollywood' and the 'Art Cinema' as a Bipolar Modeling System," *Wide Angle* 7, no. 3 (1985): 44.

49. Schrader also acknowledges the importance of Jean-Luc Godard and Robert Bresson, two "king-pins" of the art cinema, to his films, particularly to *American Gigolo*.

50. Paul Schrader, *Schrader on Schrader* (London: Faber and Faber, 1990) 160.

51. Bob Fisher, "Don Peterman and Flashdance," *American Cinematographer*, April 1984: 64.

3. High Concept and Changes in the Market for Entertainment

1. Michael Conant, "The Paramount Decrees Reconsidered," *The American Film Industry*, ed. Tino Balio (Madison: University of Wisconsin Press, 1985) 537–573.

2. See, for example, Douglas Gomery's characterization in "The American Film Industry of the 1970's: Stasis in the 'New Hollywood,'" *Wide Angle* 5, no. 4 (1982): 52–60.

3. U.S. Department of Commerce, Office of Business Economics, National Income Division, annual figures.

4. Frederic Stuart, "The Effects of Television on the Motion Picture Industry," *The American Movie Industry*, ed. Gorham Kindem (Carbondale: Southern_ Illinois University Press, 1982) 257–308.

5. Balio, *The American Film Industry* 434.

6. See "Television: The Vault of Hollywood" in Michele Hilmes, *Hollywood and Broadcasting: From Radio to Cable* (Chicago: University of Illinois Press, 1990) 140–170.

7. George Katona, *The Mass Consumption Society* (New York: McGraw Hill, 1964).

8. Elmo Roper, "The Fortune Survey," *Fortune*, March 1949.

9. Janet Staiger, "The Package-Unit System: Unit Management after 1955" in Bordwell, Staiger, and Thompson 330.

10. Tino Balio, ed., *Hollywood in the Age of Television* (Cambridge, Mass.: Unwin Hyman, 1990) 303.

11. Ibid. 34.

12. Michael Pye also notes that the deal would mean that MCA would gain access to the Universal library of film titles for use in television. At that point, MCA already owned the pre-1948 Paramount library.

13. For an interesting analysis of the motives behind this takeover, read Peter Bart, "What Hollywood Isn't Telling MCA's New Owners," *Variety*, December 3, 1990: 1.

14. Thomas Guback, "Theatrical Film," *Who Owns the Media? Concentration of Ownership in the Mass Communications Industry*, ed. Benjamin Compaine (New York: Knowledge Industry Publications, 1981) 271.

15. James Monaco, *American Film Now* (New York: New American Library, 1979) 33.

16. Robert Stanley, *The Celluloid Empire: A History of the American Movie Industry* (New York: Hastings House, 1978) 236.

17. John Douglas Eames, *The Paramount Story* (New York: Crown Publishers, 1985) 224–225.

18. Guback, "Theatrical Films" 270.

19. This reference is from Steven Bach, *Final Cut: Dreams and Disaster in the Making of Heaven's Gate* (New York: William Morrow, 1985) 53. Bach's book offers a comprehensive overview of United Artists' history, with a special emphasis on the late 1970s and the early 1980s.

20. An average of major company share of U.S.-Canadian market receipts for films earning rentals of $1 million or more; reported in *Variety*, January 5, 1975; February 11, 1976; January 18, 1978; January 10, 1979; January 28, 1981.

21. John Gregory Dunne, *The Studio* (New York: Limelight Editions, 1968) 242.

22. Among the most notorious failures are Paramount's *Darling Lili*, Fox's *Hello, Dolly!* and *Dr. Dolittle*, and Columbia's *Lost Horizon* and *1776*.

23. For a rather amusing recounting of this period see *Contemporary Film and the New Generation*, eds. Louis M. Savary and J. Paul Carrico (New York: Association Press, 1971); especially peruse part 2—"What Seems To Be the Matter in American Cinema": 53–142.

24. Peter Guber, personal interview, Los Angeles, March 24, 1988.

25. Columbia's efforts at reaching the youth audience were aided by its distribution deal with BBS, the production company operated by Bert Schneider, Bob Rafelson, and Steve Blauner. BBS was responsible for several of the youth-

oriented films, including *Head, Five Easy Pieces, Drive He Said, Easy Rider,* and *The Last Picture Show.* For an analysis of the operation of BBS, consult Teresa Grimes, "BBS: Auspicious Beginnings, Open Endings," *Movie* 31/32: 54–66; and Mitchell Cohen, "The Corporate Style of BBS: Seven Intricate Pieces," *Take One,* Winter 1974/75.

26. By the end of the decade, though, Altman's relationship with Fox became increasingly estranged, and in 1979, Fox gave Altman's film *Health* virtually no distribution.

27. Even with *O.C. & Stiggs,* Altman had to fight to prove to MGM that he wanted to make a commercial film. In his detailed biography, Patrick McGilligan recounts several amusing and disheartening exchanges between Altman, Freddie Fields, and Frank Yablans, then in charge at MGM. See Patrick McGilligan, *Robert Altman: Jumping Off the Cliff* (New York: St. Martin's Press, 1989) 528–534.

28. Gerald Mast, *A Short History of the Movies* (Indianapolis: Bobbs-Merrill Educational Publishing, 1981) 430.

29. Stuart Byron, "First Annual 'Grosses Gloss,' " *Film Comment,* March/April 1976: 31.

30. Hoberman, "1975–1985: Ten Years That Shook the World" 38.

31. Other films during this period, such as *Raise the Titanic* (1980; negative cost: $36 million; rentals: $6.8 million) and *Inchon* (1982; negative cost: $46 million; rentals: $1.9 million), were similar large-budget fiascos, but received less publicity due to each project's lack of a single, "doomed" auteur. See "Selected Theatrical Winners and Losers" in Harold L. Vogel, *Entertainment Industry Economics: A Guide for Financial Analysis* (Cambridge: Cambridge University Press, 1990) 114.

32. Monaco, *American Film Now* 149.

33. See Stuart Byron's discussion of the film in "The Third Annual 'Grosses Gloss' " from *Film Comment,* March/April 1978: 75.

34. "Cimino: If You Don't Get It Right, What's the Point?" *Films Illustrated,* October 1981: 27.

35. Ibid. 29.

36. Teri Ritzer, "MGM in Serious Discussion Concerning Buy of UA Assets," *Hollywood Reporter,* May 19, 1981: 22; and Lawrence Cohn, "1956–87 Big-Buck Scorecard," *Variety,* January 20, 1988: 64.

37. Quoted in Michael Pye, *Moguls: Inside the Business of Show Business* (New York: Holt, Rinehart and Winston, 1980) 186.

38. "Paramount's 'Fever' Passes $100,000,000, Second Only to 'Godfather' Take," *Variety,* June 7, 1978: 3.

39. For *Love Story:* "What can you say about a 25-year-old girl who dies?" and for *The Godfather:* "Make him an offer he can't refuse."

40. For an application of this argument to different forms of popular entertainment, see David A. Garvin, "Blockbusters: The Economics of Mass Entertainment," *Journal of Cultural Economics,* June 1981: 1–20.

41. Hoberman, "1975–1985: Ten Years That Shook the World" 36.

42. Monaco, *American Film Now* 394.

43. Stanley, *The Celluloid Empire* 254.

44. See Chapter 2, "The World Film Trade and the U.S. Motion Picture Industry," in Steven S. Wildman and Stephen E. Siwek, *International Trade in Films and Television Programs* (Cambridge, Mass.: Ballinger Publishing Company, 1988) 13–36.

45. Joseph D. Phillips, "Forms of Cultural Dependency: Film Conglomerate 'Blockbusters,'" *Journal of Communication* 25, no. 2 (Spring 1975): 171–182.

46. For an analysis of Paramount's involvement with the television market, consult Timothy White, "Hollywood's Attempts at Appropriating Television: The Case of Paramount Pictures," in *Hollywood in the Age of Television*, ed. Tino Balio: 145–164.

47. Douglas Gomery, "Movie Merger Mania," *On Film* 13 (Fall 1984): 5.

48. For an excellent historical overview of the institution of the new technologies, consult Bruce A. Austin's "The Film Industry, Its Audience, and New Communications Technologies," in *Current Research in Film: Audiences, Economics, and Law*, vol. 2, ed. Bruce A. Austin (Norwood, N.J.: Ablex Publishing Corporation, 1986) 80–115.

49. The majors which possess this facility include Paramount Home Video, CBS/Fox, Columbia Home Entertainment, Warner Home Video, and MCA.

50. See *Variety* issues: July 31, 1984, and December 13, 1985, respectively.

51. David Lachrenbruch, "Home Video: Home Is Where the Action Is," *Channels of Communication*, November/December 1983: 42.

52. Consult one of the few articles to discuss this significant change in practice: Alex Ben Block's "Priced to Sell?" *Forbes*, November 19, 1984: 41.

53. *Raiders of the Lost Ark*, upon release, quickly became the all-time home video champ, with 420,000 units shipped. *Flashdance* also initially sold over 200,000 units. "Fast Forward," *Time*, December 5, 1983: 74.

54. Block, "Priced to Sell?" 41.

55. See *Variety* issues: September 7, 1983 (MCA), April 17, 1984 (Disney), and April 17, 1984 (Media).

56. Tom Bierbaum, "Vid Biz Takes Some Big Steps in Sell-Thru, Sponsors," *Variety*, November 15, 1989: 2.

57. Vogel, "Selected Theatrical Winners and Losers" 83.

58. Anthony Slide, *The Television Industry* (New York: Greenwood Press, 1991) 130.

59. Stratford P. Sherman, "Coming Soon: Hollywood's Epic Shakeout," *Fortune*, April 30, 1984: 216.

60. Ibid.

61. Universal Pay-TV announced a six-year film licensing agreement with HBO on February 15, 1984; Warner Bros. signed a five-year exclusive deal in June 1985. (*Variety* issues: February 15, 1984: 1, and June 5, 1986: 1.

62. *Variety*, March 20, 1985: 1.

63. Tom Bierbaum, "Columbia Pictures, HBO and CBS Combine for New Studio," *Variety*, December 1, 1982: 19.

64. Michele Hilmes, "Pay Television: Breaking the Broadcast Bottleneck," in *Hollywood in the Age of Television*, ed. Tino Balio: 305.

65. Premiere proposed an exclusive nine-month window on films produced by its partners. This proposal prompted the antitrust action.

66. Sherman, "Coming Soon" 216.

67. Tom Bierbaum, "Movie Channel Accord Reached," *Variety*, November 12, 1982: 1.

68. The majors have also been moving into the international pay cable markets: in July 1983, MGM/UA, Paramount, and Universal, via their foreign partnership UIP, made entry into the British pay cable market; in August 1984, UIP began negotiations with German Bertelsmann about setting up pay-TV in the Federal Republic of Germany.

69. Dennis Mueller, "Mergers and Market Shares," *Review of Economics and Statistics*, Winter 1984: 259. Mueller suggests consulting David J. Ravenscraft, "Structure-Profit Relationships at the Line of Business Level," *Review of Economics and Statistics*, February 1983.

70. The following analysis in this chapter considers the contemporary period until the end of 1989.

71. For the market share charts, MGM/UA includes releases from both MGM and UA during the periods when the two companies were not officially merged.

72. Tony Schwartz's article "Hollywood's Hottest Stars" (*New York*, July 30, 1984: 25–33) offers some very interesting anecdotes about the Diller regime at Paramount, including some interviews with Paramount executives.

73. Marc Frons and Cynthia Green, "Barry Diller: The Man Who Has To Make It All Happen," *Business Week*, May 20, 1985: 107.

74. Schwartz, "Hollywood's Hottest Stars" 27.

75. Mardi Marans, personal interview, Los Angeles, April 15, 1988.

76. Frons and Green, "Barry Diller" 107.

77. For the changes at Gulf & Western brought about by Martin Davis, see "Gulf & Western: From Grab Bag to Lean, Mean, Marketing Machine," *Business Week*, September 14, 1987: 152+.

78. Ellen Farley, "Paramount Pictures, The Turnaround: A Frank Mancuso Production," *Business Week*, March 24, 1986: 83.

79. Martin S. Davis blames Paramount's poor 1985 showing upon a list of pictures (e.g., *The River Rat, Joy of Sex, Top Secret!*) instituted by Diller, not Mancuso. For more information on the transition from Diller to Mancuso, see Farley's article (above) and Jeffrey Trachtenberg's "G&W after Bludhorn," *Forbes*, December 3, 1984: 39–40.

80. In July 1987, the exclusive cable rights were renegotiated. Paramount ended up with a $500 million–85 film deal with HBO (see *Broadcasting*, July 20, 1987: 21).

81. "Now Playing: Multiplexes and More Movies," *New York Times*, January 10, 1988: H-26.

82. The *Star Trek* films were based on the Paramount television series from the 1960s. In 1986, the company developed *Star Trek: The Next Generation* as a series for first-run syndication.

83. Joe Mandese, "Hollywood's Top Gun," *Marketing & Media Decisions*, March 1988: 110.

84. Diana Widom, telephone interview, Los Angeles, February 21, 1988.

85. See Douglas Gomery, "Corporate Ownership and Control in the Contemporary US Film Industry," *Screen* 25, no. 4/5 (1984): 62, for more information on Warner's losses.

86. Robert Gustafson, "What's Happening to Our Pix Biz? From Warner Brothers to Warner Communications Inc.," in Balio, *The American Film Industry* 579.

87. Richard Gold, "Time Inc. Not for Sale, Affirm Execs at Meet," *Variety*, July 5, 1989: 1.

88. Balio, *Hollywood in the Age of Television* 265.

89. Richard Gold, "Time's Move of the Year: Vaults to Media Pinnacle," *Variety*, March 8, 1989: 1.

90. Ibid.

91. Richard Gold and Paul Harris, "Time Marches On, Grabs Warner, Outpaces Par," *Variety*, July 26, 1989: 1.

92. "Lucas Crusades for Time/Warner," *Variety*, July 19, 1989: 6.

93. During January 1988, Paramount lost its lead to Disney due to the phenomenally successful *Three Men and a Baby* and *Good Morning, Vietnam*.

94. Stephen Koepp, "Do You Believe in Magic?" *Time*, April 25, 1988: 68–69.

95. This strategy was repeated four years later when Disney formed a third production arm, Hollywood Pictures, to be run separately from both Disney and Touchstone; see Jane Galbraith, "Disney Sprouts Third Pic Production Arm," *Variety*, December 7, 1988: 4.

96. Disney's venture into pay cable has proven its expertise at media other than theatrical film. With Eisner's strong endorsement, the Disney Channel has grown in strength to outperform all other pay cable services with over 1.6 million subscribers in its first year (see *Daily Variety*, January 25, 1985). Under the supervision of Jim Jimmiro, Disney Home Video has parlayed its film library into an extremely lucrative enterprise (DHV's *Lady and the Tramp* is the best-selling video of all time).

97. Claudia Eller, "Disney's Decade to Spread the Magic," *Variety*, January 17, 1990: 3.

98. Ronald Grover, "Lights, Camera, Auction," *Business Week*, December 10, 1990: 27.

99. Bart, "What Hollywood Isn't Telling MCA's New Owners" 8.

100. Patrick McGilligan, "Breaking Away Mogul Style," *American Film*, June 1980: 30.

101. For an account of the Frank Yablans regime at MGM starting in 1983, see Peter Bart, *Fade Out: The Calamitous Final Days of MGM* (New York: William Morrow, 1990).

102. Douglas Gomery focuses on these mergers in "Corporate Ownership and Control" 60–69.

103. "Marvin Davis' New Scenario for Fox," *Business Week*, May 30, 1983: 38.

104. Kathryn Harris, "Diller's Hands-On Efforts Pull Firm off the Critical List," *Los Angeles Times*, April 19, 1987: part IV, 1.

105. John Huey and Stephen J. Sansweet, "Coca-Cola to Pay Over $820 Million for Movie Firm," *Wall Street Journal,* January 20, 1982: 2.

106. Gomery, "Movie Merger Mania" 7.

107. Tom Bierbaum, "Col-HBO-CBS Studio: Agreement Dramatically Alters Rapidly Changing FeeVee Feature Landscape," *Variety,* December 1, 1982: 2.

108. Ibid. 1.

109. Ibid. 2.

110. Charles Kipps, "Sony and Columbia: A Tidy Case of Hardware Meeting Software," *Variety,* October 3, 1989: 5.

111. Peter Bart, "Col's Billion Dollar Man Sets New Standard in H'wood," *Variety,* November 29, 1989: 1.

112. See Stan Berkowitz, "Is 3-D Just Another Fad?" *Los Angeles,* March 1983: 120.

113. Interestingly, the studios' attempts at this type of film (the classics divisions) have largely failed. As of 1988, only Orion Classics was still in existence.

114. Richard J. Pietschmann, "The New Little Kings of Hollywood," *Los Angeles,* December 1987: 244–254.

115. Anne Thompson, "Field of Dreams," *Film Comment,* March/April 1990: 62.

116. Laurie Halpern Smith, "Cinecom: East Indie," *Movieline,* November 6, 1987: 57.

117. Pietschmann, "The New Little Kings" 247.

118. As Shep Gordon, co-chairman of Alive Films, which released *The Whales of August,* comments: "If it was strictly making money, I wouldn't be making pictures with Lillian Gish and Bette Davis. No one who's strictly looking at the bottom line would choose to do a picture where the youngest actor is 76."

119. Jerry Bruckheimer, telephone interview, Los Angeles, October 26, 1987. Bruckheimer produced *Flashdance* with partner Don Simpson.

120. Nancy Goliger, personal interview, Los Angeles, March 16, 1988.

121. See, for example, Peter R. Dickson and James L. Ginter, "Market Segmentation, Product Differentiation, and Marketing Strategy," *Journal of Marketing* 51 (1987): 1–10.

122. Ibid. 1.

123. Jack Hirshleifer, *Price Theory and Applications,* 2d ed. (Englewood Cliffs, N.J.: Prentice Hall, 1980): 385.

124. For a fuller discussion of the bases for differentiation, consult Kenneth Clarkson and Roger LeRoy Miller, "Market Structure and Performance," *Industrial Organization* (New York: McGraw-Hill, 1982) 84–104.

125. Joseph Dominick, "Film Economics and Film Content: 1964–1983," *Current Research in Film: Audiences, Economics, and Law,* vol. 3, ed. Bruce A. Austin (Norwood, N.J.: Ablex Publishing Corporation, 1987) 138.

126. Additionally, as I have shown earlier in the chapter, the oligopolization of the industry has become polarized, as opposed to a tight union among all the majors.

127. Edward Chamberlain, *The Theory of Monopolistic Competition* (Cambridge, Mass.: Harvard University Press, 1965).

128. Clarkson and Miller, *Industrial Organization* 326.

129. For a brief explanation of "the high-tech style" in design, see Alan Johnson's entry in *What's What in the 1980s*, ed. Christopher Pick (Detroit: Gale Research Company, 1982) 150–151.

130. Peter McAlevey, personal interviews, Los Angeles, January 13 and March 17, 1988; and Ansen and McAlevey, "The Producer Is King Again," 86.

131. Although demographics on this cross-over trend are not available, films such as *Top Gun* and *Rambo: First Blood Part II* are frequently discussed as opening to a fairly specific audience and broadening out later.

132. Schwartz, "Hollywood's Hottest Stars" 27.

133. Some obvious exceptions would include the films *Ragtime, Reds*, and *Heartburn*—all of which deviated from traditional genre definitions and also were positioned as key products for the company.

134. Kilday, "Strip Show" 63.

135. Quoted in Pollock, "Flashfight" Calendar section, 1 +.

136. Among others, see David Ansen and Peter McAlevey, "The Mouse That Roared," *Newsweek*, March 3, 1986: 63.

137. Ray Loynd, "Disney Unfurls a New Banner: Touchstone Films to Handle Non-Traditional Product," *Variety*, February 16, 1984: 1.

138. Janet Maslin, "Touchstone Has a Recognizable Touch," *New York Times*, November 5, 1989: 17.

4. Marketing the Image: High Concept and the Development of Marketing

1. Seth Cagin and Philip Dray, *Hollywood Films of the Seventies: Sex, Drugs, Rock'N'Roll and Politics* (New York: Harper and Row, 1984) 223–224.

2. Richard Kahn, "The Day Film Marketing Came of Age," *Variety*, October 30, 1979: 38.

3. Richard Albarino, "'Billy Jack' Hits Reissue Jackpot," *Variety*, November 7, 1973: 1.

4. Kahn, "The Day Film Marketing Came of Age" 38.

5. Syd Silverman, "U.S. Four-Walling: Boon or Threat?" *Variety*, May 8, 1974: 64.

6. Ibid.

7. Kahn, "The Day Film Marketing Came of Age" 92.

8. Byron, "First Annual 'Grosses Gloss'" 30.

9. Addison Verrill, "'Kong' Wants 'Jaws' Boxoffice Crown," *Variety*, December 22, 1976: 1.

10. A. D. Murphy, "June Breaks Hot: Await Staying Power," *Variety*, June 22, 1977: 3.

11. "725 Gets Heretic," *Variety*, June 8, 1977: 3.

12. Byron, "First Annual 'Grosses Gloss'" 30.

13. Hoberman, "1975–1985: Ten Years That Shook the World" 34–60.

14. Ibid. 36.

15. Charles O. Glenn, "In Reality, Nothing Just Happens," *Variety*, October 28, 1975: 62.

16. Mason Wiley and Damien Bona, "Altman Goes Country," *Inside Oscar* (New York: Ballantine Books, 1988) 511.

17. For an interesting critical discussion of the film's reception and social impact, see Charles Michener, "Altman's Opryland Epic," *Newsweek*, June 30, 1975: 46–50.

18. Interview with Nancy Goliger, Los Angeles, March 16, 1988.

19. Interestingly, director Paul Schrader devised this campaign himself after several proposed campaigns from Paramount's marketing department: "[Schrader] was heavily involved with all aspects of the ad campaign for *American Gigolo*, at one point getting authorization from Paramount to spend an additional $15,000 to develop his own print campaign when he felt those being proposed didn't work." From "Schrader Deep in 'Gigolo' Ad Plan: Trailer Taken from Original Neg," *Variety*, February 27, 1980: 43.

20. Myron Meisel, "The Sixth Annual Grosses Gloss," *Film Comment*, March/April 1981: 66.

21. Ibid.

22. Quoted in Dan Yakir, "Campaigns and Caveat," *Film Comment*, March/April 1980: 74.

23. For exact reproductions of these ads, see Gregory J. Edwards, *The International Film Poster* (London: Columbus Books, 1985). Edwards's book also offers a very interesting comparison between poster images from different national cinemas and their sources.

24. On this strategy, producer Jerry Bruckheimer comments, "A movie doesn't have the shelf life of a soft drink, so you must establish its identity quickly and effectively. Don and I like to do that with a strong, singular image—Jennifer Beals in her off-the-shoulder sweater in the print ad for *Flashdance*, Eddie Murphy sitting on the hood of the red Mercedes for *Beverly Hills Cop* and giving the okay sign at the very end of the TV spot." Jerry Bruckheimer, telephone interview, Los Angeles, October 27, 1987.

25. For more information on the development of these campaigns, consult William Daniels, "Film Ad Art Is No Easy Task," *Variety*, October 30, 1984.

26. Yakir, "Campaigns and Caveat" 76.

27. Richard Gold, "Create New Print Ad Campaigns to 'Freshen' Three Summer Pics," *Variety*, June 18, 1986: 34.

28. In Britain, the term "berk" refers to a stupid, incompetent person. For a discussion of these campaigns, see Peter Schmideg, "Tailor-Made," *Cinema Papers*, July 1985: 45–46.

29. The film used a different campaign in Europe, where it received very strong business.

30. Quoted in Tom Matthews, "The Lure of the Movie Poster," *Boxoffice*, June 1986: 13.

31. Richard Gold, "Majors Tune in Tube, Stint on Print," *Variety*, December 20, 1989: 4.

32. William Severini Kowinski, "The Malling of the Movies," *American Film*, September 1983: 56.

33. Quoted in Jay Padroff, "Rock'N'Reel," *Millimeter*, November 1985: 12.

34. Doty, "Music Sells Movies" 74.

35. Interview with Peter Guber, Los Angeles, March 24, 1988.

36. John Gregory Dunne, "Gone Hollywood," *Esquire*, September 1976: 30.

37. Doty, "Music Sells Movies" 76.

38. "A Hit Is Born and Made," *Variety*, February 9, 1977: 124.

39. "The Key Art Awards: Past Winners," *Hollywood Reporter*, June 21, 1988: 58.

40. *Eyes of Laura Mars* also features several modular set pieces scored to the disco soundtrack (e.g., the sequence in which the crew shoots to the tune of "Let's All Chant"). In some ways, this modular structure anticipates the more advanced modularity in films such as *Flashdance* or *Top Gun*.

41. Steven Ginsberg, "Jon Peters Org Develops 16 Features," *Variety*, August 2, 1978: 7.

42. Many of the photographs used in the film were shot by Helmut Newton, famous at the time for his provocative and marketable shots of decadence and violence. Perhaps the only tie-in *not* developed by Peters was a book of photographs used in the film.

43. Indeed, music seems to be at the very heart of the Peters projects; he even announced plans for a film based on the hit Barbra Streisand–Neil Diamond song "You Don't Bring Me Flowers" ("Jon Peters' 3 Pics for Orion, One Inspired by Streisand Tune," *Variety*, December 12, 1979: 4).

44. Quoted in Shaun Considine, *Barbra Streisand: The Woman, The Myth, The Music* (New York: Dell Publishing, 1985) 322.

45. From the pressbook for *Sgt. Pepper's Lonely Hearts Club Band*, Universal City Studios, 1978.

46. Pye, *Moguls* 236.

47. Anthony Haden-Guest, "Robert Stigwood Has the Stomach," *New York*, January 30, 1978: 52.

48. Pye, *Moguls* 245–249; and Haden-Guest, "Robert Stigwood Has the Stomach" 53.

49. Pye, *Moguls* 253.

50. Ibid. 255.

51. Tony Schwartz, "Stigwood's Midas Touch," *Newsweek*, January 23, 1978: 40.

52. Denisoff and Romanowski, *Risky Business* 219.

53. Charles Michener, "The New Movie Musicals," *Newsweek*, March 24, 1975: 59.

54. The film's campaign was based upon an unusual shot of Tommy (Roger Daltrey) undergoing science experiments. His plugged mouth, nose, and eyes were juxtaposed with the copy "Your senses will never be the same."

55. Doty, "Music Sells Movies" 76.

56. Steve Pond, "Night Fever, Ten Years After," *Premiere*, December 1987: 98; and Ben Fong-Torres, "Al Coury Owns Number One," *Rolling Stone*, October 5, 1978: 17, 40–43.

57. A quote from the Paramount Press Book and Merchandising Manual for *Saturday Night Fever*: "John is rapidly gaining recognition in the record world. His first album 'John Travolta' which included the giant hit single 'Let Her In'

gained him the Billboard award for new pop male vocalist of the year. His new album 'Can't Let You Go' is reaching a wider audience and is regarded as an artistic achievement."

58. The Travolta print image is spoofed in two other Paramount films, *Airplane!* and *Footloose*, while the image from *A Star Is Born* even became the centerpiece for a Carol Burnett skit.

59. While the film failed at the boxoffice, the soundtrack album sold over 3 million copies — an amazing figure for a film with such a low level of audience interest.

60. Ansen, "Rock Tycoon Robert Stigwood" 43.

61. Olen J. Earnest, "Star Wars: A Case Study of Motion Picture Marketing," *Current Research in Film: Audiences, Economics, and Law*, vol. 1, ed. Bruce A. Austin (Norwood, N.J.: Ablex Publishing Corporation, 1983) 16.

62. Guber even authored a book (*Inside the Deep*) about the making of the film, and released the book in conjunction with the film's national opening. See Peter Guber, *Inside the Deep* (New York: Bantam Books, 1977) xvii.

63. Pye, *Moguls* 193.

64. Ibid. 195.

65. Pollock, "Flashfight" Calendar section, 10.

66. Jerry Bruckheimer, telephone interview, Los Angeles, October 26, 1987.

67. Lewis, "Purple Rain: Music Video Comes of Age" 22.

68. Martin A. Grove, "Special Report: Licensing and Merchandising," *Hollywood Reporter*, June 10, 1986: s-3.

69. James Greenberg, "Product Merchandising Helps Hype a Film at B.O. But You Need a Winner," *Variety*, October 30, 1984: 64.

70. Several Disney features have spawned successful merchandising, including *Pinocchio, Fantasia, Dumbo, Bambi*, and *Snow White*. Other early successful merchandising ventures include the *Planet of the Apes, Pink Panther*, and James Bond series. Greenberg's article, as well as Mike Reynolds's "Licensing Yesterday" and Cliff Rothman's "Disney: A Merchandising World Leader" (*Hollywood Reporter*, June 10, 1986) all offer information on these early merchandising efforts.

71. Ali MacGraw recounts the story behind Evans's merchandising scheme in her autobiography *Moving Pictures* (New York: Bantam Books, 1991) 13.

72. Mark Litwack, *Reel Power* (New York: Morrow, 1986) 241.

73. "Ready or Not, Here Comes Gatsby," *Time*, March 18, 1974: 87.

74. Ibid.

75. Ibid. 88.

76. Paramount Press Book and Merchandising Manual for *King Kong*, 1976.

77. Vincent Coppola, David T. Friendly, Janet Huck, "Now, It's Superhype," *Newsweek*, October 9, 1978: 91; and Kenneth Turan, "Superman! Supersell!" *American Film*, December-January 1978: 49–52.

78. Turan, "Superman! Supersell!" 49.

79. "E.T. and Friends Are Flying High," *Business Week*, January 10, 1983: 77.

80. Dale Pollock, *Skywalking: The Life and Films of George Lucas* (New York: Harmony Books, 1983) 194.

81. Turan, "Superman! Supersell!" 49.

82. Greenberg, "Product Merchandising" 66.

83. Interview with Sid Kaufman, Leisure Concepts Incorporated, Culver City, Calif., May 26, 1988.

84. "Audits and Surveys Inc. for Licensing Industry Merchandiser's Association," Fall 1987.

85. Bill George, "What's Wrinkled, Bug-Eyed, and Worth Billions," *Cinefantastique* 2/3 (1982): 17.

86. Aljean Harmetz, "Movie Merchandise: The Rush Is On," *New York Times*, June 14, 1989: C19.

87. "Ninja Turtle Power — Or How to Ride Out a Runaway," *Variety*, June 13, 1990: 48.

88. Michael Fleming, "Turtles, 'Toons and Toys Are In," *Variety*, April 18, 1990: 8.

89. See, for example, Susan Cheever Cowley, "The Travolta Hustle," *Newsweek*, May 29, 1978: 97; and Langway and Reed, "Flashdance, Flashfashions" 55.

90. This trend might be changing — studios are becoming increasingly aware of possible fashion trends, and are entering into more licenses with fashion manufacturers.

91. Mark Humphrey, "Licensing and Merchandising: Adding More Business to Showbusiness," *Hollywood Reporter*, June 7, 1988: 38.

92. Ronald Grover, "You Don't Know Them — But They Know Moviegoers," *Business Week*, May 25, 1987.

93. Advance ad, *Weekly Variety*, May 1, 1974: 8–9.

5. High Concept and Market Research: Movie Making by the Numbers

1. Bordwell, Staiger, and Thompson, *The Classical Hollywood Cinema* 144.

2. Hy Hollinger, "Hollywood's View of Research Depends on Just Who's Being Asked, What Methods Are Used," *Variety*, January 12, 1983: 36.

3. Janet Staiger, "Announcing Wares, Winning Patrons, Voicing Ideals: Thinking About the History and Theory of Film Advertising," *Cinema Journal* 29, no. 3 (1990): 18.

4. Bruce A. Austin, *Immediate Seating: A Look at Movie Audiences* (Belmont, Calif.: Wadsworth Publishing Company, 1989) 5.

5. Hollinger, "Hollywood's View of Research" 36.

6. Gregg Kilday, "Two or Three Things We Know About . . . The Eighties," *Film Comment*, November/December 1989: 60.

7. Julie Salamon, *The Devil's Candy* (Boston: Houghton Mifflin Company, 1991) 365.

8. "Del Belso at WB," *Variety*, February 27, 1980: 45.

9. Peter J. Boyer, "Risky Business," *American Film*, January/February 1984: 14.

10. Kahn, "The Day Film Marketing Came of Age" 38.

11. Anne Thompson, "Reporting the Numbers," *LA Weekly*, July 24, 1992: 29.

12. As Thompson notes, a studio reporting boxoffice figures to *Variety* or *The Hollywood Reporter* may actually be reporting number of theaters, not number of

screens. Thompson claims, therefore, that *Batman Returns*, for example, opened on 3,600 screens in 2,644 theaters. Consequently, the necessity for a solid opening becomes even more pressing, since the studio is actually supporting more seats through playing on more than one screen in some multiplexes.

13. For an analysis of platform vs. saturation release strategies and the accompanying advertising costs, see Lee Beaupre and Anne Thompson, "Eighth Annual Grosses Gloss," *Film Comment*, March/April 1983: 68.

14. Steven Knapp and Barry L. Sherman, "Motion Picture Attendance: A Market Segmentation Approach," *Current Research in Film: Audiences, Economics, and Law*, vol. 2, ed. Bruce A. Austin (Norwood, N.J.: Ablex Publishing Corporation, 1986) 35–36.

15. Neal Koch, "She Lives! She Dies! Let the Audience Decide," *New York Times*, April 19, 1992: H11.

16. Thomas Simonet, "Market Research: Beyond the Fanny of the Cohn," *Film Comment*, January/February 1980: 68.

17. Ibid. 69.

18. Hollinger, "Hollywood's View of Research" 36.

19. Elaine Dutka, "The Man Who Makes You King," *Los Angeles Times*, July 12, 1992: Calendar section, 86.

20. Caryn James, "Test Screenings of New Movies Put Demographics over Creativity," *New York Times*, March 9, 1988: C17.

21. As a perfect example of this problem, James describes a sneak preview of *Made in Heaven* in which the market researchers told director Alan Rudolph, "Remember, you have to reach every dummy in the audience." To which Rudolph replied, "Why not get a more intelligent audience?"

22. In addition, there is a certain bias introduced by showing the movie free of charge; the audience has an incentive to be more forgiving than if they had paid for the film.

23. Thomas Simonet, "Conglomerates and Content: Remakes, Sequels, and Series in the New Hollywood," *Current Research in Film: Audiences, Economics, and Law*, vol. 3, ed. Bruce A. Austin (Norwood, N.J.: Ablex Publishing Corporation, 1987) 154.

24. Pat H. Broeske, "Hollywood's '91 Focus: A Good Story," *Los Angeles Times*, January 8, 1991: F12.

25. In this type of analysis a model is formulated by positing a relationship between a dependent variable and one or more explanatory variables. I will specify a model with boxoffice revenue as the dependent variable, several quantifiable explanatory variables, and a sample of all films released from 1983 through 1986. Regression analysis indicates the relative influence of each explanatory variable toward the constitution of the dependent variable. Therefore, from the regression equation, one can gauge the effect of each explanatory variable: the coefficient attached to each explanatory variable shows the size of the effect and whether the variable has a negative or positive effect on the dependent variable. Certain statistical tests can demonstrate the significance of each of the explanatory variables, that is, whether each explanatory variable is significantly different from zero (i.e., that the variable has any explanatory power

whatsoever). In addition, correlation analysis illustrates the relative strength of an association between any two variables, without specifying causality.

26. Austin's study (London: Scarecrow Press, 1983) offers a comprehensive overview of prior research and methodologies utilized in this area. Using Austin's study as a starting point, the research can be broadly divided into three different categories: (1) material relating to psychological research and uses and gratification research, (2) sociological and demographic work, and (3) economic research.

27. Barry R. Litman, "Predicting Success of Theatrical Movies: New Empirical Evidence," National Convention of the Association for Education in Journalism, Boston, August 13, 1980.

28. Ibid. 2.

29. Ibid. 16.

30. Ibid. 12.

31. See, for example, Bruce A. Austin, "A Longitudinal Test of the Taste Culture and Elitist Hypotheses," *Journal of Popular Film and Television* 4 (1983): 156–165; or " . . . But Why This Movie?" *Boxoffice*, February 1984: 16–18.

32. Austin, "But Why This Movie?" 18.

33. Austin, "A Longitudinal Test" 162.

34. Thomas Simonet and Kenneth Harwood, "Identified Auteurs among Top-Grossing American Film Directors, 1945–1969," Society for Cinema Studies Conference, University of Vermont, 1976; and Thomas Simonet and Kenneth Harwood, "Popular Favorites and Critics' Darlings among Film Directors in American Release," Society for Cinema Studies Conference, Northwestern University, 1977.

35. Simonet, "Market Research" 91.

36. David Ogilvy, "Ogilvy Comes to New York, Ogilvy Goes to Hollywood," *New York*, February 6, 1978: 58.

37. Gorham Kindem, "Hollywood's Movie Star System: A Historical Overview," *The American Movie Industry: The Business of Motion Pictures*, ed. Gorham Kindem (Carbondale: Southern Illinois University Press, 1982) 79–93.

38. Ibid. 92.

39. As quoted in D. K. McLeod, "Bankability Reconsidered," *Movieline*, September 25, 1987: 23.

40. Bruce A. Austin, "Do Movie Ratings Affect a Film's Performance at the Ticket Window?" *Boxoffice*, March 1983: 40–42; and Bruce A. Austin, Mark J. Nicolich, and Thomas Simonet, "MPAA Ratings and the Box Office: Some Tantalizing Statistics," *Film Quarterly* 35 (1981): 28–30.

41. This study was constructed before the PG-13 rating was instituted in 1984.

42. Since the sample covers four consecutive years, the price of admission during this period does not remain constant. The annual *Motion Picture Almanac* offers figures on admission prices, and, indeed, the price did gradually increase: 1983 – $3.15, 1984 – $3.34, 1985 – $3.51, 1986 – $3.67. To adjust the revenue for this increase in admission price, an index for admission was devised with 1983 as the base year (1984 – 1.06, 1985 – 1.11, 1986 – 1.17), and then the grosses

were deflated by this index. Due to this adjustment, the number of observations in the sample (i.e., those films which have grossed at least $1 million) fell from 518 to 512. The observations themselves skew positively as a result of the extraordinary grosses of several films—for example, *Return of the Jedi* ($252.3m), *Ghostbusters* ($208.3m adj.), and *Beverly Hills Cop* ($216.8m adj.) tower above the mean gross of $18.8 million.

43. I have included a binary variable (i.e., a variable taking on the value of either 0 or 1) set to 1 if the film is distributed by a major (or mini-major), and 0 if distributed by an independent.

44. Richard Natale, "Summer Plugs Clog P&A Pipe Dreams," *Variety*, June 1, 1992: 88.

45. For instance, *Indiana Jones and the Temple of Doom* grossed $33.8 million opening on May 23, 1984, and *Rambo: First Blood Part II* opened to a $25.1 million gross on May 22, 1985; *Rocky IV* (opening at $19.9 million on November 27, 1985) and *Star Trek IV: The Voyage Home* (opening at $16.8 million on November 26, 1986) both had strong openings during the Thanksgiving holiday weekend.

46. This variable is binary with the value 1 = film with star, 0 = no star.

47. As with the star variable, the value is 1 for a film with a marketable director, 0 otherwise.

48. Conversion of the Maltin ratings followed this method: M (Maltin) 4 – C (Converted) 5.0; M3.5 – C4.5; M3.0 – C4.0; M2.5 – C3.5; M2.0 – C3.0; M1.5 – C2.5; M1.0 – C2.0; M Bomb – C1.0.

49. Litman's method is somewhat problematic, since the press tends to favor reporting high-cost or above-budget films, rather than reporting medium- or low-budget projects.

50. Tests of variable significance and correlation also locate those variables which have a greater effect on revenue.

51. As a measure of this relation, the correlation coefficient ranges between − 1 and + 1: a correlation of − 1 indicates perfect negative correlation between two variables (i.e., as one variable increases in value, the other variable decreases proportionately), a correlation of 0 indicates no correlation (i.e., linear independence) between the variables, and a correlation of + 1 indicates perfect positive correlation (i.e., both variables move together perfectly).

52. In statistical terms, all the variables, except Academy Awards, are significantly different from 0 at the 5 percent level. As Damodar Gujarati states, "It can be shown that adjusted R-squared will increase if the t value of the coefficient of the newly added variable is larger than 1 in absolute value, where the t value is computed under the hypothesis that the population value of the said coefficient is zero." The quote is from Damodar Gujarati, *Basic Econometrics* (New York: McGraw Hill, 1978).

53. The adjusted R-squared for the best linear regression model is 0.45.

54. The best linear model includes a variable which is the size of cost squared. This variable was included in the model, since the relationship between boxoffice revenue and size of cost may be of a nonlinear form. Indeed, the variable is significant at the 5 percent level. As an interesting note to the model, the

"optimal" cost of a film can be derived by differentiating the equation given by the model and setting the result equal to 0. This equation yields the maximum of revenue with respect to cost. Using the coefficients from the best linear model, the optimal film cost is equal to $4.179/2_{(0.058)}$, or 36.025. This indicates that, given a high-budget film (i.e., $15 million or over), revenue is maximized at $36.025 million. All other factors being held equal, additional cost expenditure decreases total revenue at the boxoffice.

55. Restricted models were run to limit the number of these outliers. One model considered films with a gross between $10 million and $60 million (214 observations); another model considered films with a gross between $5 million and $65 million (334 observations). The former model had few significant variables and a low explained sum of squares; the latter model replicated the results from the larger sample, with a smaller R-squared adjusted.

56. Other films with unclear concepts fitting this pattern in the model include *Videodrome* (1983), *Prizzi's Honor* (1985), *Heartburn* (1986), *Out of Bounds* (1986), and *The Adventures of Buckaroo Banzai* (1984).

57. Modeling boxoffice revenue through long-run market research projects is thorny due to the inherent unpredictability of the market for film. Trends in taste and entertainment options are difficult to incorporate in any model. While genre can be included as a variable, trends in audience taste appear to have a large influence on revenue: for example, in the late '70s, *Star Wars* and *Halloween* revived the science fiction and horror genres, respectively, thereby instituting a greater output of both types of film. The genre itself could not account for this revival; rather, the reconfiguration of the genre in these films sparked the new interest.

Data specification and quantification in these market research models also present several concerns. In pursuing an institutional problem through statistical analysis, researchers are faced with data sets designed previously for other uses. This type of analysis, referred to as secondary analysis, in most cases depends on the testing of hypotheses through using a data set which has been generated independently of the research interests of the current project. For a discussion of the costs and benefits of secondary analysis as a research tool, consult Lee B. Becker, "Secondary Analysis," *Research Methods in Mass Communication*, eds. Guido H. Stempel and Bruce H. Westley (Englewood Cliffs, N.J.: Prentice-Hall, 1981) 240–254. Consequently, the analyst usually has only a limited understanding of the origins of the data set and the extent to which the data has been "massaged" in the creation of a full, cohesive data set. Data can be massaged in a variety of ways, such as the interpolation of missing values or the averaging of values to derive quarterly or yearly figures. Such interpolation adds to the uncertainty in measurement and, therefore, the estimation of the coefficients already inherent in such aggregated, industry-sponsored data.

Model building utilizing regression analysis also remains very sensitive to the specification of the independent variables. A strong relationship between two variables might actually be due to the influence of a third variable omitted from the model ("the third-variable effect"). Of course, in many cases, the omission of a significant variable in a regression equation occurs because the variable may not be readily quantifiable or even identifiable. The omission of a variable mis-specifies the entire model, including the significance or insignificance of the remaining independent variables. Even if a variable is included, many aspects of the film medium cannot be quantified directly; instead a proxy variable must be utilized. For instance, attempting to quantify the advertising support behind each film is virtually impossible, since studios do not release such data. Specify-ing the studio variable in the model, in some respects, can be viewed as a proxy for the probable level of support, in terms of advertising and distribution, which a studio allocates for a film. The level of support also varies between films within a single studio, so the studio variable certainly is not a perfect proxy to capture the level of advertising support.

58. Herbert Marcuse, *One-Dimensional Man: Studies in the Ideology of Ad-vanced Industrial Society* (Boston: Beacon Press, 1966) 8.

59. Dutka, "The Man Who Makes You King" Calendar section, 7.

60. Koch, "She Lives! She Dies!" H11; and John Horn, "Audiences Make the Final Cut," *Dallas Morning News*, September 13, 1991: C10.

61. Of course, "narrowcasting," or targeting a well-defined subdemographic, works along a similar pattern: to maximize the satisfaction of the greatest num-ber *within that subdemographic*, rather than within the population at large.

62. David Ehrenstein, "Two Snaps Down," *Advocate*, November 3, 1992: 78.

63. Dutka, "The Man Who Makes You King" Calendar section, 81.

64. Ibid.

65. Martin A. Grove, "Hollywood Report: Future Films and Future Focus," *Hollywood Reporter*, August 19 and 21, 1991: 2.

66. David J. Fox, "Unraveling a Hollywood Mystery," *Los Angeles Times*, Au-gust 21, 1991: C1.

67. Future Films press release, August 1991, Future Films, 3900 West Alameda Suite 1700, Burbank, Calif. 91505.

68. Marcuse, *One-Dimensional Man* 13.

69. Russ W. Baker, "Putting the Cult Back in Culture," *Village Voice*, Novem-ber 12, 1991: 41.

70. Broeske, "Hollywood's '91 Focus" F12.

71. Charles Fleming, "Pitching Costs out of Control," *Variety*, June 27, 1990: 1.

72. Lawrence Cohn, "MegaPix for '91 Late to Gate," *Variety*, July 11, 1990: 85.

73. Fleming, "Pitching Costs" 29.

74. Ibid.

75. Marcy Magiera, "Disney Adds to Tie-ins," *Advertising Age*, February 11, 1991: 5.

76. Claudia Eller, " 'Tracy' Cost Put at $101mil," *Variety*, October 22, 1990: 3.

77. Jeffrey Katzenberg, "The World Is Changing: Some Thoughts on Our Business," reprinted in *Variety*, January 31, 1991: 18+.

78. Ibid. 19.

79. Ibid.

80. Ibid.

81. Leo Bogart, "What Forces Shape the Future of Advertising Research?" *Journal of Advertising Research*, February/March 1986: 100.

82. Judith Waldrop, "The Baby Boom Turns 45," *American Demographics*, January 1991: 2.

83. Betsy Sharkey, "Spotlight on Entertainment," *Adweek*, March 18, 1991: 33.

84. Joseph Helgot, Michael Schwartz, Frank Romo, and Jaime Korman, "Aging Baby Boomers and Declining Leisure-Time: Strategic Implications for the Movie Industry," MarketCast Reports, 1988.

85. Sharkey, "Spotlight on Entertainment" 32.

86. Marcy Magiera, "Madison Avenue Hits Hollywood," *Advertising Age*, December 10, 1990: 24.

87. Dennis H. Tootelian and Ralph M. Gaedeke, "The Teen Market: An Exploratory Analysis of Income, Spending, and Shopping Patterns," *Journal of Consumer Marketing* 9.4 (Fall 1992): 38.

88. Gold, "Majors Tune In Tube" 4.

89. Robert March, "Roth: Instincts, Not Voodoo, Key to Future Fox Films," *Hollywood Reporter*, February 21, 1990: 1.

6. Conclusion: High Concept and the Course of American Film History

1. Steve McQueen actually starred in this project in 1976. The film was never released theatrically.

2. Mast, *A Short History of the Movies* 424.

3. Graham Fuller, "Movies Highlight: Robert Altman," *Interview*, May 1992: 31.

4. Altman received a late career boost outside the mainstream film industry through making the independent hit films *The Player* (1992) and *Short Cuts* (1993) for Fine Line.

5. Robin Wood even describes *Cruising* as an "incoherent text" in which the ideological constraints of mainstream society struggle against the personal beliefs of the film artist to create a narratively fragmented work. See Chapter 4, "The Incoherent Text: Narrative in the 70s" in *Hollywood from Vietnam to Reagan* (New York: Columbia University Press, 1986) 46–69.

6. For a discussion of Coppola's new "studio" and the role played by *One from the Heart* in its development, see Bygrave and Goodman, "Meet Me in Las Vegas" 38–45.

7. Of course, eventually Scorsese was able to direct this film, sponsored by Cineplex-Odeon and Universal, in 1988.

8. Allen's work base in New York further augments his freedom from the Los Angeles–based studios.

9. Timothy Corrigan, *A Cinema without Walls: Movies and Culture after Vietnam* (New Brunswick, N.J.: Rutgers University Press, 1991) 23.

10. For the connection between high concept and the made-for-TV movie, see Edgerton, "High Concept, Small Screen" 114–127.

11. Andrew Britton, "Blissing Out: The Politics of Reaganite Entertainment," *Movie* 31/32: 3.

12. Wood, *Hollywood from Vietnam to Reagan* 164.

13. The argument of Britton and Wood is also replicated, with a slightly different slant, by Robert Ray. Ray describes the movement from the New Hollywood in terms of Right vs. Left films; see "The Left and Right Cycles" in Robert Ray, *A Certain Tendency of the Hollywood Cinema, 1930–1980* (Princeton, N.J.: Princeton University Press, 1985) 296–325.

14. Wood, *Hollywood from Vietnam to Reagan* 166.

15. David E. James, *Allegories of Cinema: American Film in the Sixties* (Princeton, N.J.: Princeton University Press, 1989) 23.

16. Ibid. 22–25.

17. Bordwell, Staiger, and Thompson, *The Classical Hollywood Cinema* 110.

18. Richard B. Woodward, "A Dark Lens on America," *New York Times Magazine*, January 14, 1990: 30.

19. Ibid. 43.

20. Natale, "Summer Plugs Clog P&A Pipe Dreams" 88.

21. For a discussion of the determinants of the rise in African-American cinema, see Anne Thompson, "Altered States: Hollywood in Transition," *LA Weekly*, November 20, 1992: 41.

Index

High Concept

Lightning Source UK Ltd.
Milton Keynes UK
UKHW01f0654051018

330049UK00001B/2/P